CHILDREN OF THE WHALES

Story

Volume

13

# Characters

## On the Mud Whale

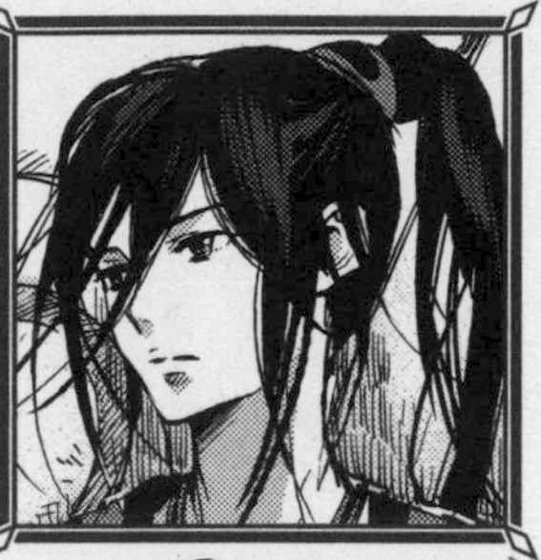

### Ouni
(Marked, 16 years old)

A very powerful thymia user. His daímonas power is awakening, but he is still defeated by Orca and captured.

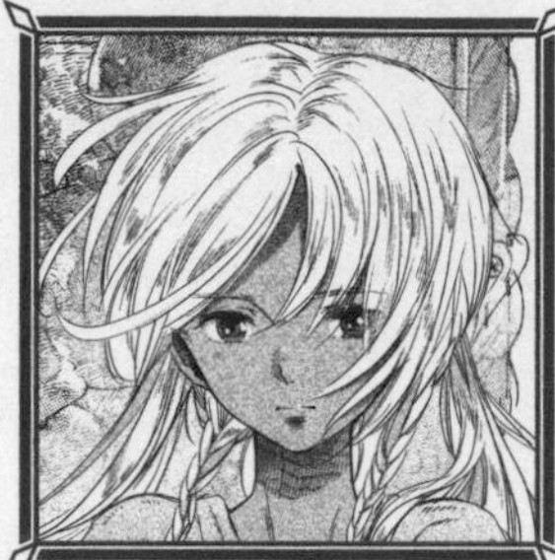

### Lykos
(Marked, 14 years old)

A girl from the Allied Empire who drifted into the Mud Whale. She runs into Liontari in Amonlogia and is captured.

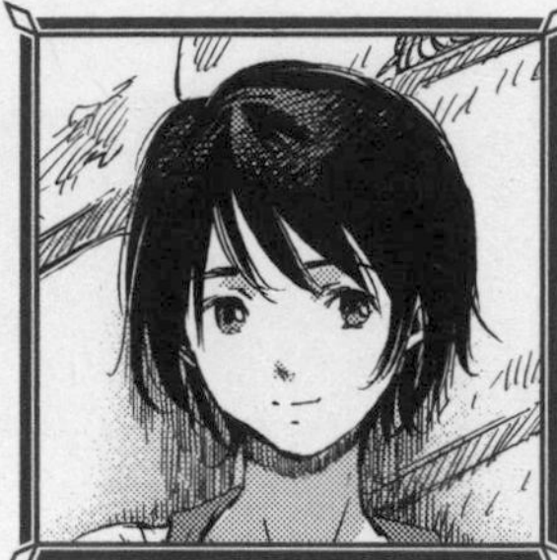

### Chakuro
(Marked, 14 years old)

The young archivist of the Mud Whale. In order to save the hostage Unmarked, he and a group of Marked infiltrate Amonlogia.

Allied Empire

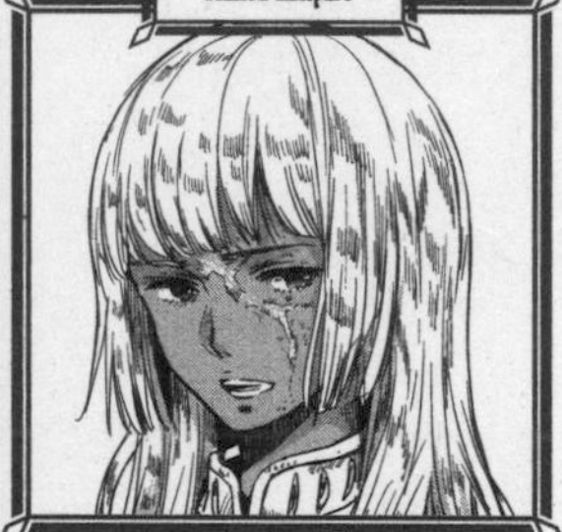

### Orca
(Marked)

A high-ranking official from the Allied Empire and Lykos's brother. He invades Amonlogia and seizes the island's guardian, Kýma.

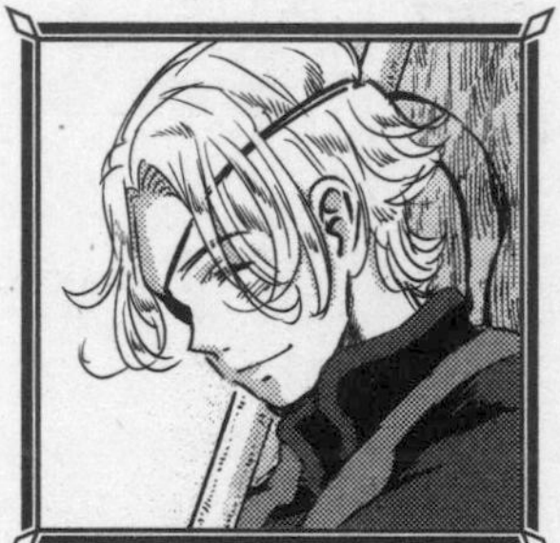

### Shuan
(Marked, 26 years old)

Former commander of the Vigilante Corps. He takes on Orca in an attempt to save Ouni, but is no match for the imperial commander.

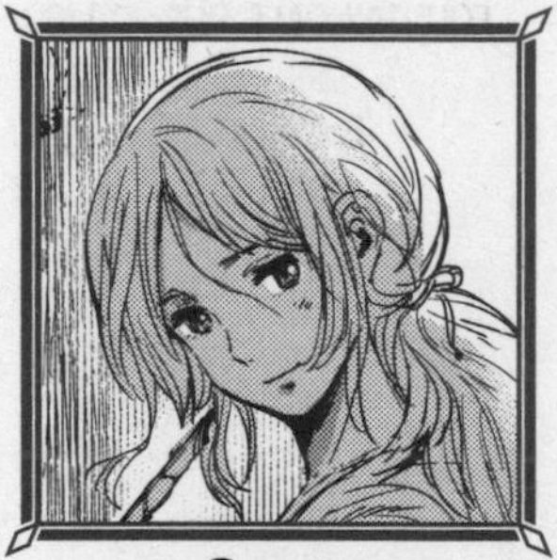

### Suou
(Unmarked, 17 years old)

Mayor of the Mud Whale. Was being held prisoner with the rest of the Unmarked, but they have since been rescued.

Amonlogia

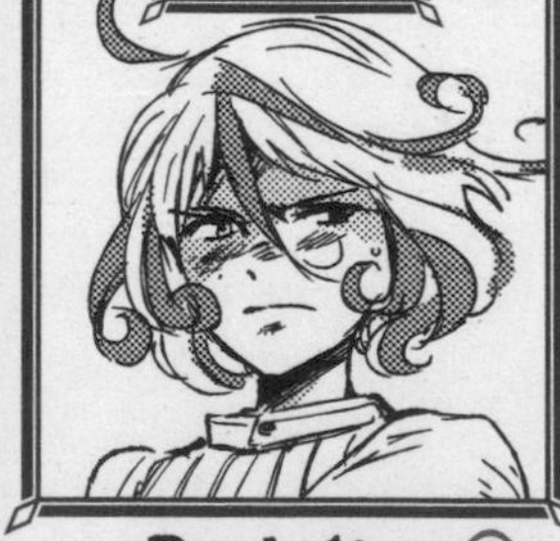

### Rochalízo
(?, 17 years old)

The youngest son of the Duke of Amonlogia. He is considered useless by his family, but he has decided to save the Mud Whale.

Amonlogia

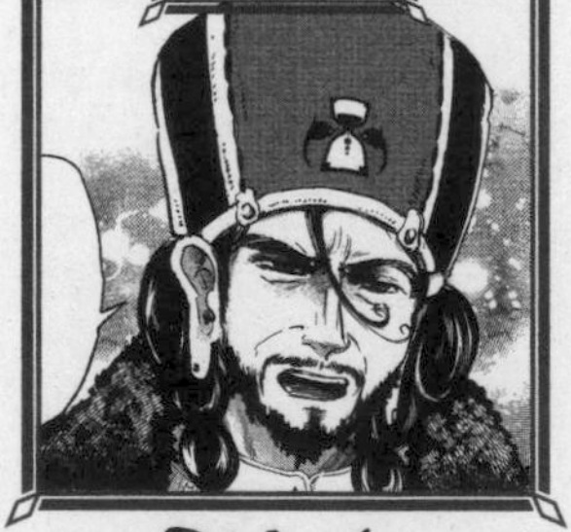

### Dáchtyla

Duke of Amonlogia and Rochalízo's father. His greatest fear, the capture of the guardian Kýma, has come to pass.

Allied Empire

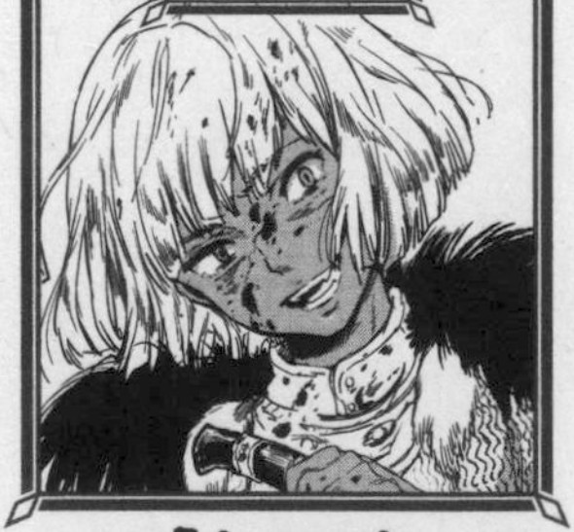

### Liontari
(Marked)

Joined the invasion of Amonlogia as Orca's jester. He faces off against Lykos and Chakuro.

# Glossary of the Sea of Sand

| The Mud Whale | A huge, drifting island-ship. Those in the empire who resisted giving up their emotions were exiled here, along with all their descendants. |
| Thymia | Telekinetic power derived from emotions. |
| The Marked | The 90 percent of the Mud Whale population who are thymia users. They are all short-lived. |
| The Unmarked | The members of the Mud Whale population who cannot use thymia. Unlike the Marked, they are long-lived. |
| Nous | A unique organism that obtains energy from peoples' emotions and gives people the power of thymia in return. |
| Nous Fálaina | A Nous that dwells deep within the Belly of the Mud Whale. Unlike other Nouses, it consumes the life force of humans rather than their emotions. |
| The Allied Empire | A large nation on the Sea of Sand that controls its citizenry through the Nouses and their absorption of emotions. |
| Daímonas | A legend from the empire. A being said to be able to destroy a Nous. |

# A Record of the Mud Whale and the Sea of Sand

Year 93 of the Sand Exile.

The Mud Whale drifts endlessly through the Sea of Sand, home to about 500 people who know nothing of the outside world.

The Mud Whale has been rocked by crisis, and the Amonlogian capitol is the stage of a violent clash between local and imperial troops. Chakuro, Ouni and the other Marked who rescued the hostage Unmarked are planning their escape, but Orca, commander of the imperial troops, stands in their way. Shuan and Ouni try to counter him, but they are swiftly defeated by his overpowering thymia. They are captured along with Lykos, who was defeated by Liontari.

"The Mud Whale was our entire world."

# Table of Contents

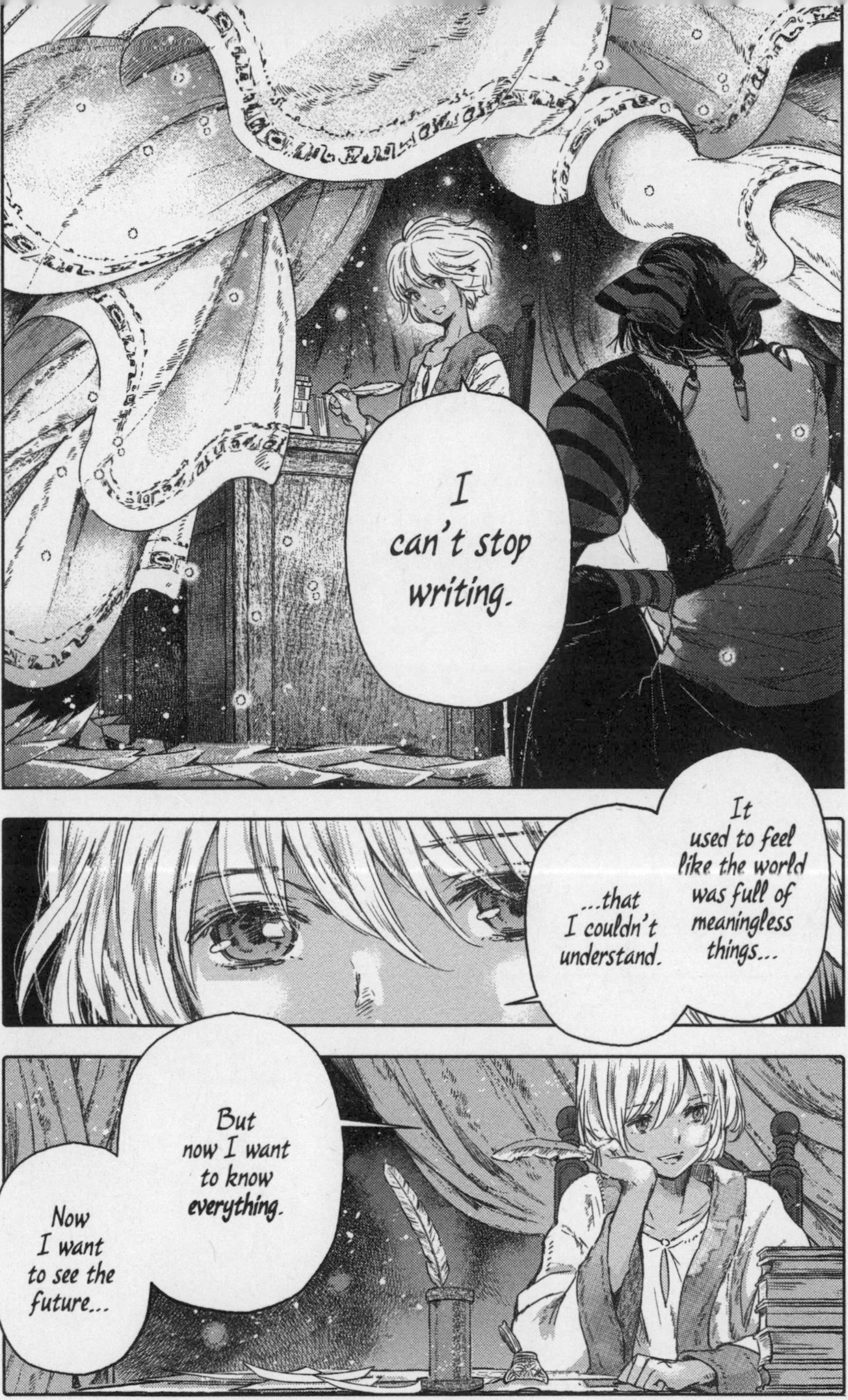
I can't stop writing.
It used to feel like the world was full of meaningless things...
...that I couldn't understand.
But now I want to know everything.
Now I want to see the future...

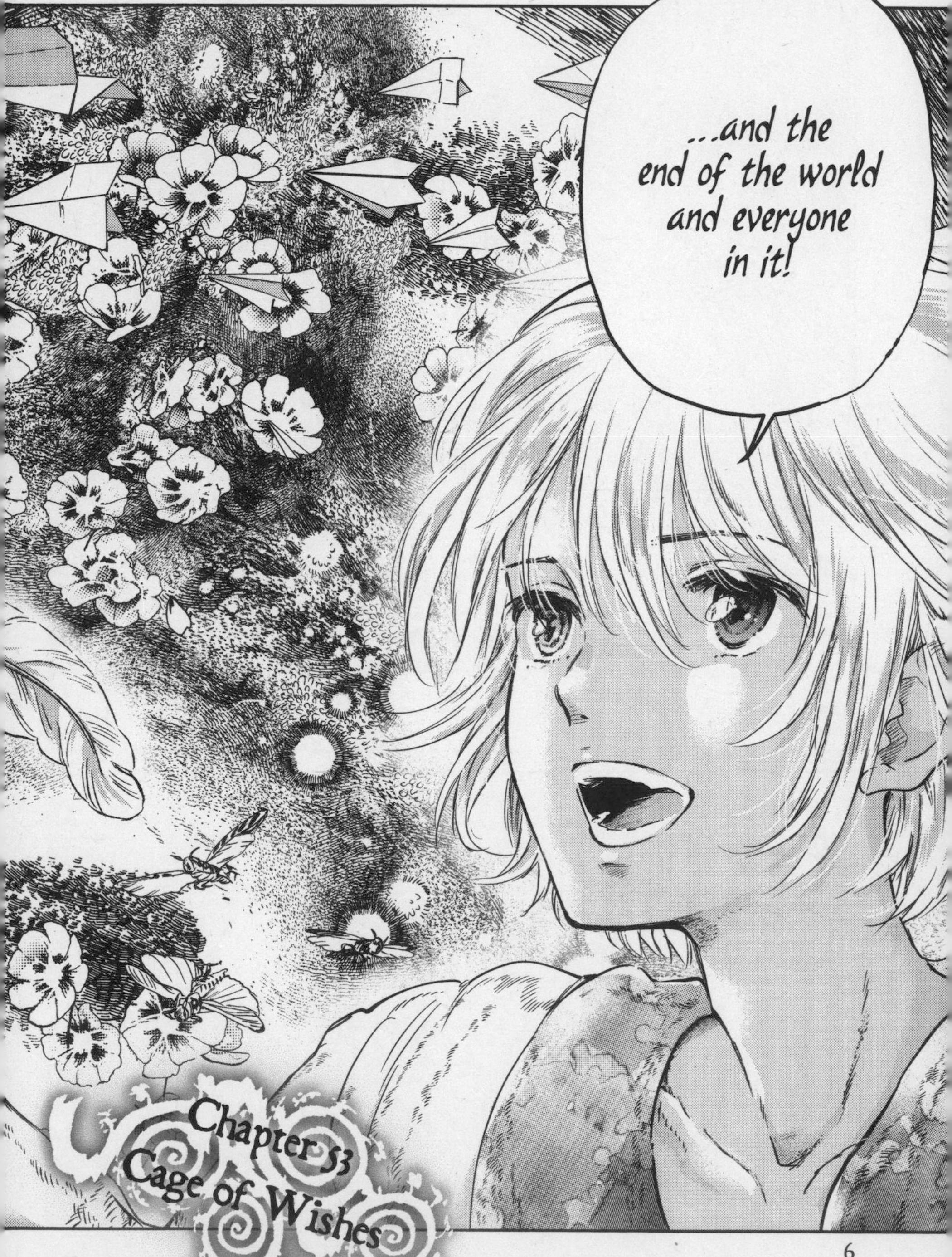
...and the end of the world and everyone in it!
Chapter 53 Cage of Wishes

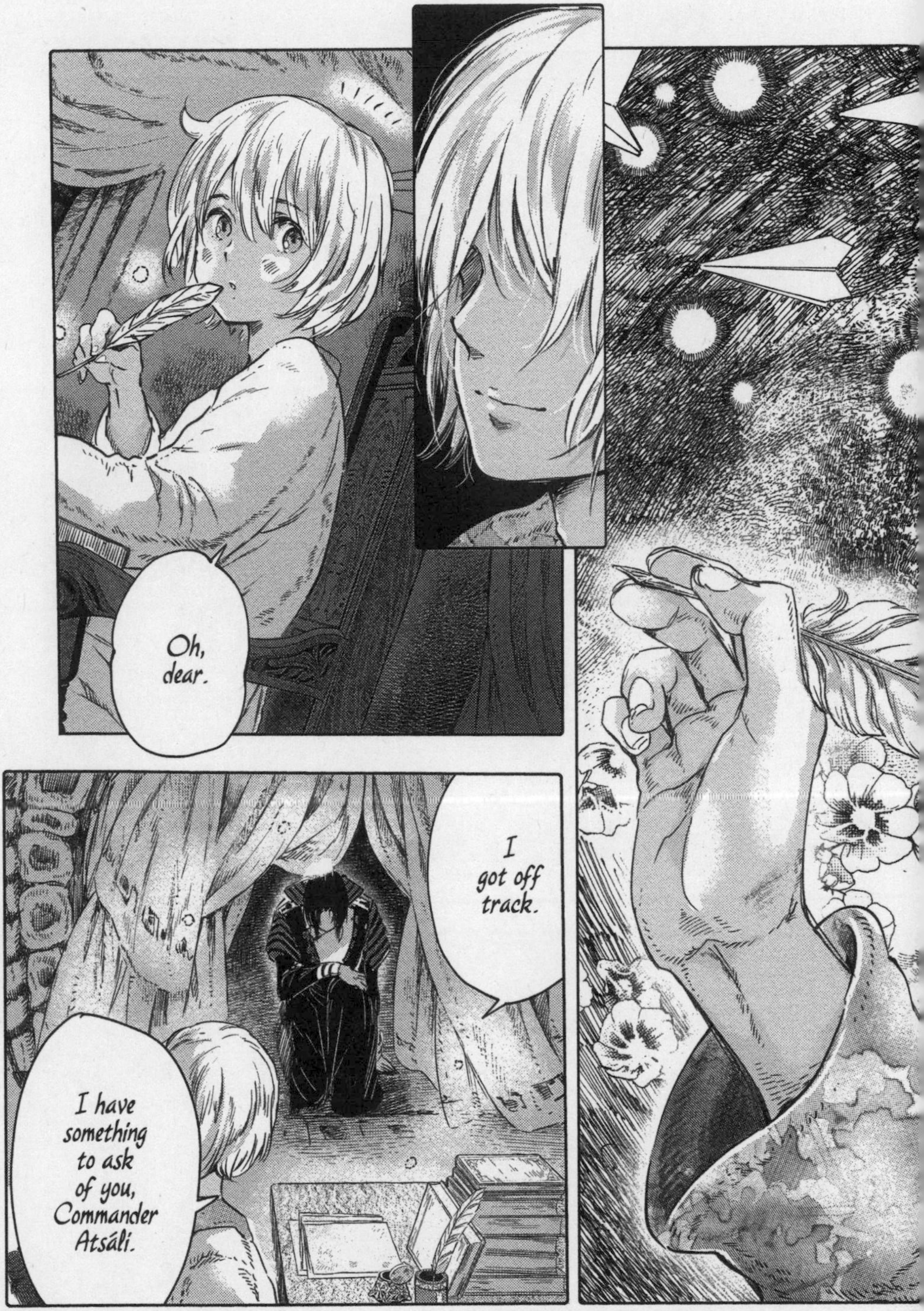
Oh, dear.
I got off track.
I have something to ask of you, Commander Atsáli.

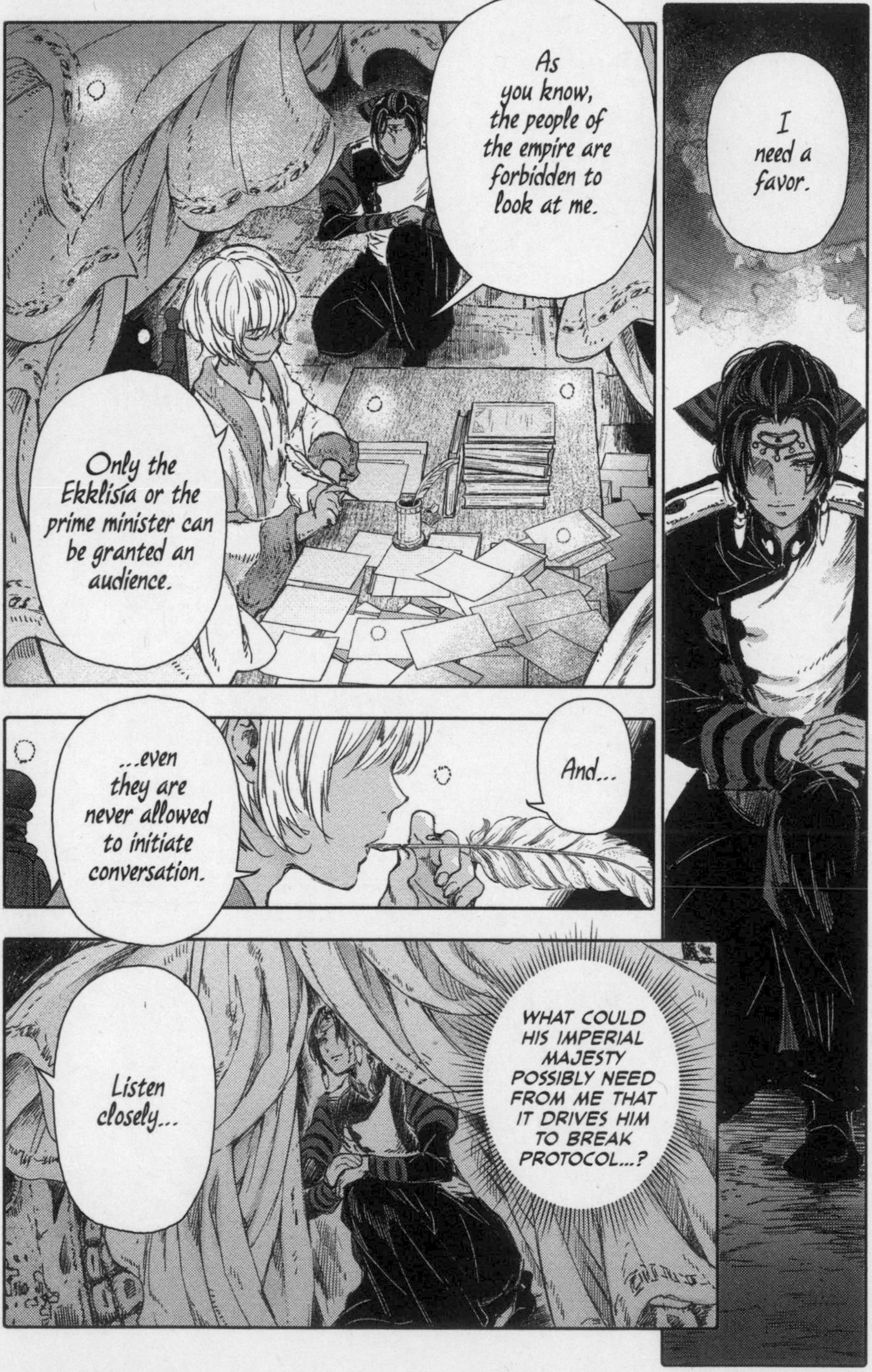
I need a favor.
As you know, the people of the empire are forbidden to look at me.
Only the Ekklisia or the prime minister can be granted an audience.
And...
...even they are never allowed to initiate conversation.
WHAT COULD HIS IMPERIAL MAJESTY POSSIBLY NEED FROM ME THAT IT DRIVES HIM TO BREAK PROTOCOL...?
Listen closely...

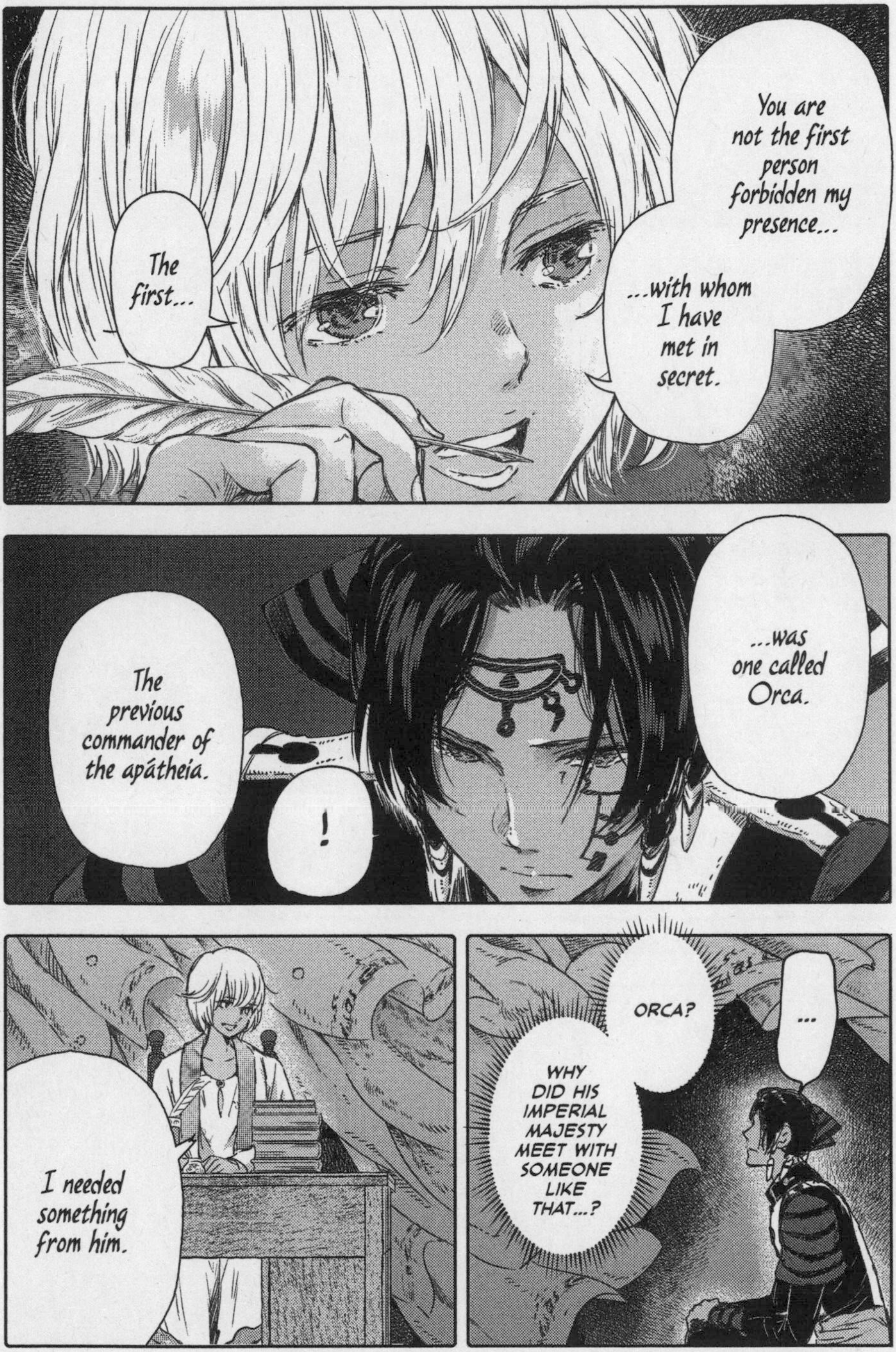

You are not the first person forbidden my presence...
...with whom I have met in secret.
The first...
...was one called Orca.
The previous commander of the apátheia.
!
...
ORCA?
WHY DID HIS IMPERIAL MAJESTY MEET WITH SOMEONE LIKE THAT...?
I needed something from him.

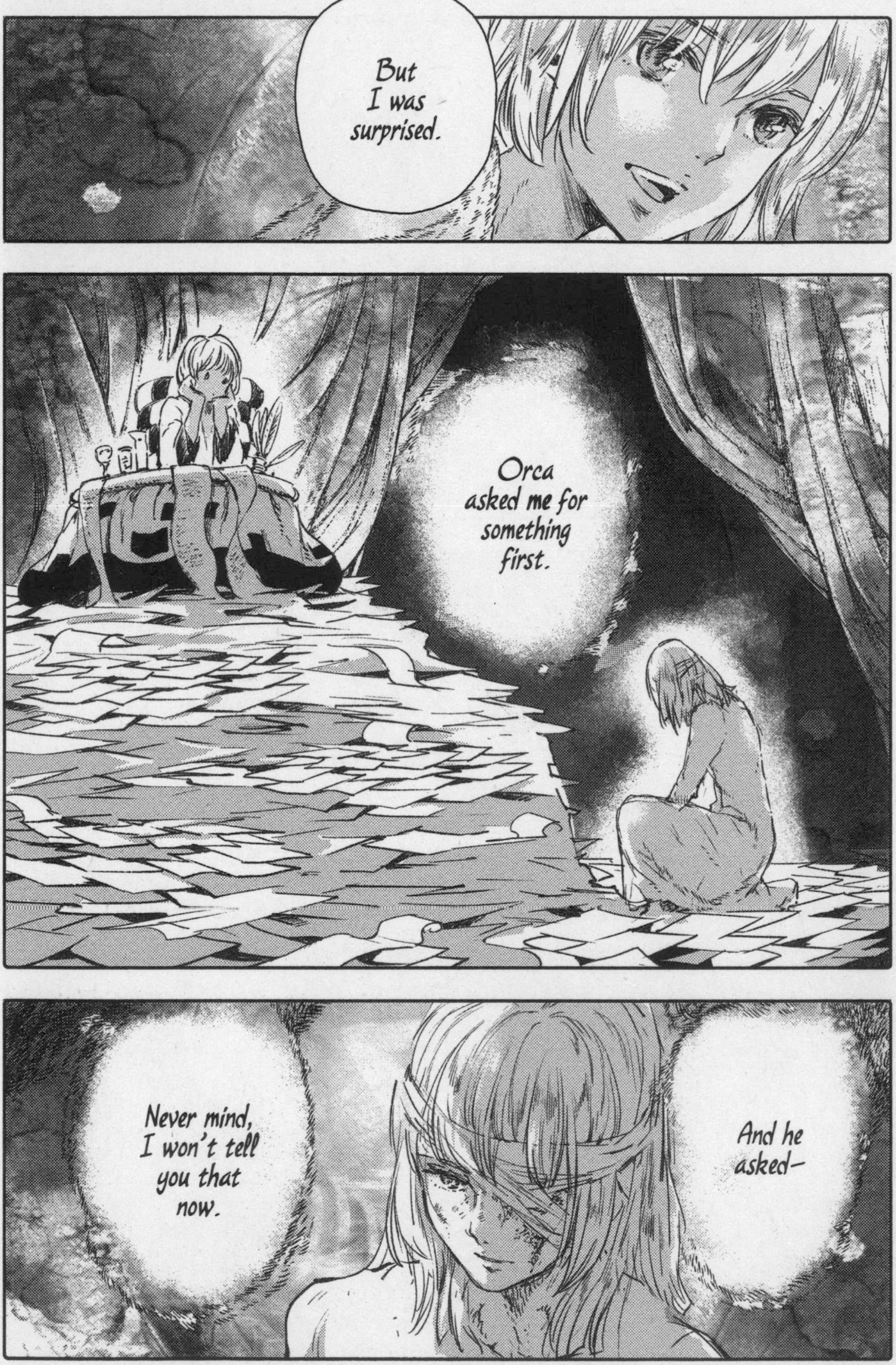
But I was surprised.
Orca asked me for something first.
And he asked—
Never mind, I won't tell you that now.

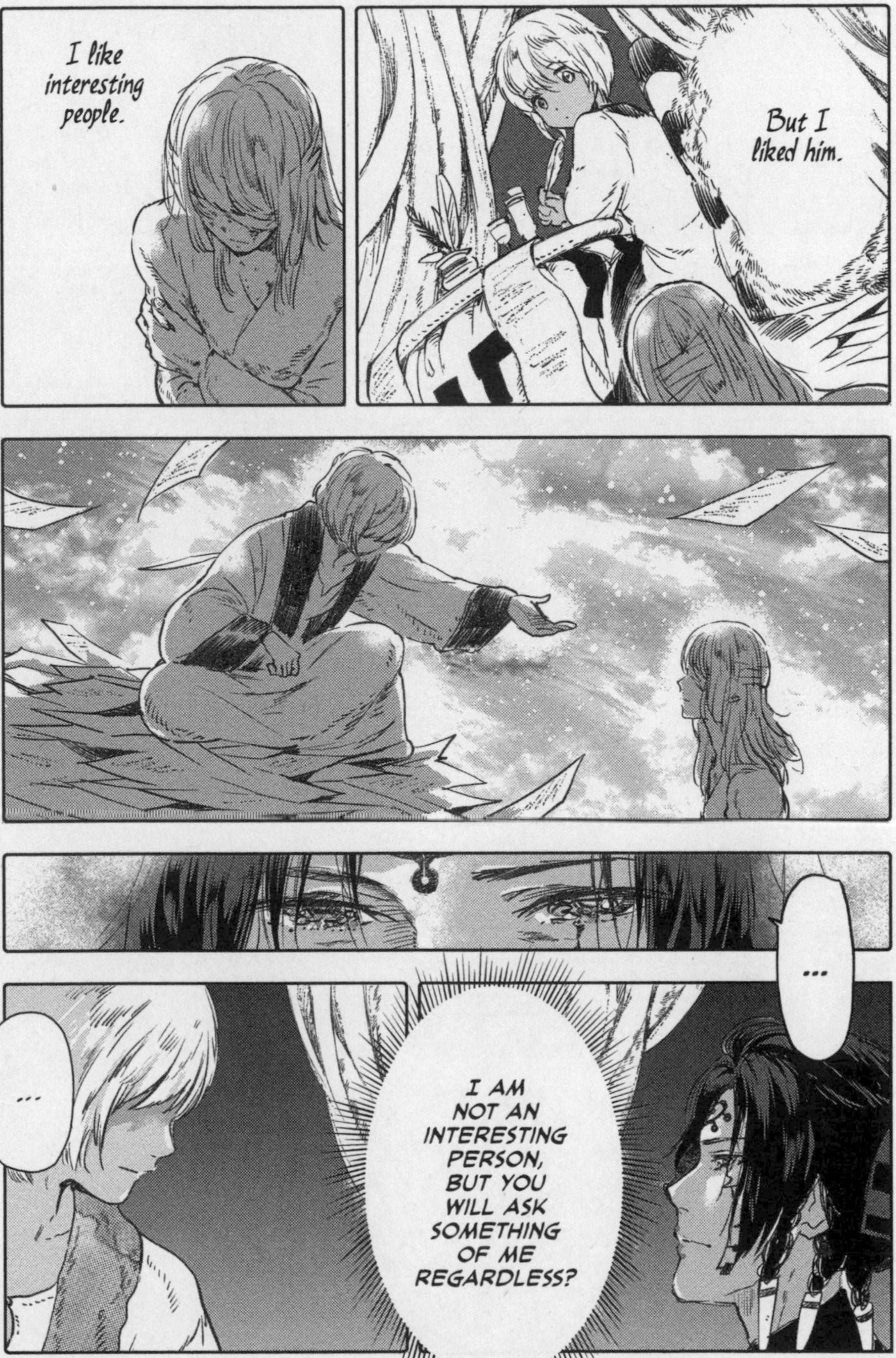
But I liked him.
I like interesting people.
...
I AM NOT AN INTERESTING PERSON, BUT YOU WILL ASK SOMETHING OF ME REGARDLESS?
...

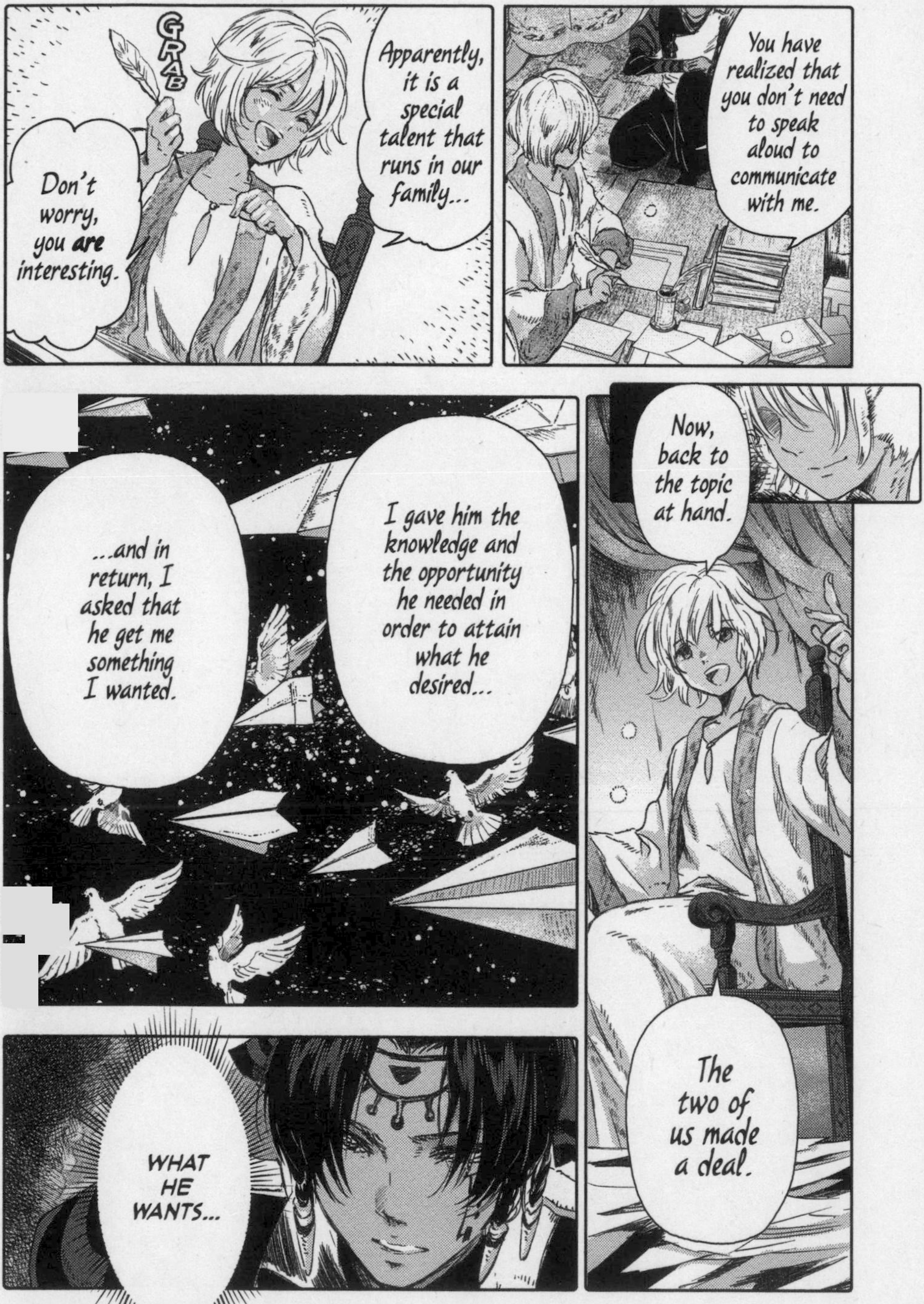
You have realized that you don't need to speak aloud to communicate with me.
Apparently, it is a special talent that runs in our family...
GRAB
Don't worry, you **are** interesting.
Now, back to the topic at hand.
The two of us made a deal.
I gave him the knowledge and the opportunity he needed in order to attain what he desired...
...and in return, I asked that he get me something I wanted.
WHAT HE WANTS...

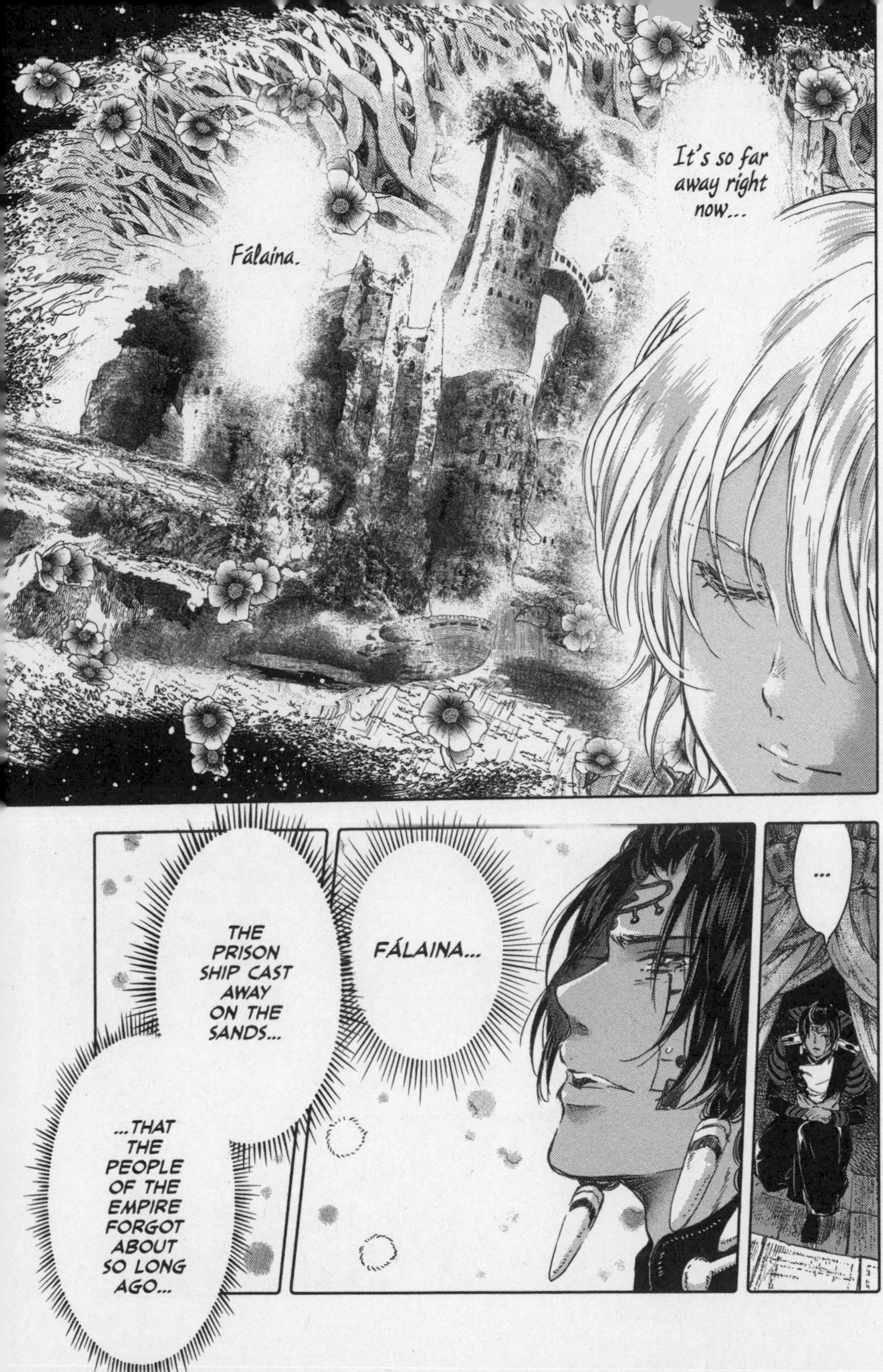
It's so far away right now...
Fálaina.
...
FÁLAINA...
THE PRISON SHIP CAST AWAY ON THE SANDS...
...THAT THE PEOPLE OF THE EMPIRE FORGOT ABOUT SO LONG AGO...

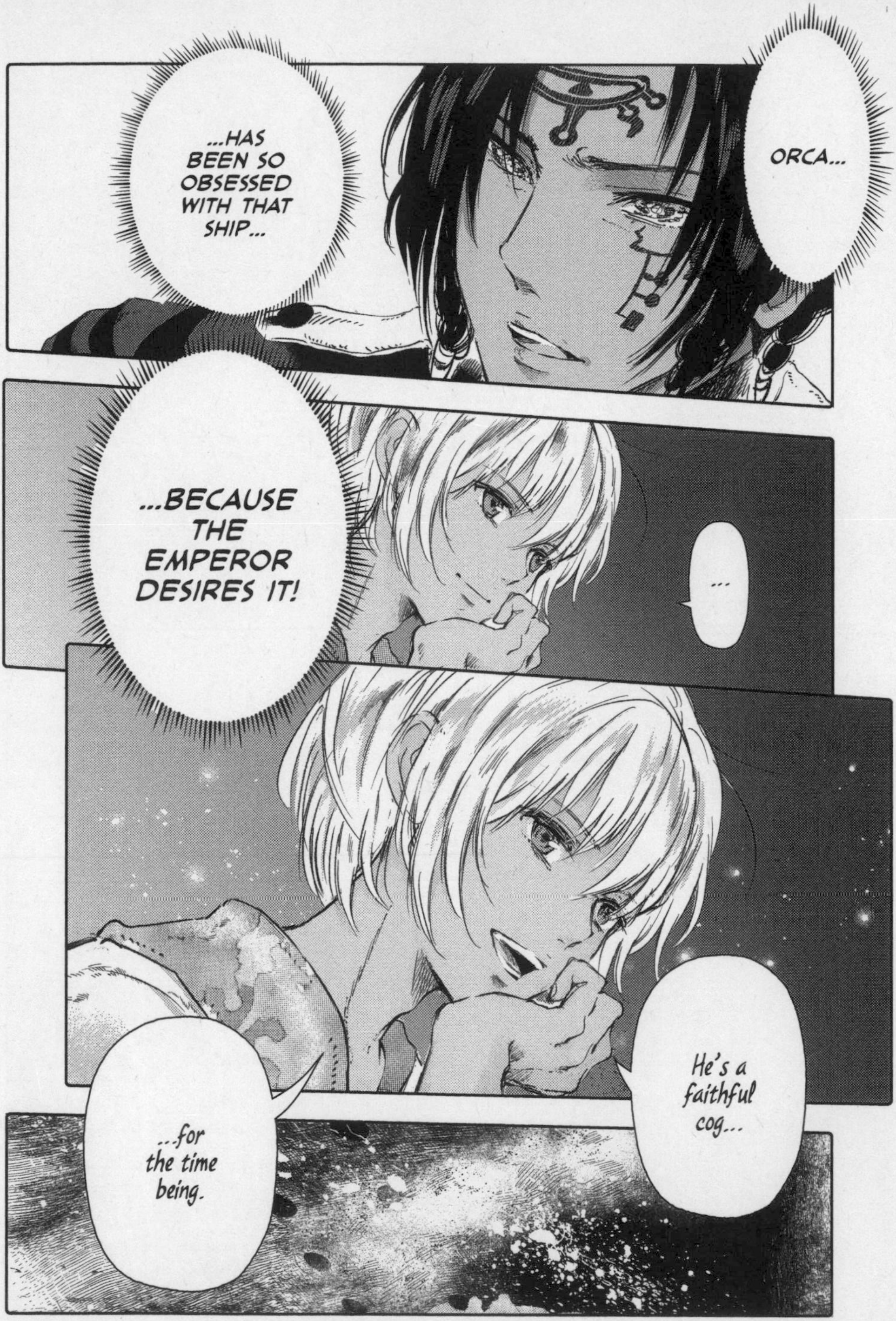
ORCA...
...HAS BEEN SO OBSESSED WITH THAT SHIP...
...BECAUSE THE EMPEROR DESIRES IT!
...
He's a faithful cog...
...for the time being.

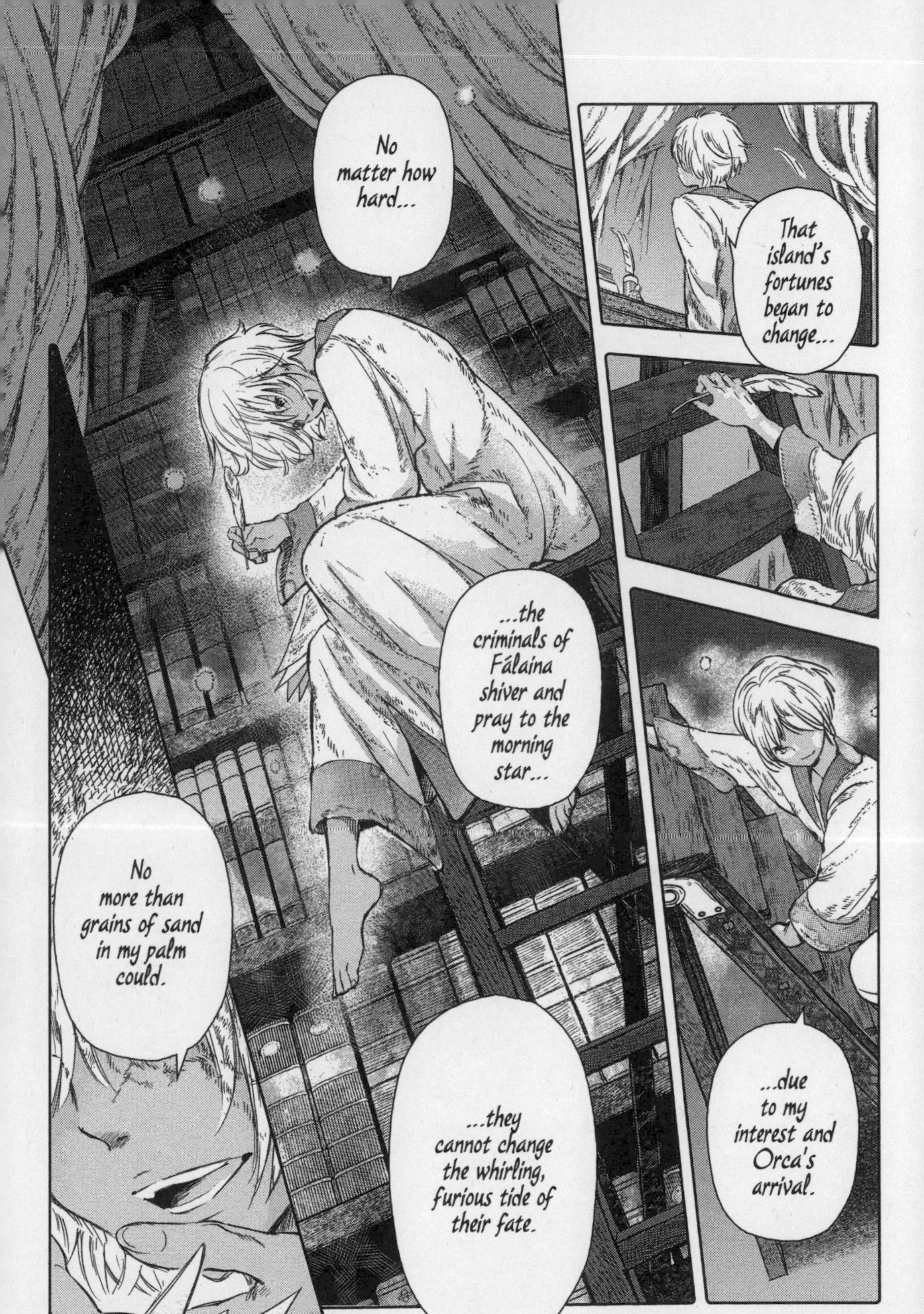
That island's fortunes began to change...
...due to my interest and Orca's arrival.
No matter how hard...
...the criminals of Fálaina shiver and pray to the morning star...
...they cannot change the whirling, furious tide of their fate.
No more than grains of sand in my palm could.

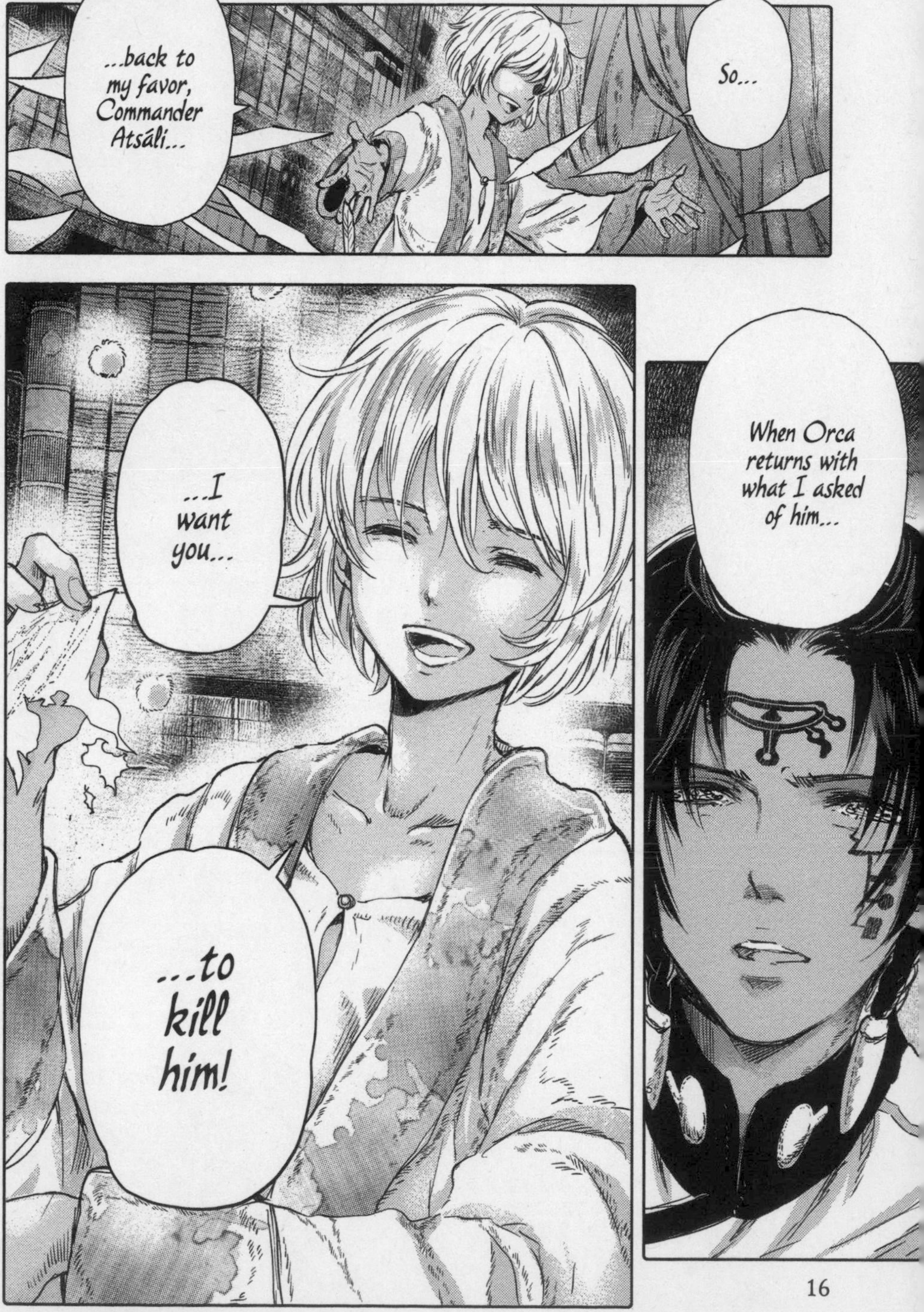
So...
...back to my favor, Commander Atsáli...
When Orca returns with what I asked of him...
...I want you...
...to kill him!

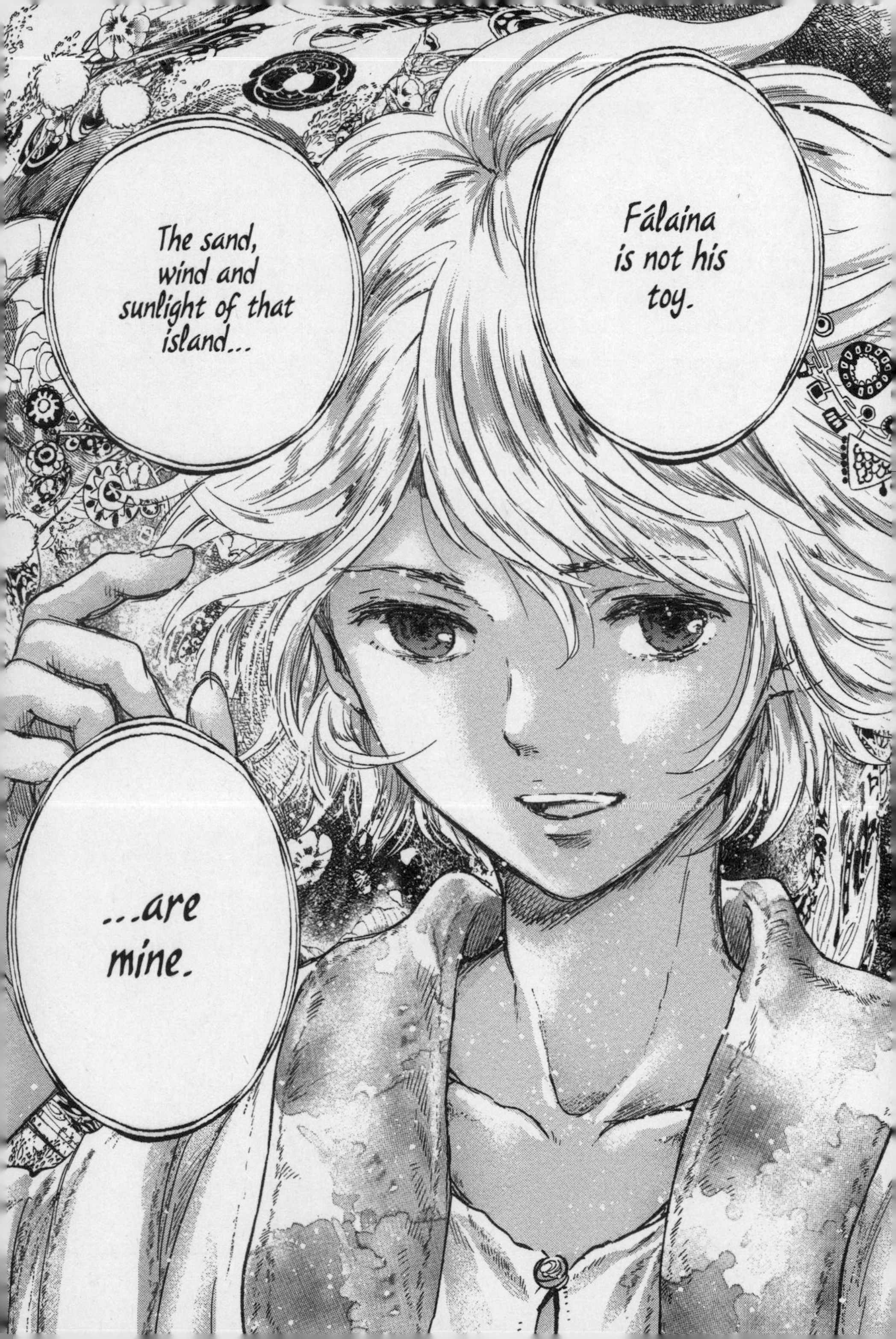
Fálaina is not his toy.
The sand, wind and sunlight of that island...
...are mine.

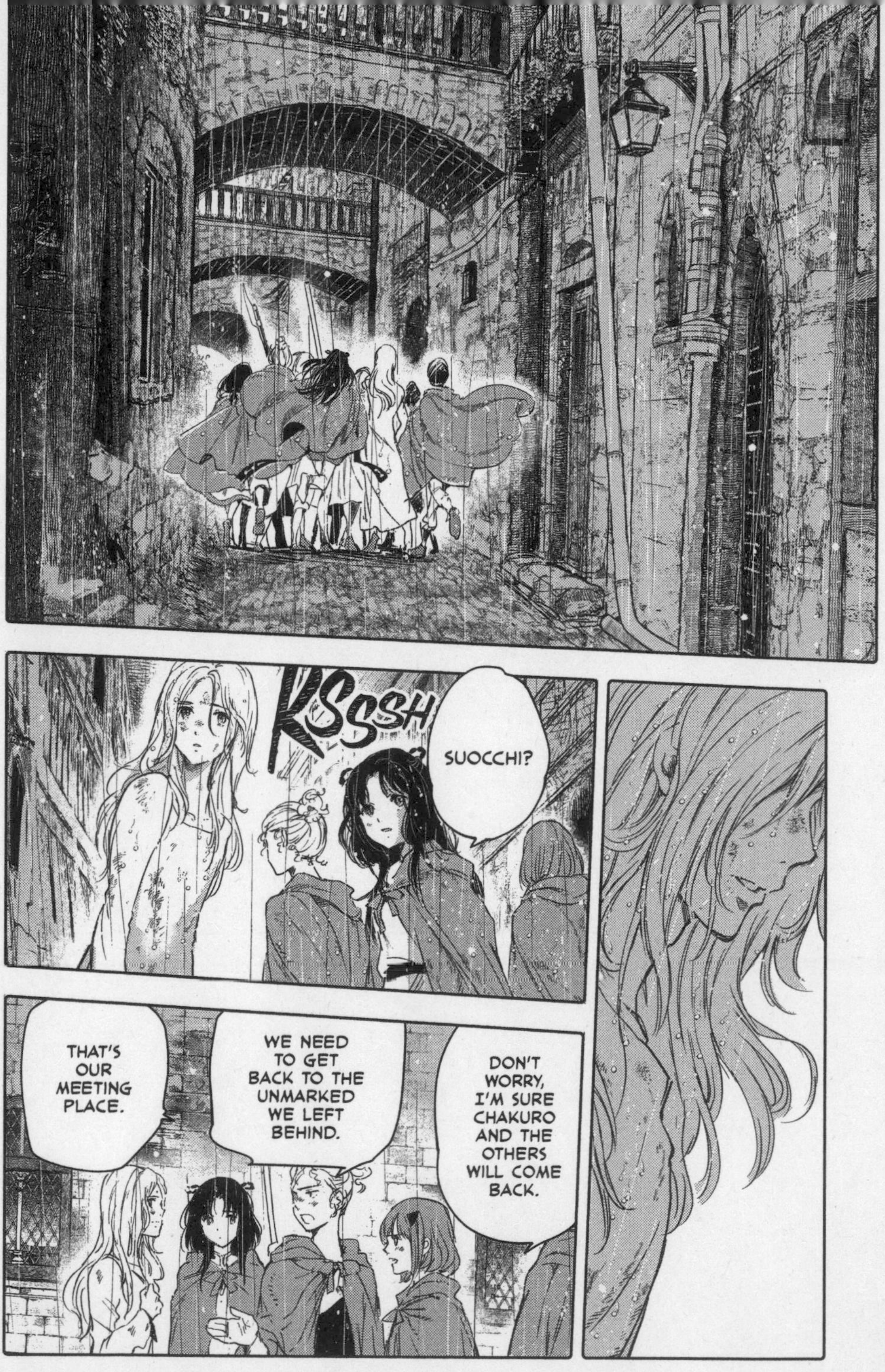
KSSSH
SUOCCHI?
DON'T WORRY, I'M SURE CHAKURO AND THE OTHERS WILL COME BACK.
WE NEED TO GET BACK TO THE UNMARKED WE LEFT BEHIND.
THAT'S OUR MEETING PLACE.

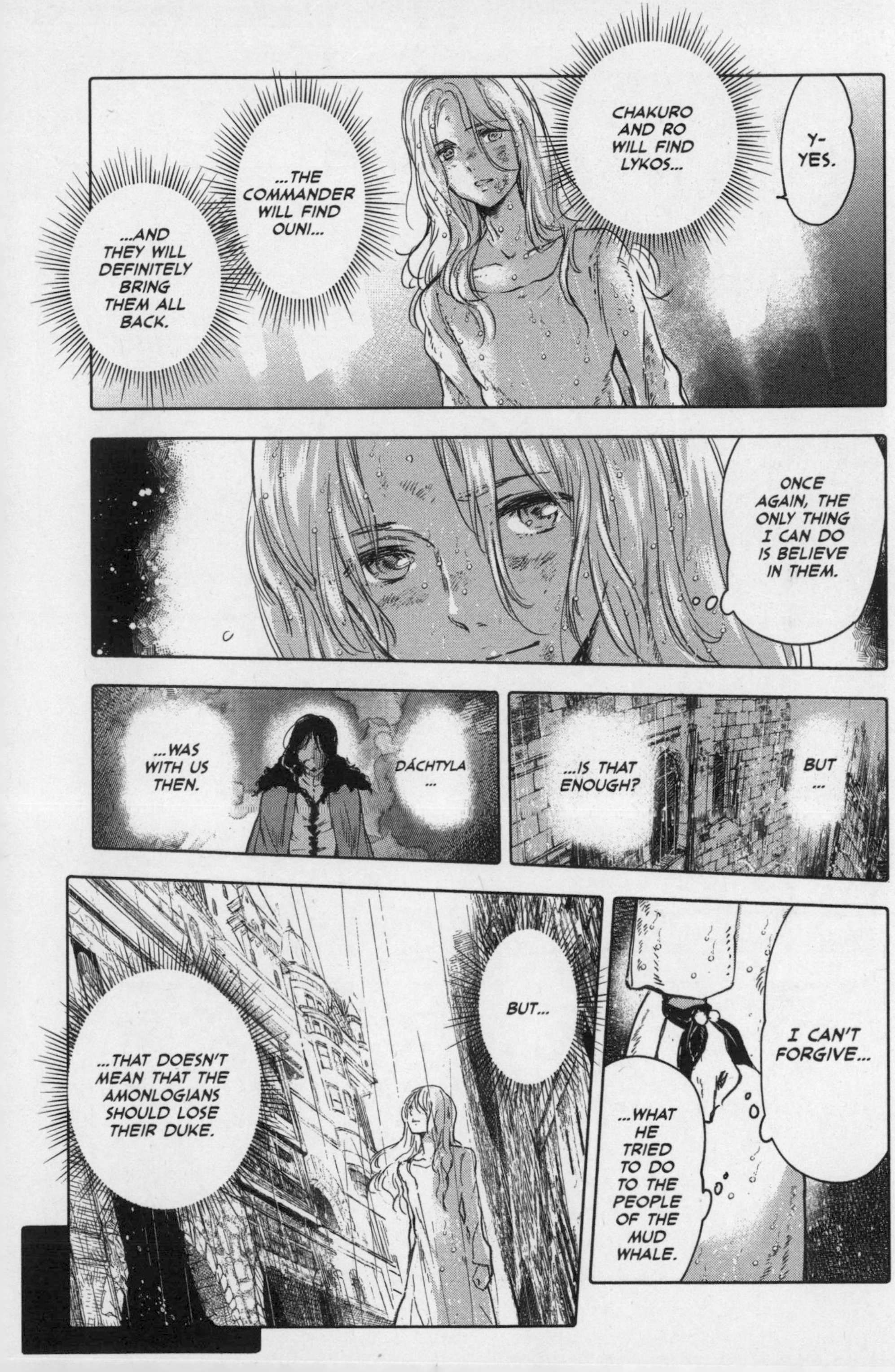
Y- YES.
CHAKURO AND RO WILL FIND LYKOS...
...THE COMMANDER WILL FIND OUNI...
...AND THEY WILL DEFINITELY BRING THEM ALL BACK.
ONCE AGAIN, THE ONLY THING I CAN DO IS BELIEVE IN THEM.
BUT ...
...IS THAT ENOUGH?
DÁCHTYLA ...
...WAS WITH US THEN.
I CAN'T FORGIVE...
...WHAT HE TRIED TO DO TO THE PEOPLE OF THE MUD WHALE.
BUT...
...THAT DOESN'T MEAN THAT THE AMONLOGIANS SHOULD LOSE THEIR DUKE.

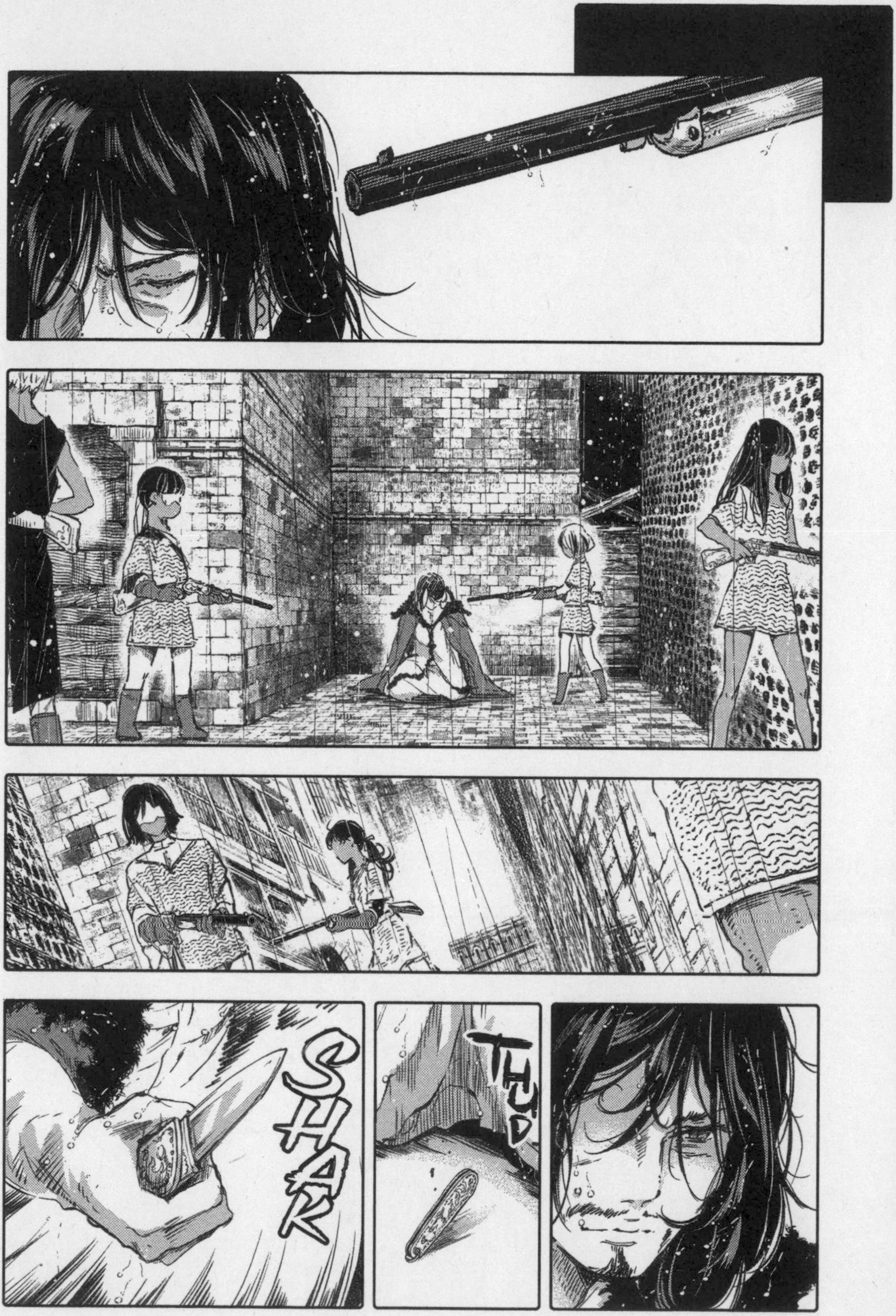
THUD
SHAR

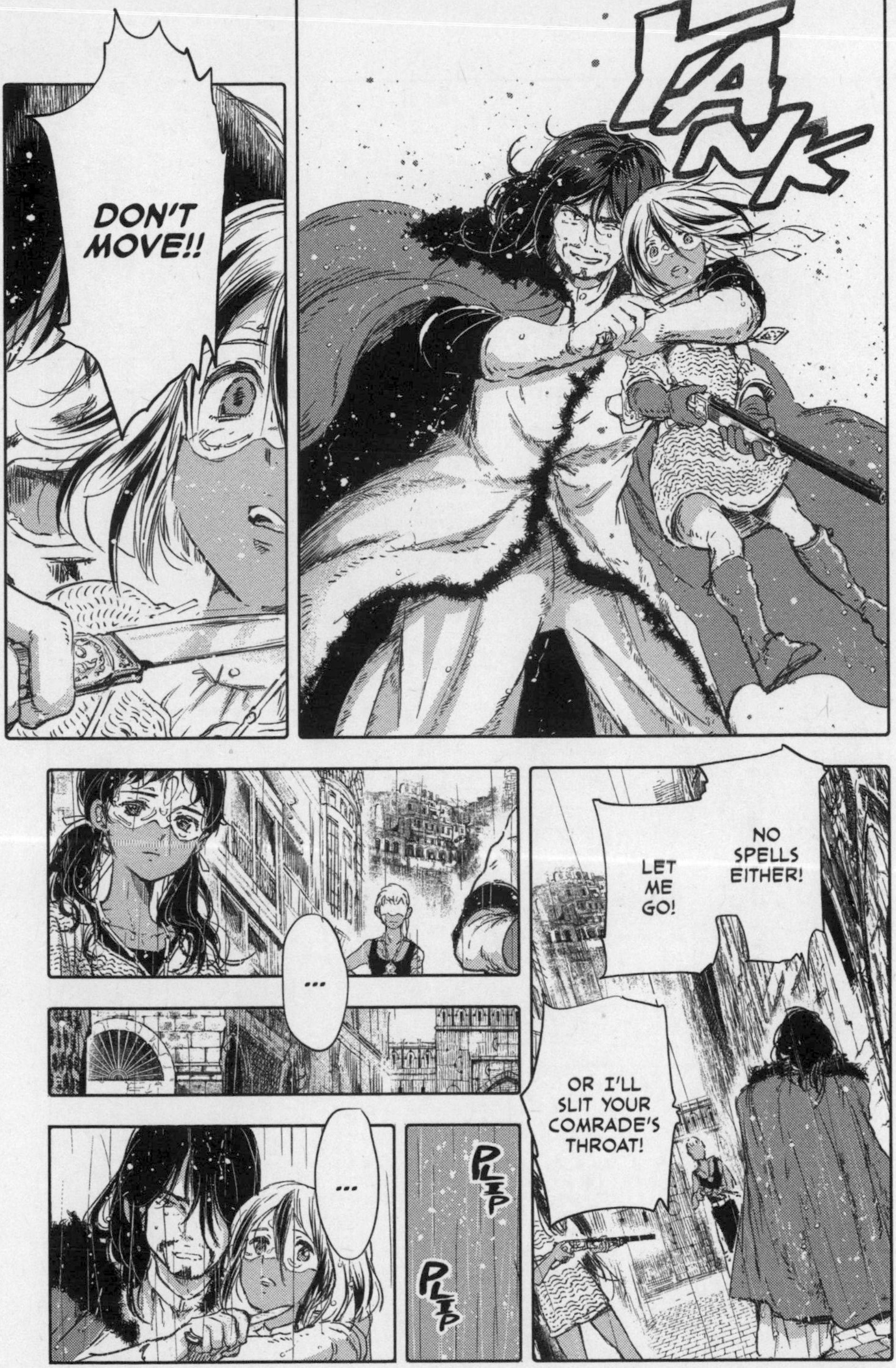
YANK
DON'T MOVE!!
NO SPELLS EITHER! LET ME GO!
OR I'LL SLIT YOUR COMRADE'S THROAT!
...
PLIP
PLIP
...

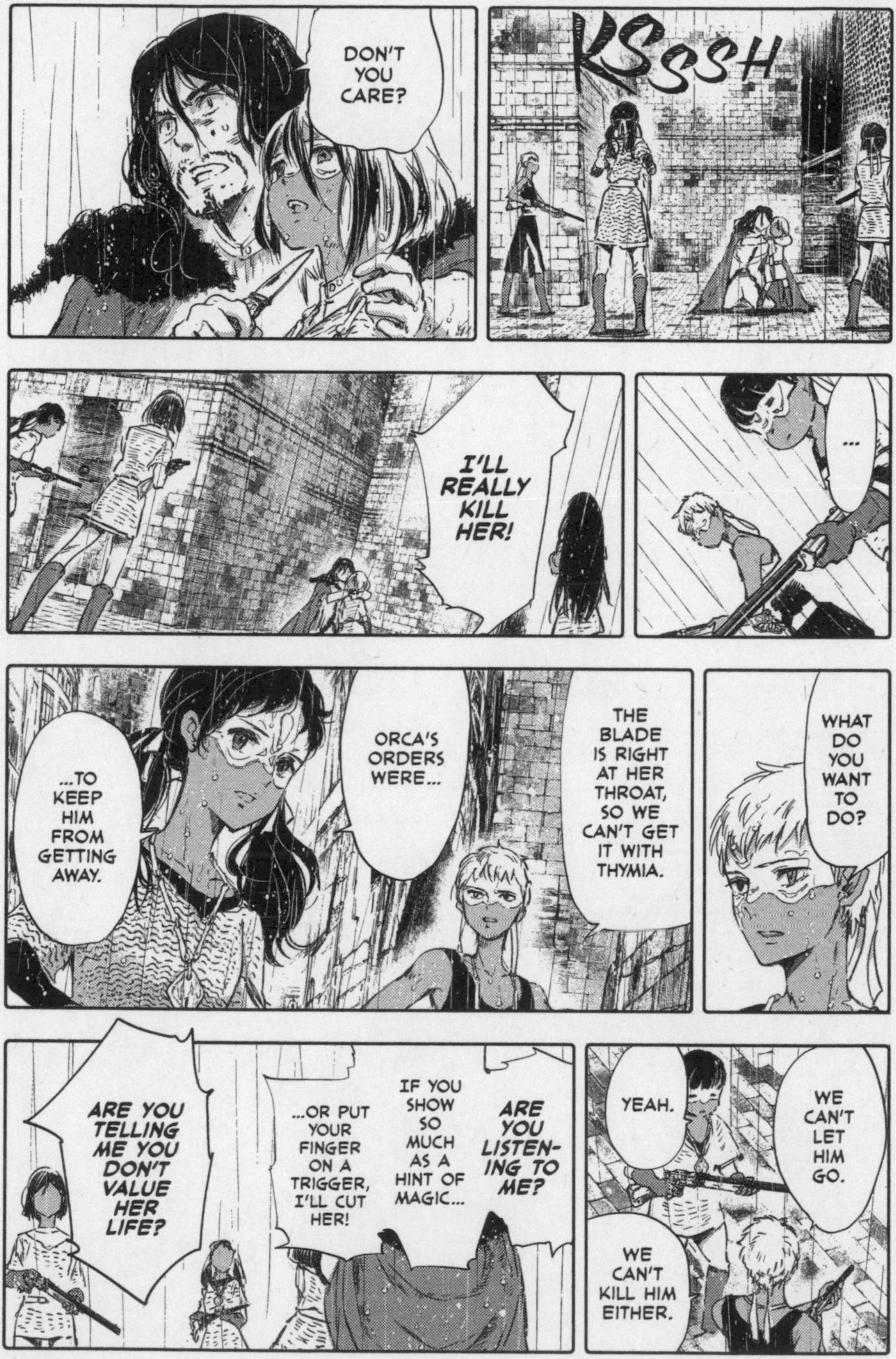
KSSSH
DON'T YOU CARE?
...
I'LL REALLY KILL HER!
WHAT DO YOU WANT TO DO?
THE BLADE IS RIGHT AT HER THROAT, SO WE CAN'T GET IT WITH THYMIA.
ORCA'S ORDERS WERE...
...TO KEEP HIM FROM GETTING AWAY.
WE CAN'T LET HIM GO.
YEAH.
WE CAN'T KILL HIM EITHER.
ARE YOU LISTENING TO ME?
IF YOU SHOW SO MUCH AS A HINT OF MAGIC...
...OR PUT YOUR FINGER ON A TRIGGER, I'LL CUT HER!
ARE YOU TELLING ME YOU DON'T VALUE HER LIFE?

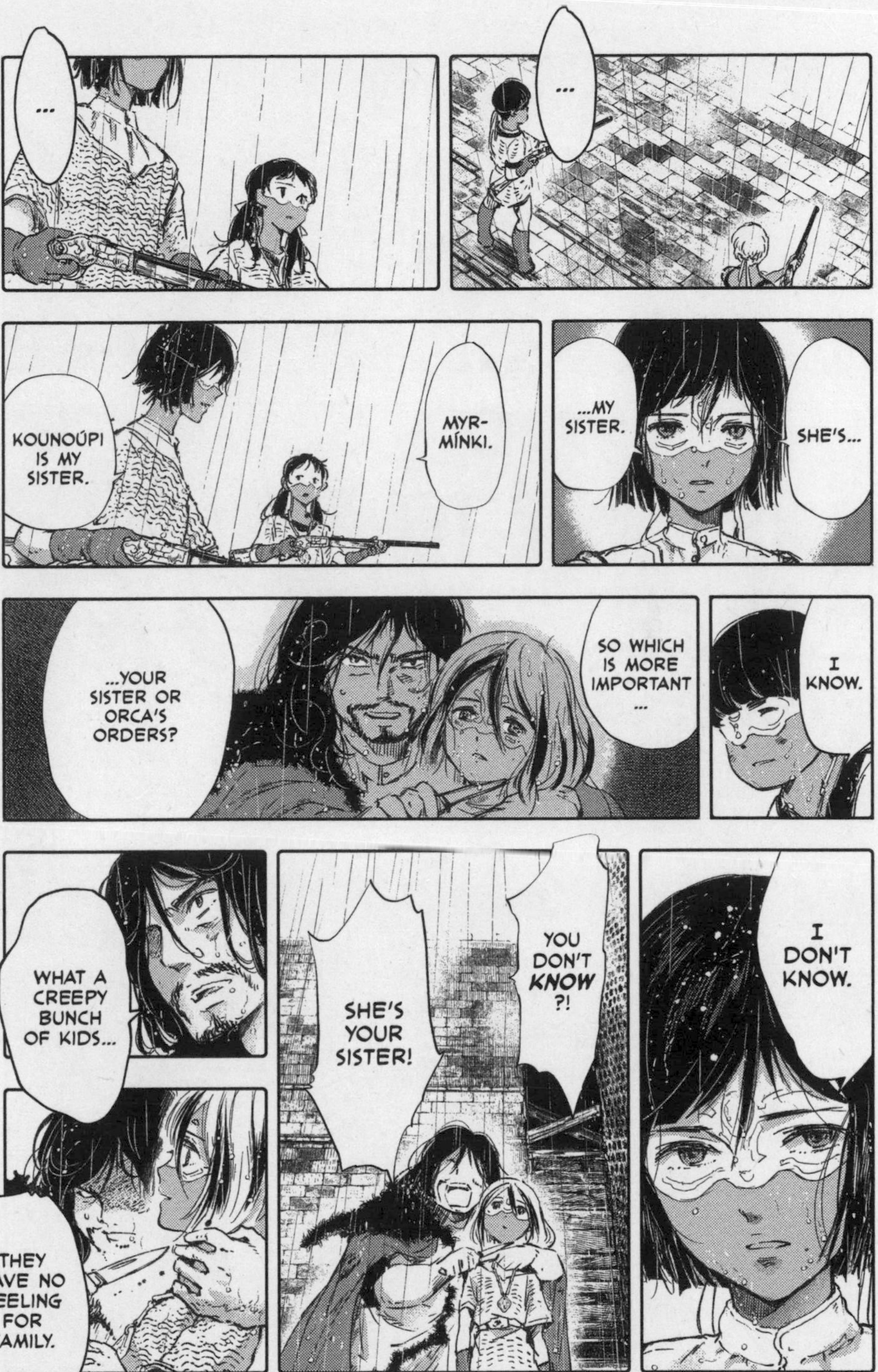
...
...
SHE'S...
...MY SISTER.
MYR-MÍNKI.
KOUNOÚPI IS MY SISTER.
I KNOW.
SO WHICH IS MORE IMPORTANT ...
...YOUR SISTER OR ORCA'S ORDERS?
I DON'T KNOW.
YOU DON'T *KNOW*?!
SHE'S YOUR SISTER!
WHAT A CREEPY BUNCH OF KIDS...
THEY HAVE NO FEELING FOR FAMILY.

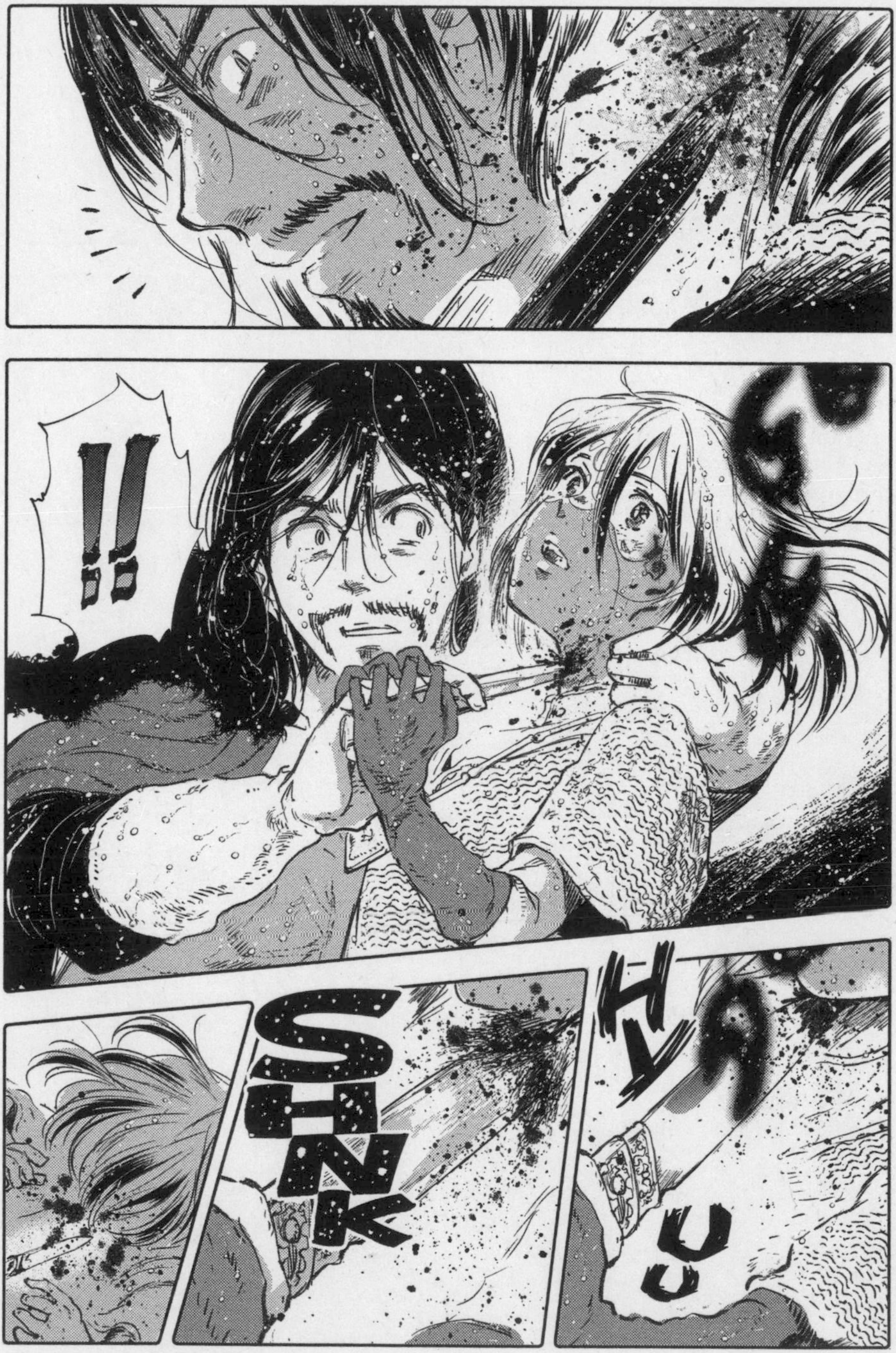
!!
HYUU
SHINK

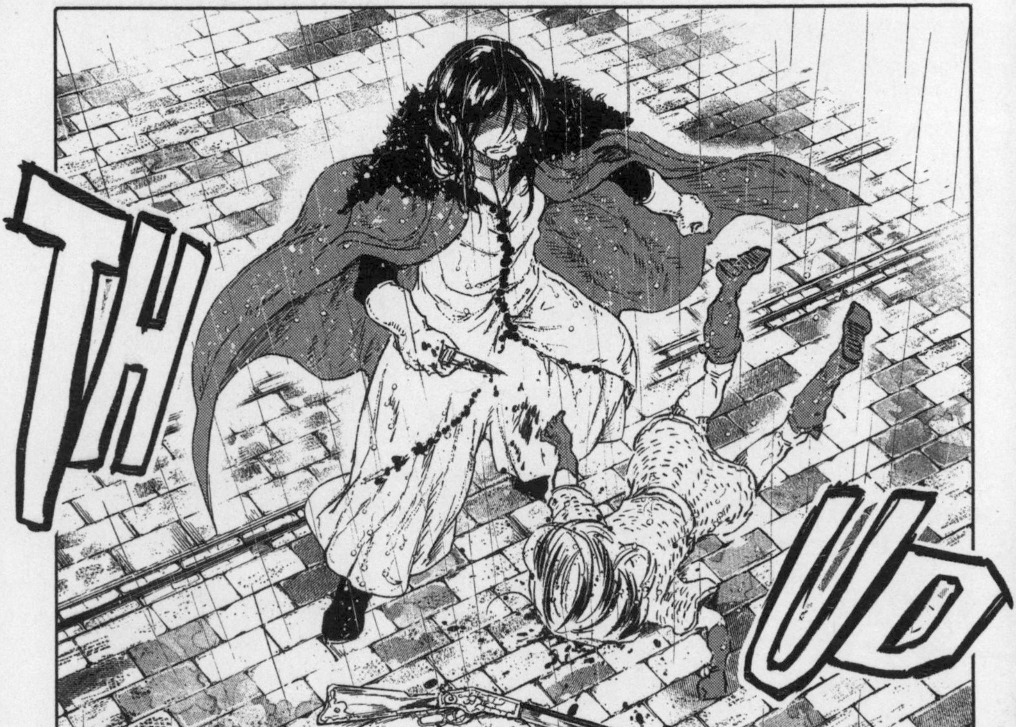
THUD
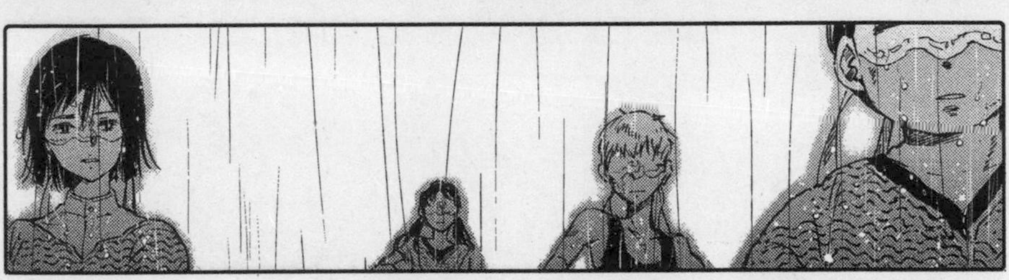
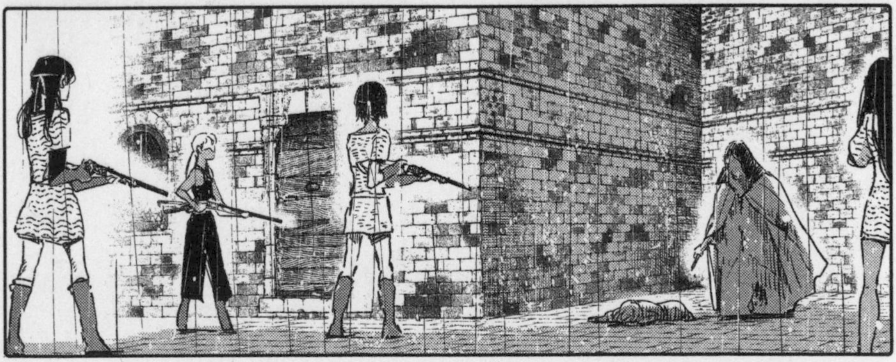

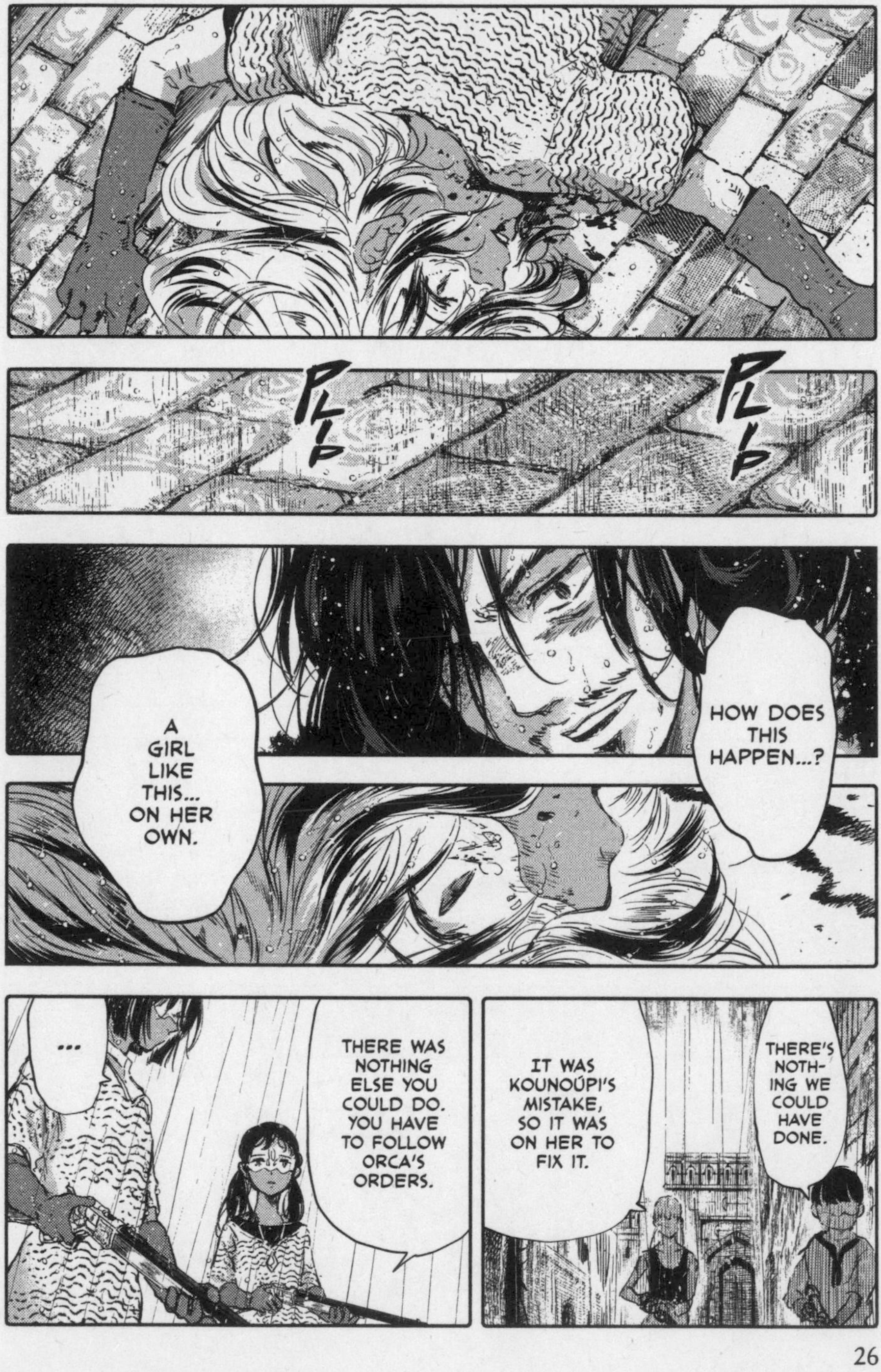
PLIP
PLIP
HOW DOES THIS HAPPEN...?
A GIRL LIKE THIS... ON HER OWN.
THERE'S NOTHING WE COULD HAVE DONE.
IT WAS KOUNOÚPI'S MISTAKE, SO IT WAS ON HER TO FIX IT.
THERE WAS NOTHING ELSE YOU COULD DO. YOU HAVE TO FOLLOW ORCA'S ORDERS.
...

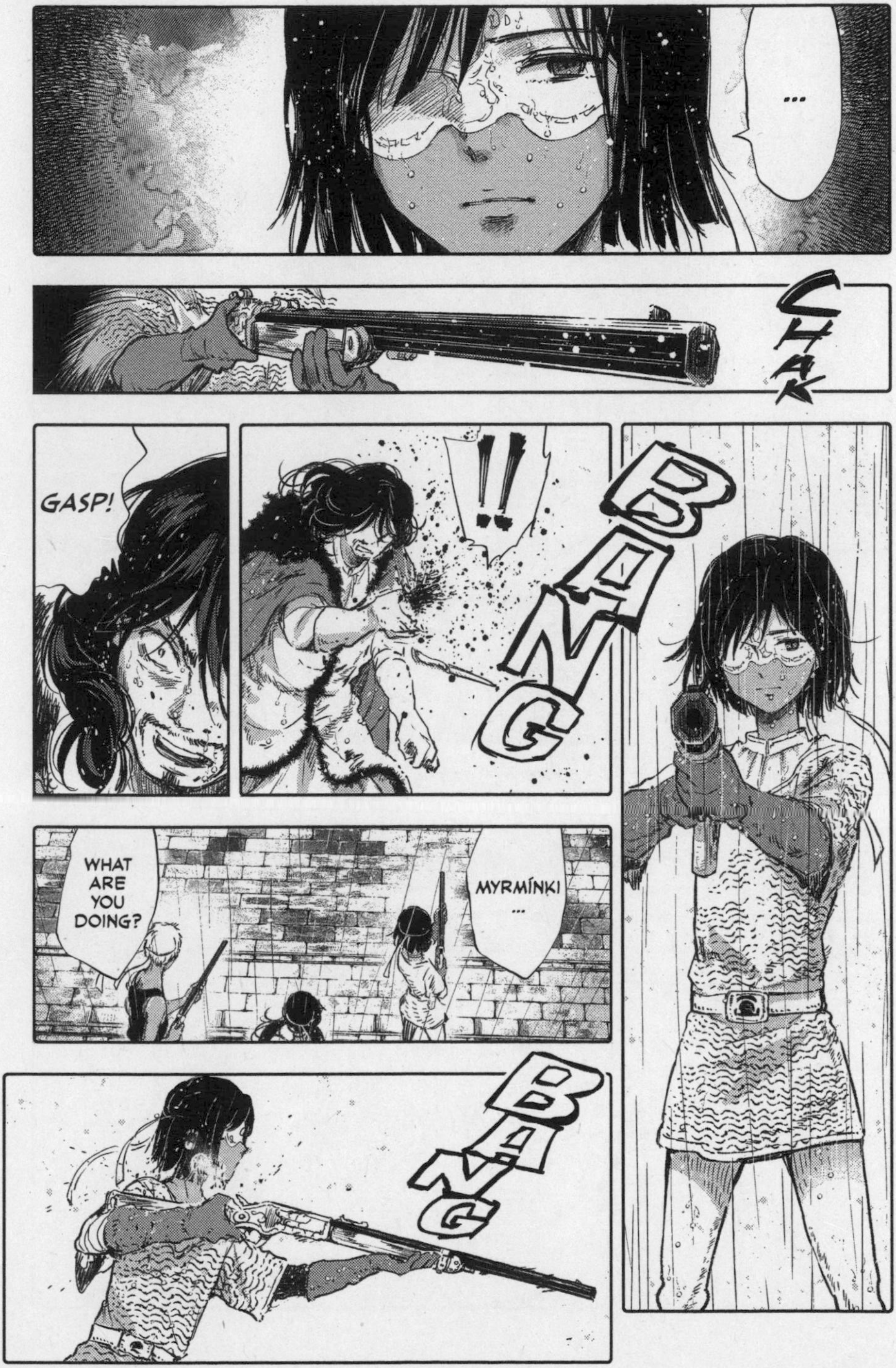
...
CHAK
BANG
!!
GASP!
MYRMÍNKI ...
WHAT ARE YOU DOING?
BANG

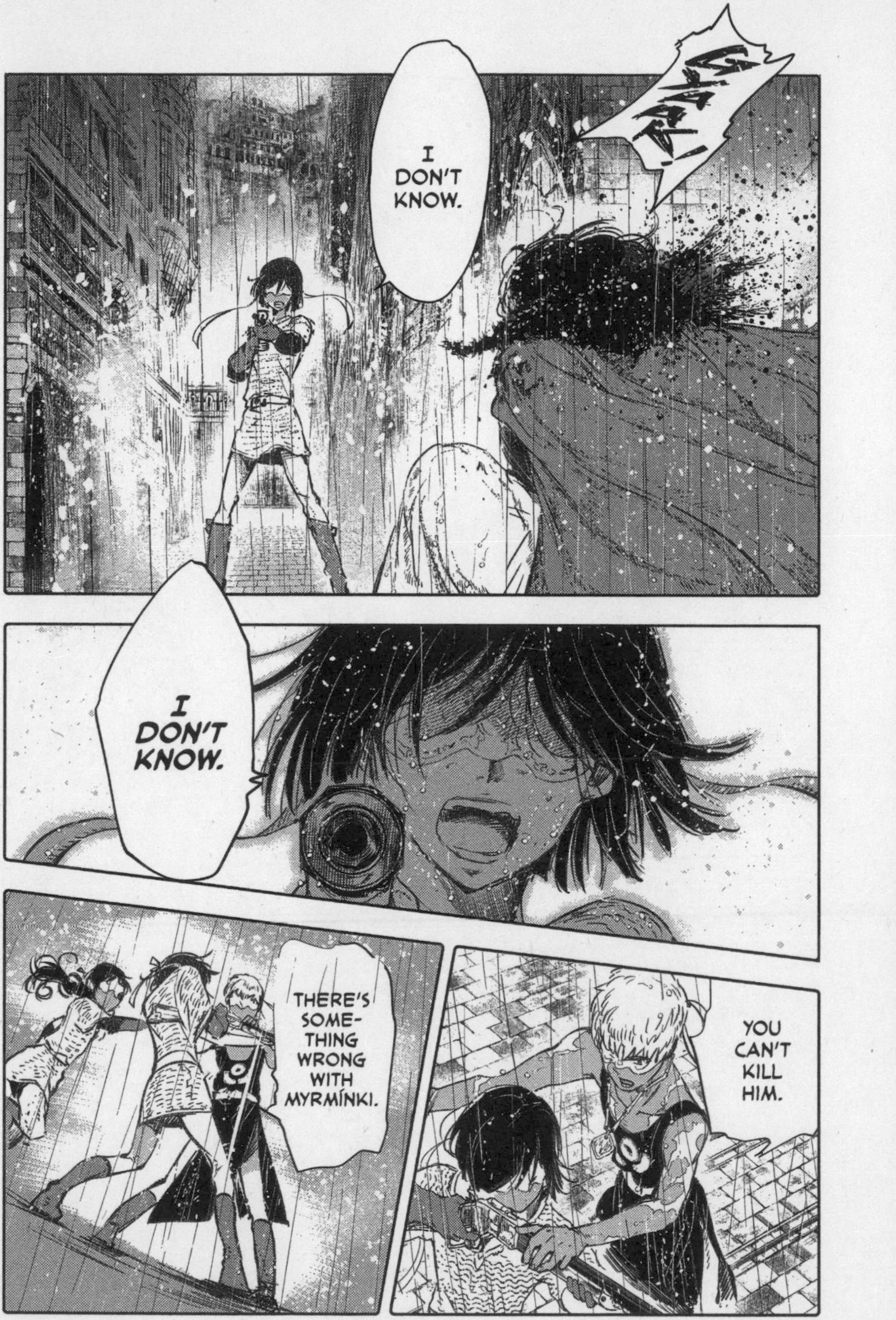
I DON'T KNOW.
I DON'T KNOW.
YOU CAN'T KILL HIM.
THERE'S SOME-THING WRONG WITH MYRMÍNKI.

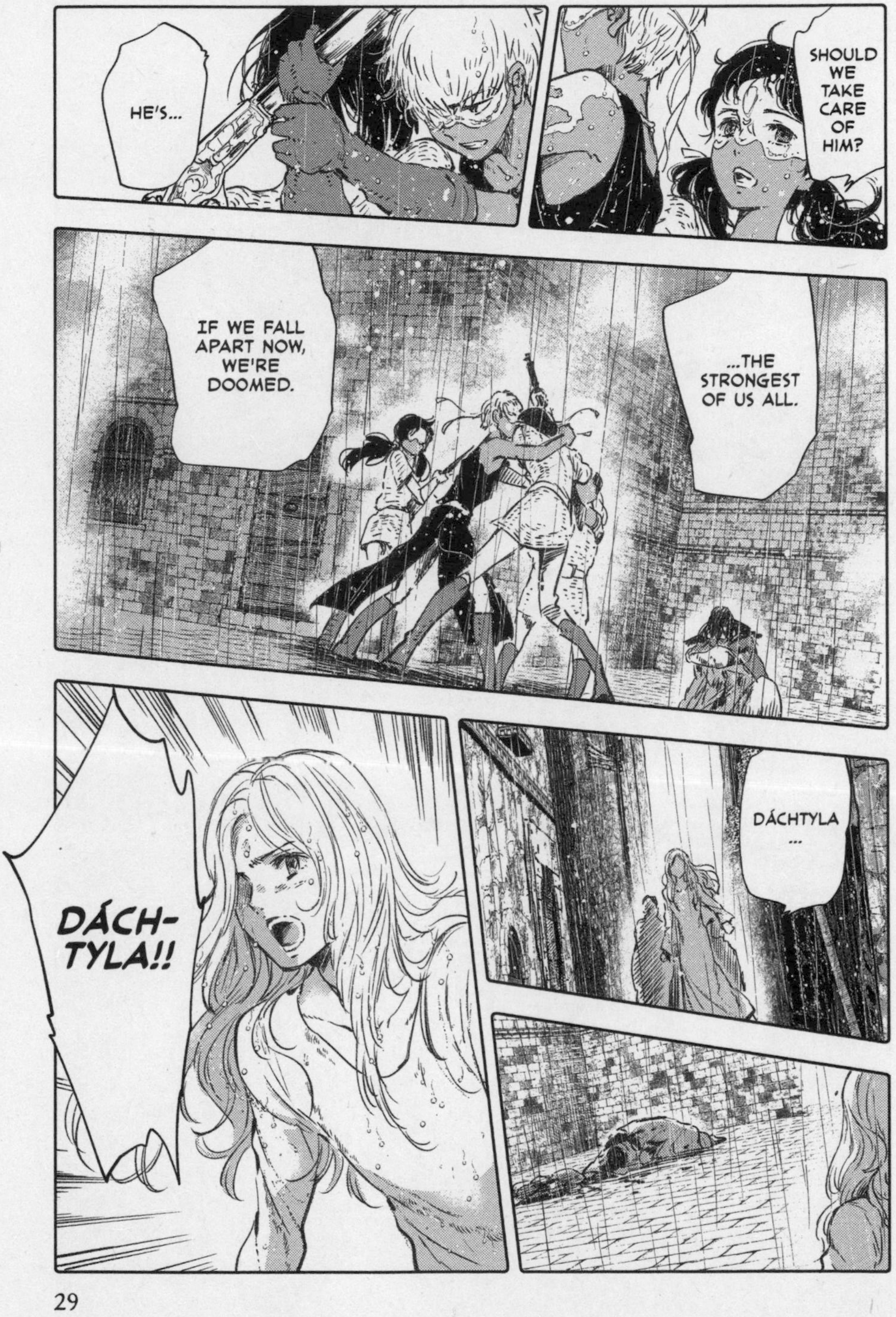
SHOULD WE TAKE CARE OF HIM?
HE'S...
...THE STRONGEST OF US ALL.
IF WE FALL APART NOW, WE'RE DOOMED.
DÁCHTYLA ...
DÁCH-TYLA!!

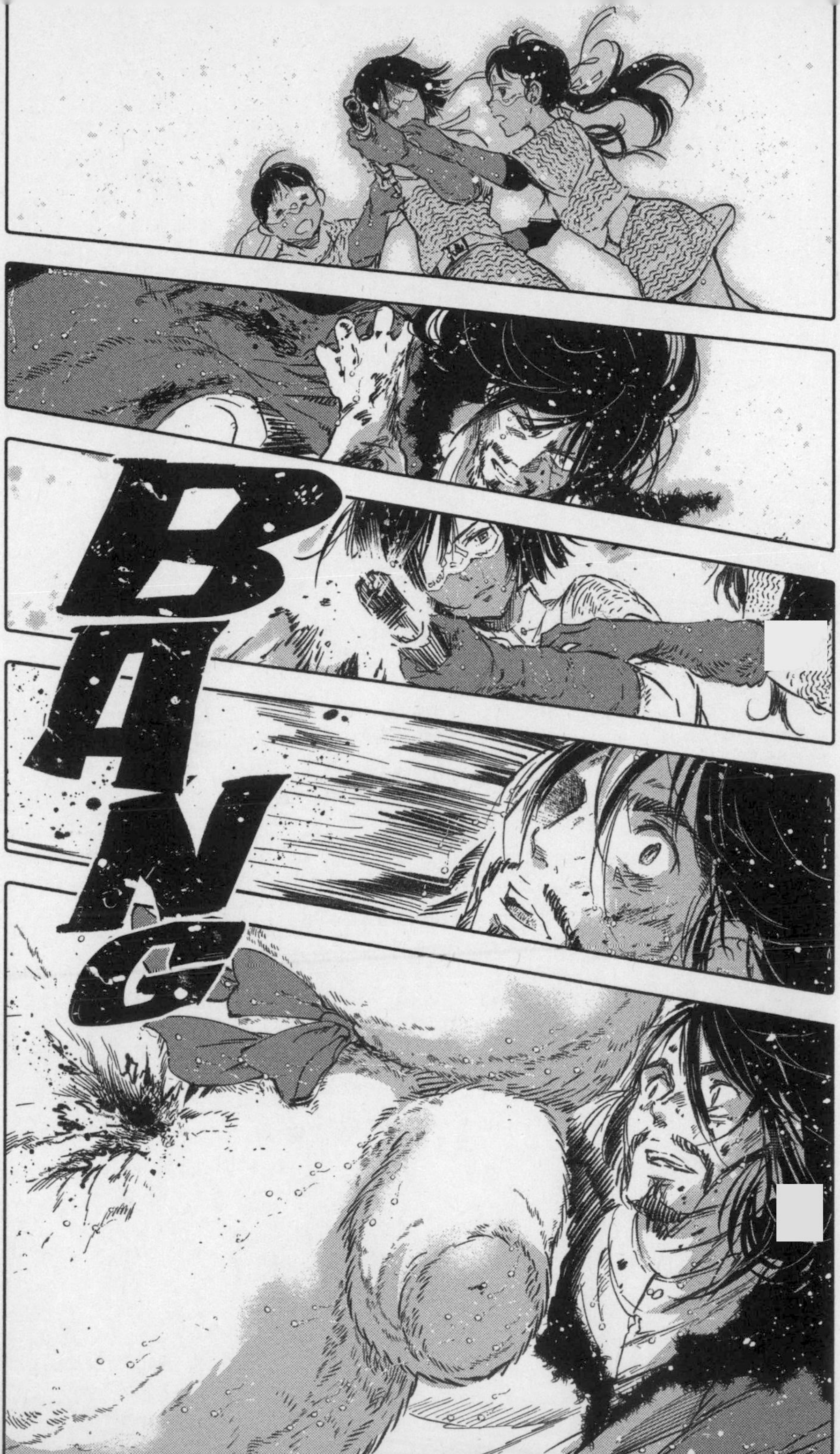
BANG

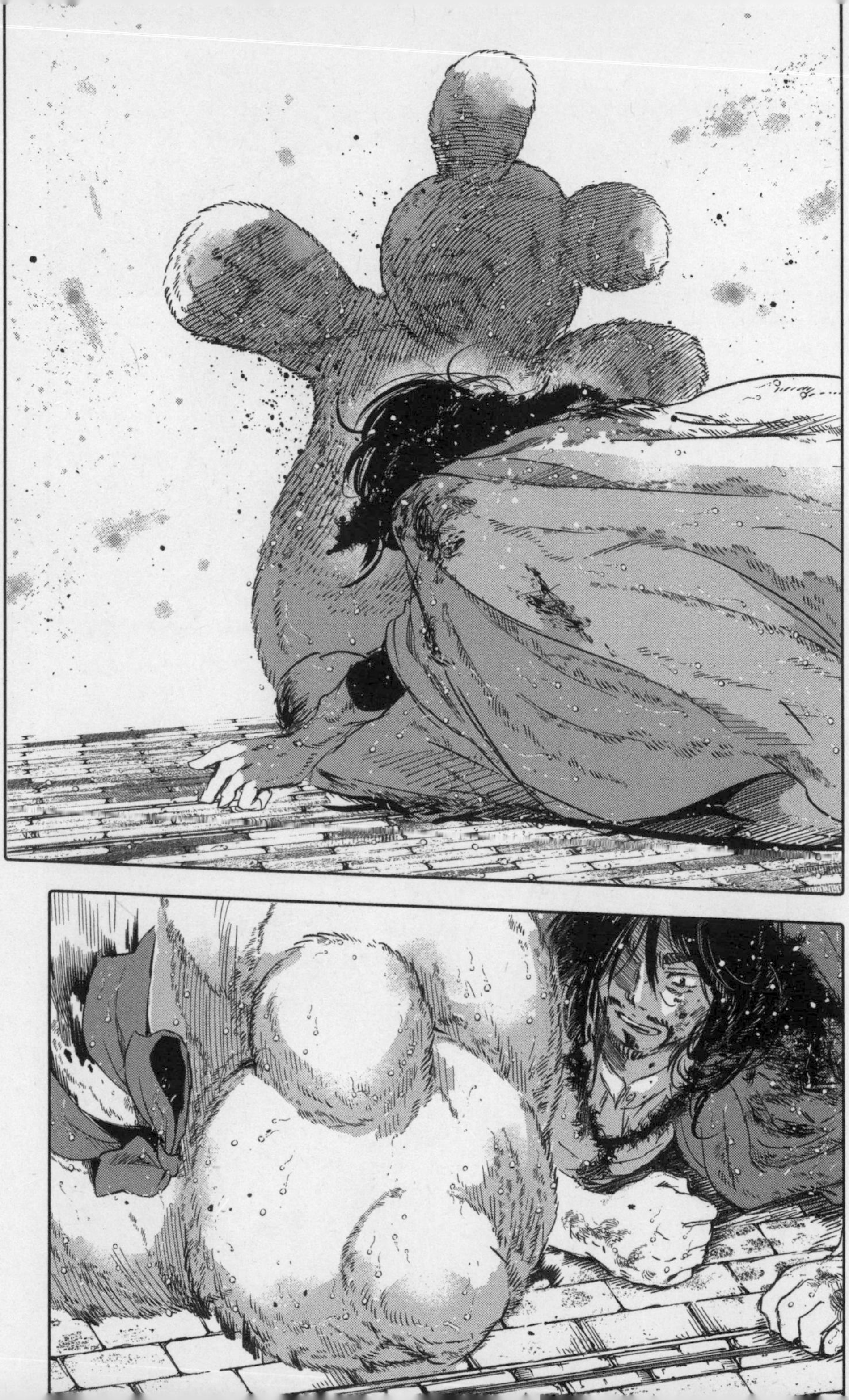

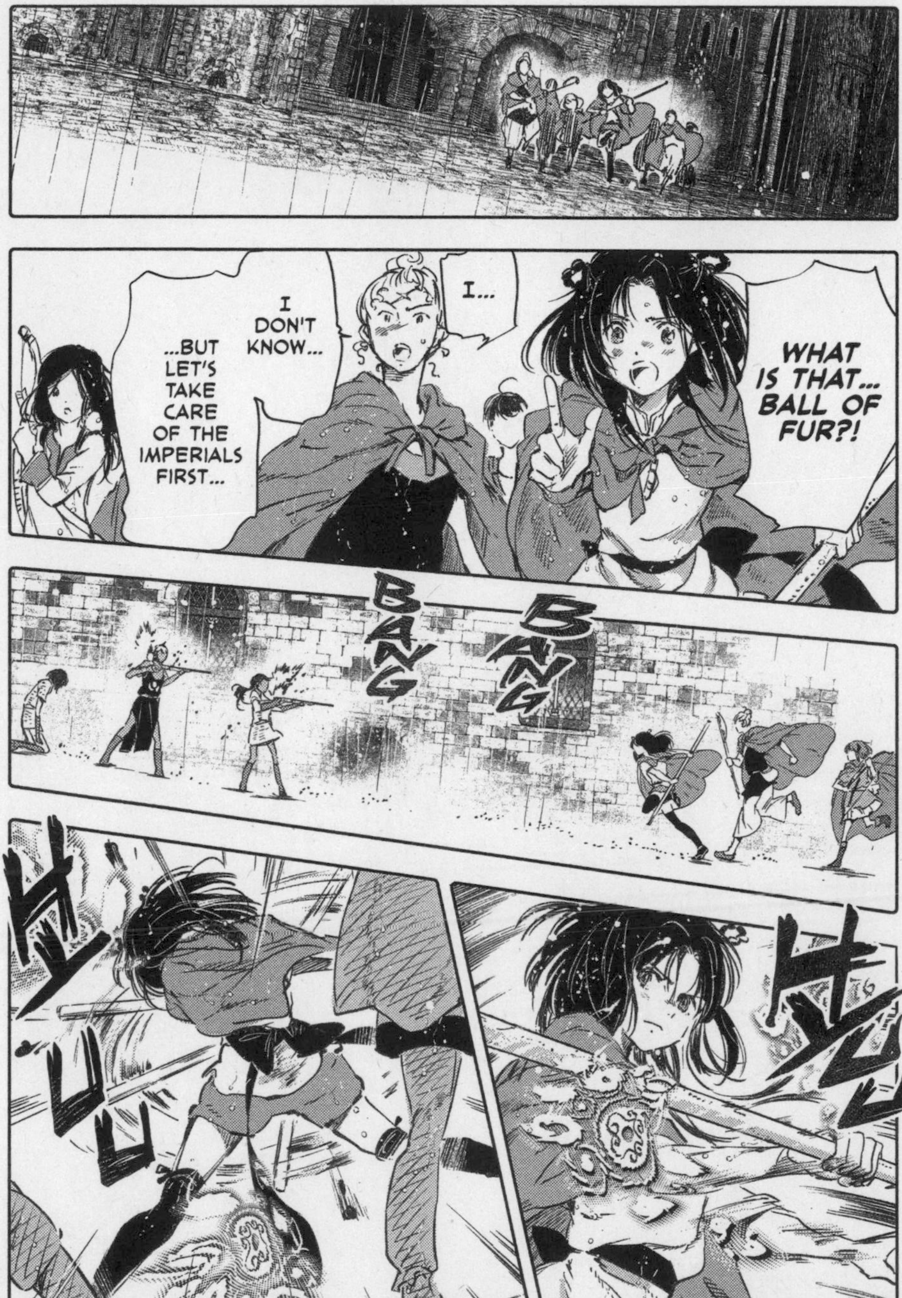
WHAT IS THAT... BALL OF FUR?!
I...
I DON'T KNOW...
...BUT LET'S TAKE CARE OF THE IMPERIALS FIRST...
BANG
BANG

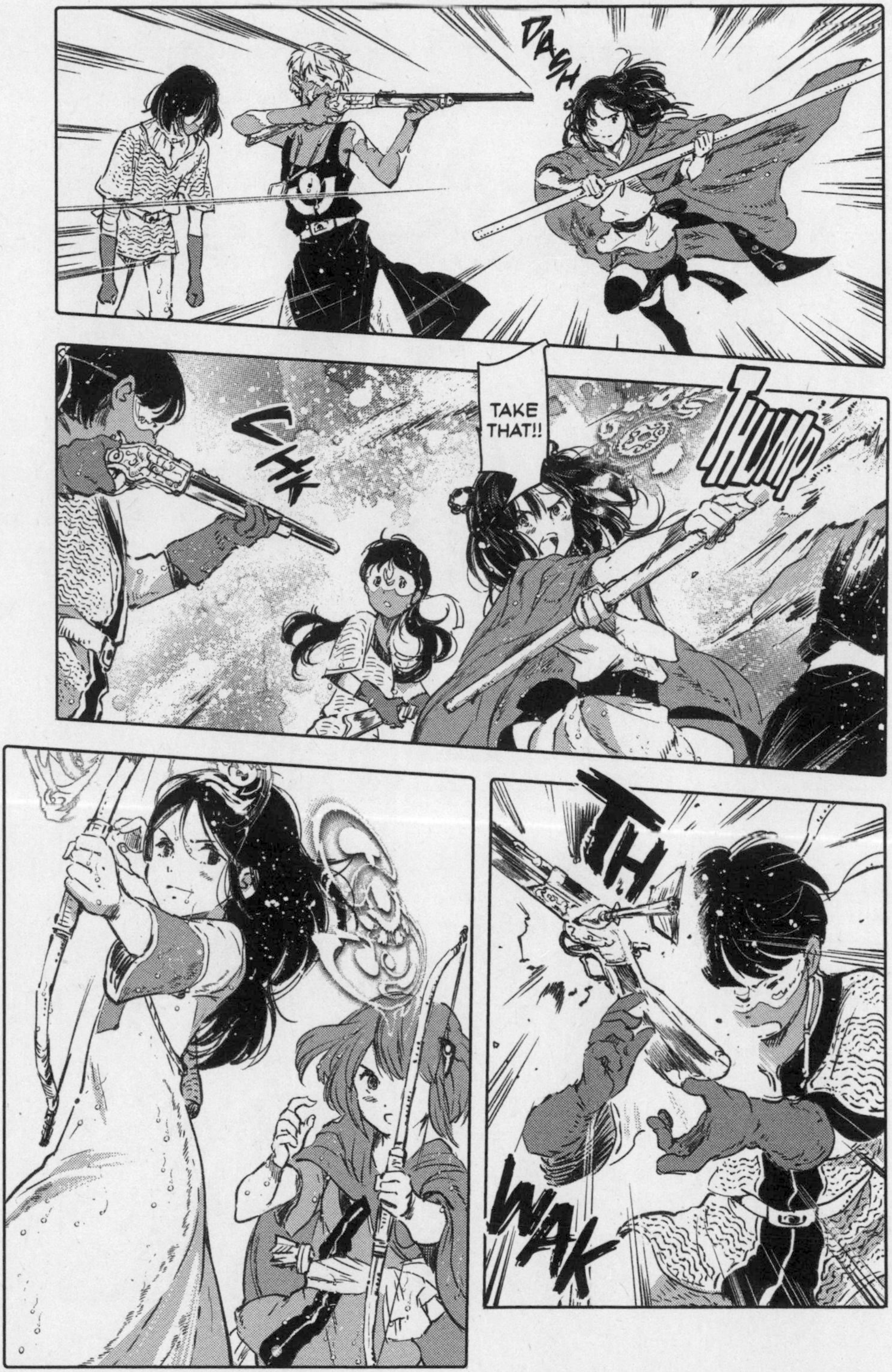
DASH
THUMP
TAKE THAT!!
CHK
TH
WAK

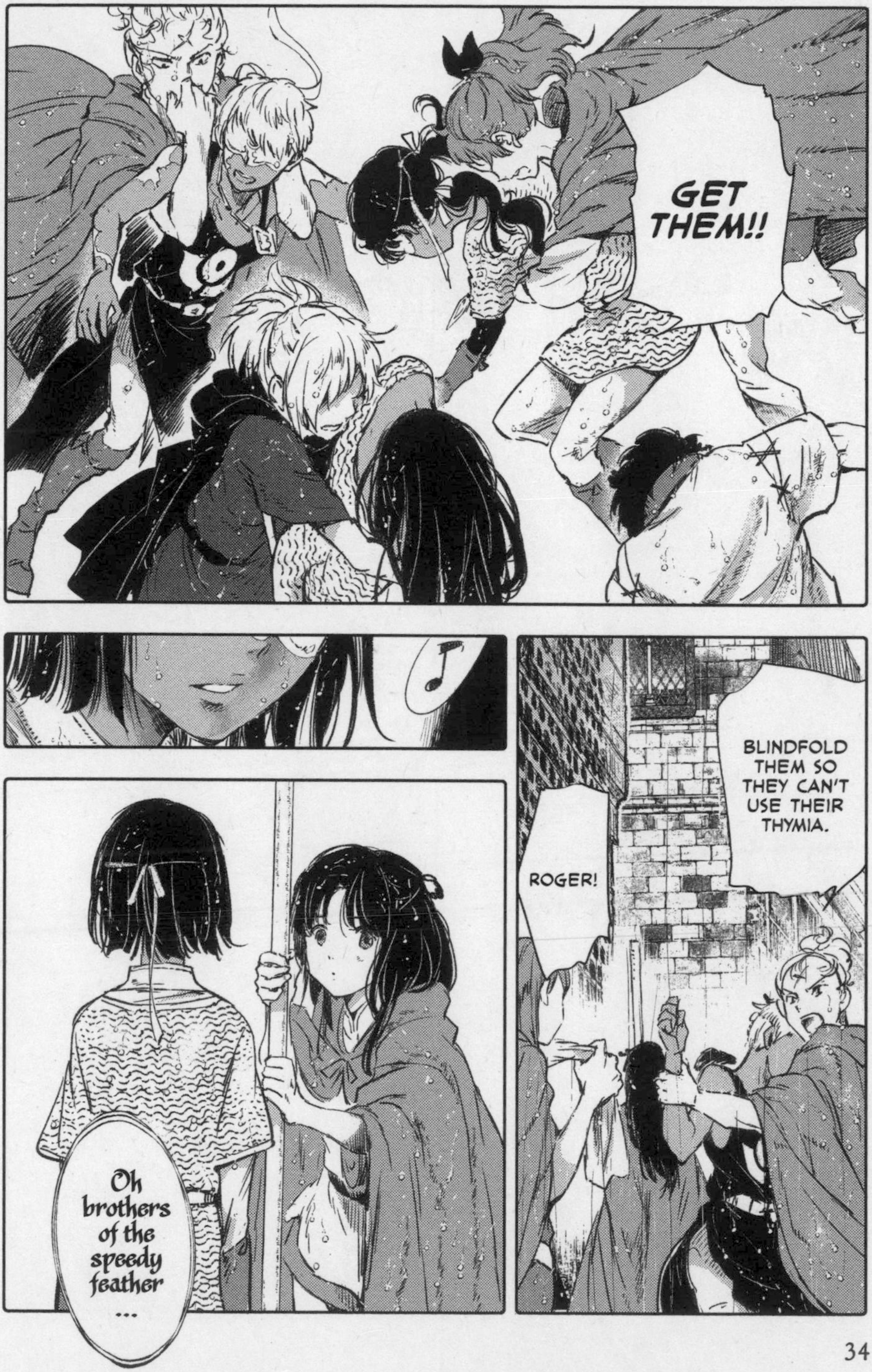
GET THEM!!
BLINDFOLD THEM SO THEY CAN'T USE THEIR THYMIA.
ROGER!
Oh brothers of the speedy feather ...

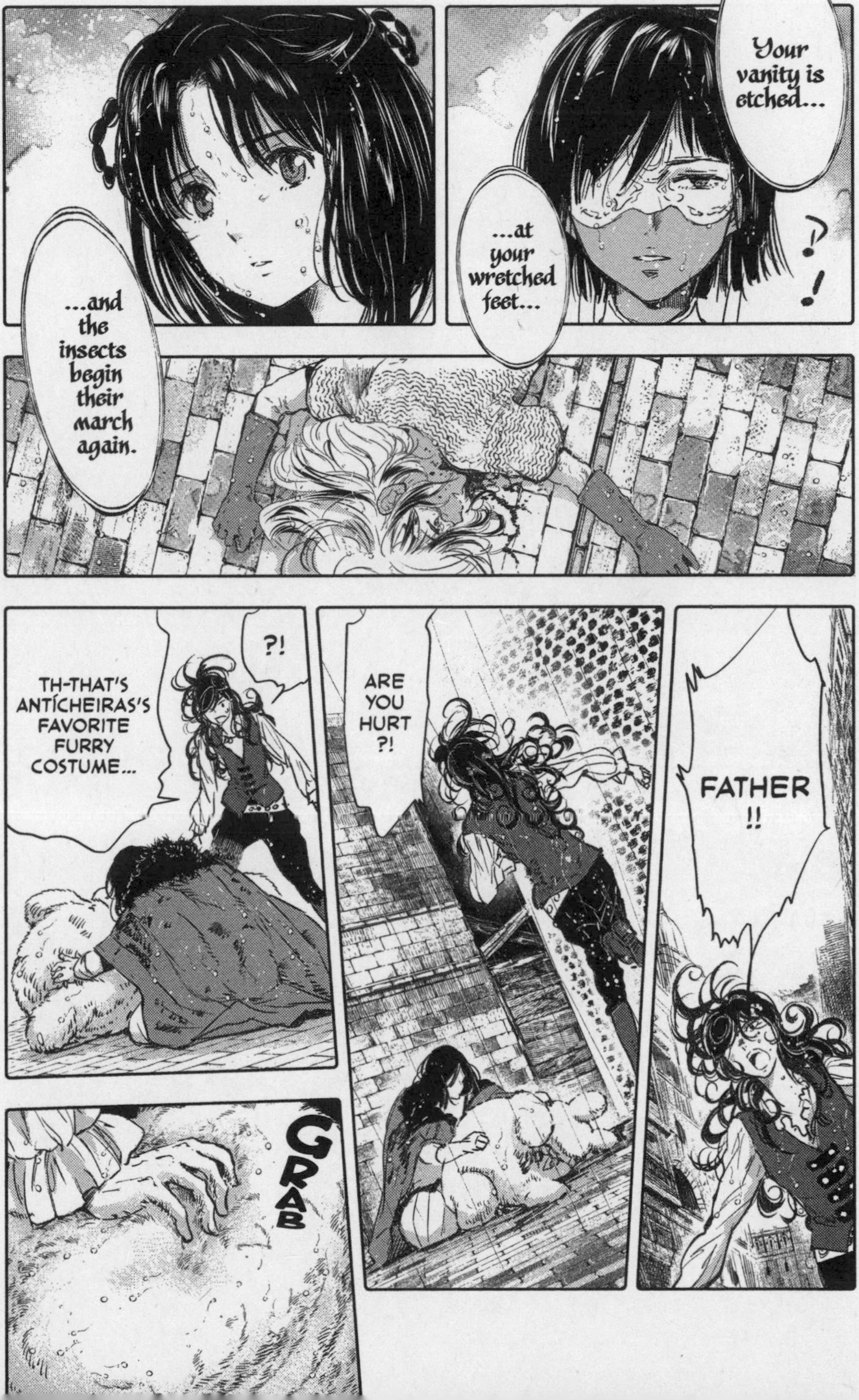
Your vanity is etched...
...at your wretched feet...
?!
...and the insects begin their march again.
FATHER!!
ARE YOU HURT?!
?!
TH-THAT'S ANTÍCHEIRAS'S FAVORITE FURRY COSTUME...
GRAB

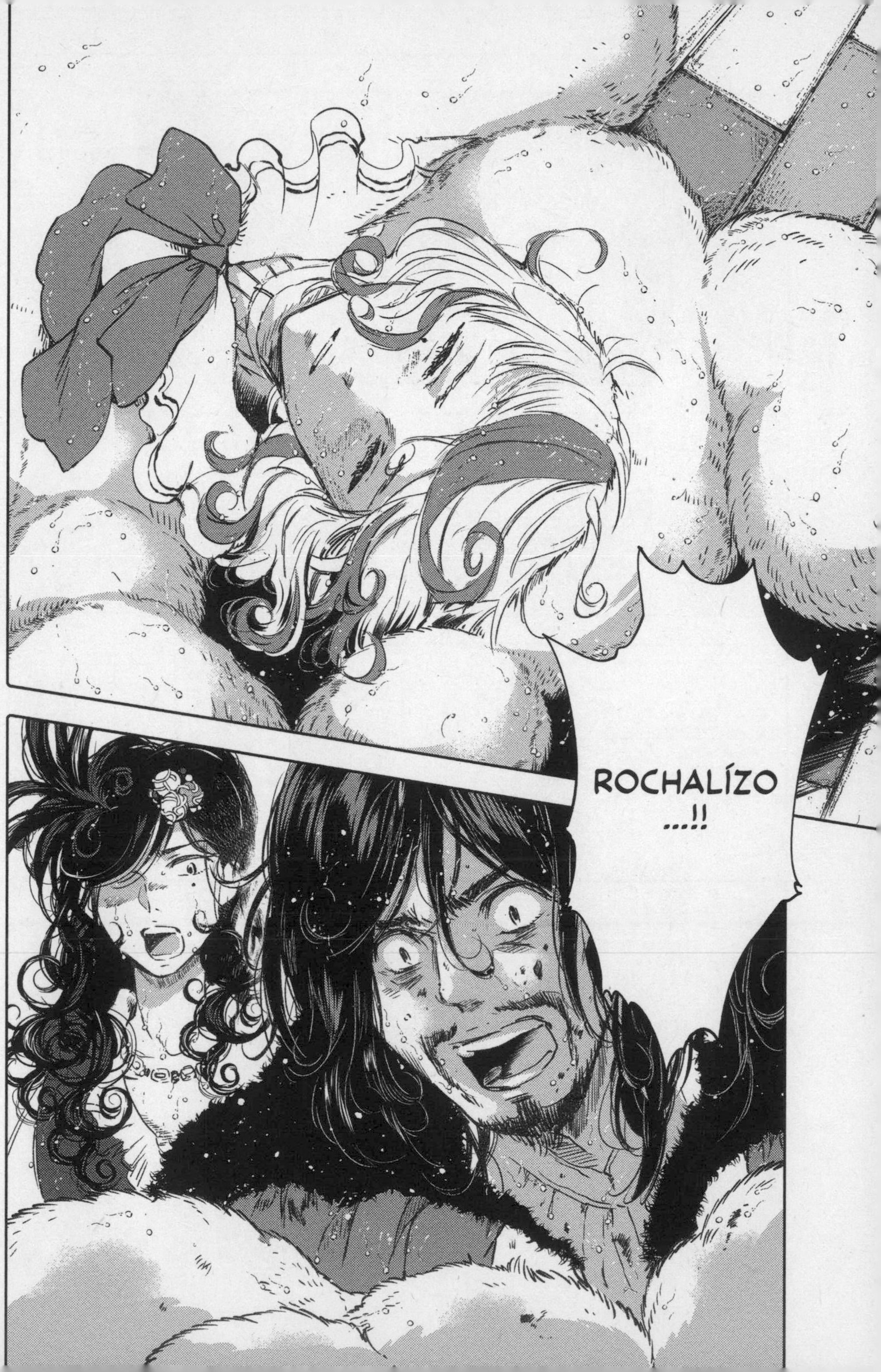
ROCHALÍZO
...!!

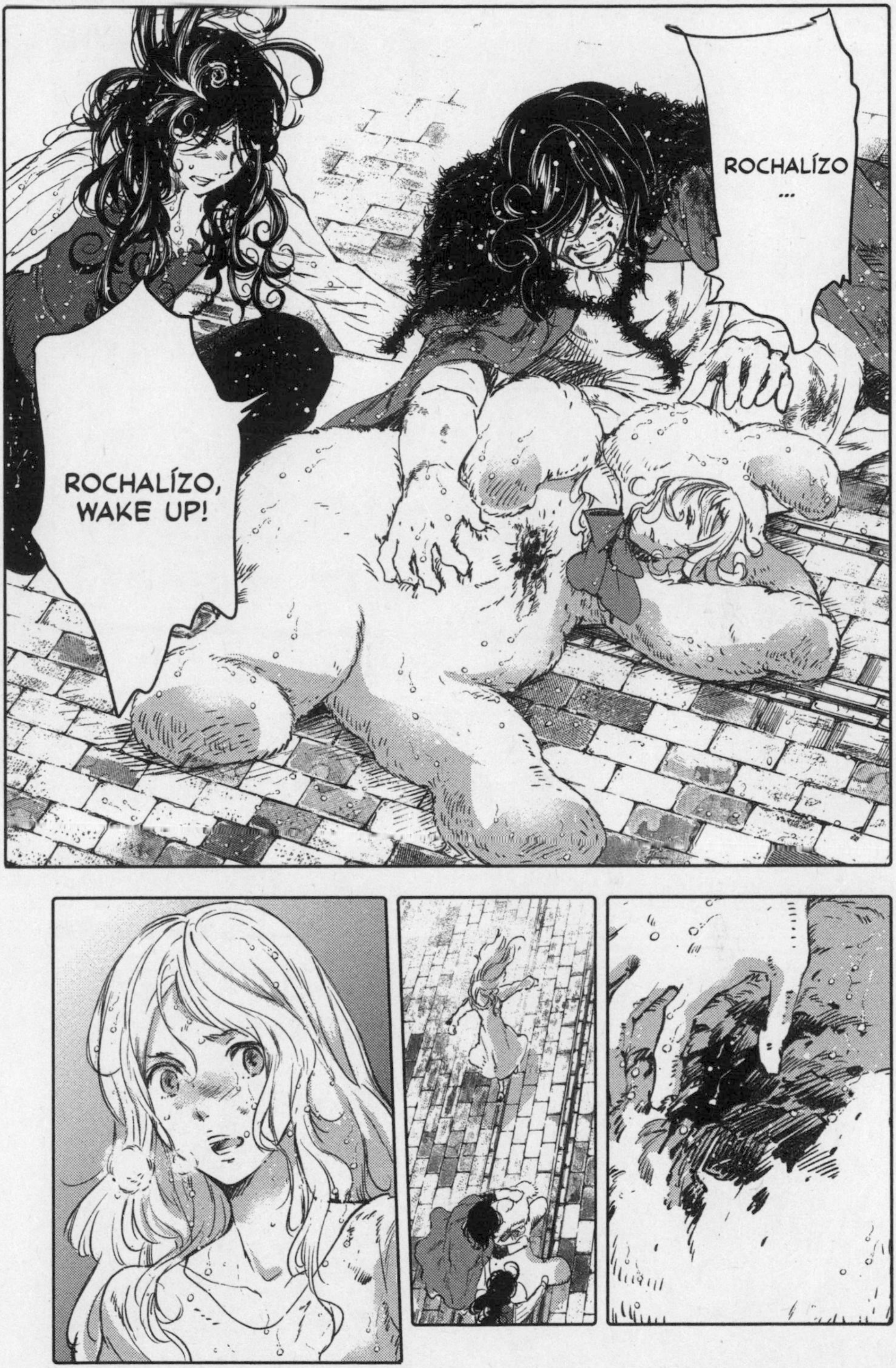
ROCHALÍZO ...
ROCHALÍZO, WAKE UP!

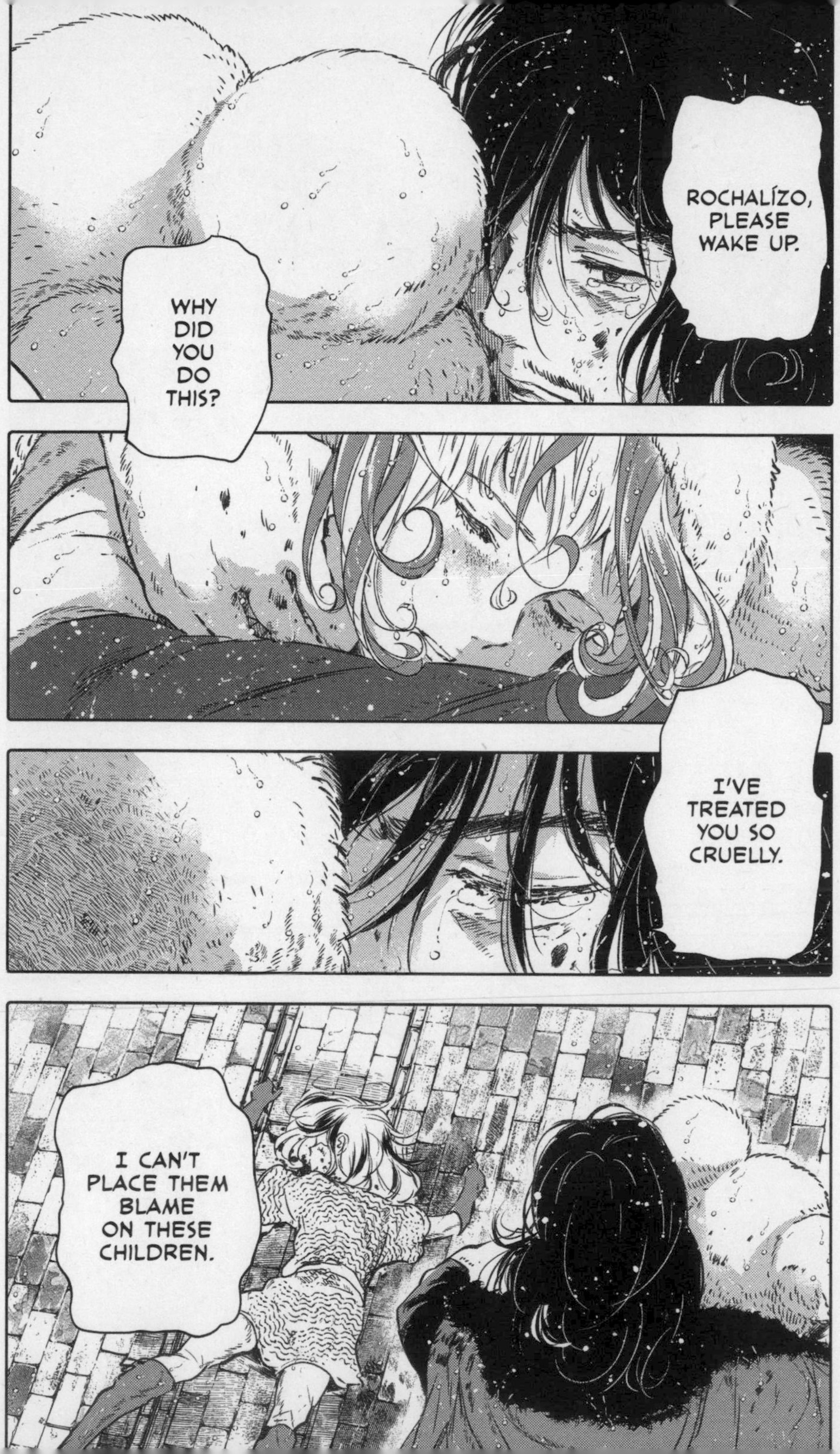
ROCHALÍZO, PLEASE WAKE UP.
WHY DID YOU DO THIS?
I'VE TREATED YOU SO CRUELLY.
I CAN'T PLACE THEM BLAME ON THESE CHILDREN.

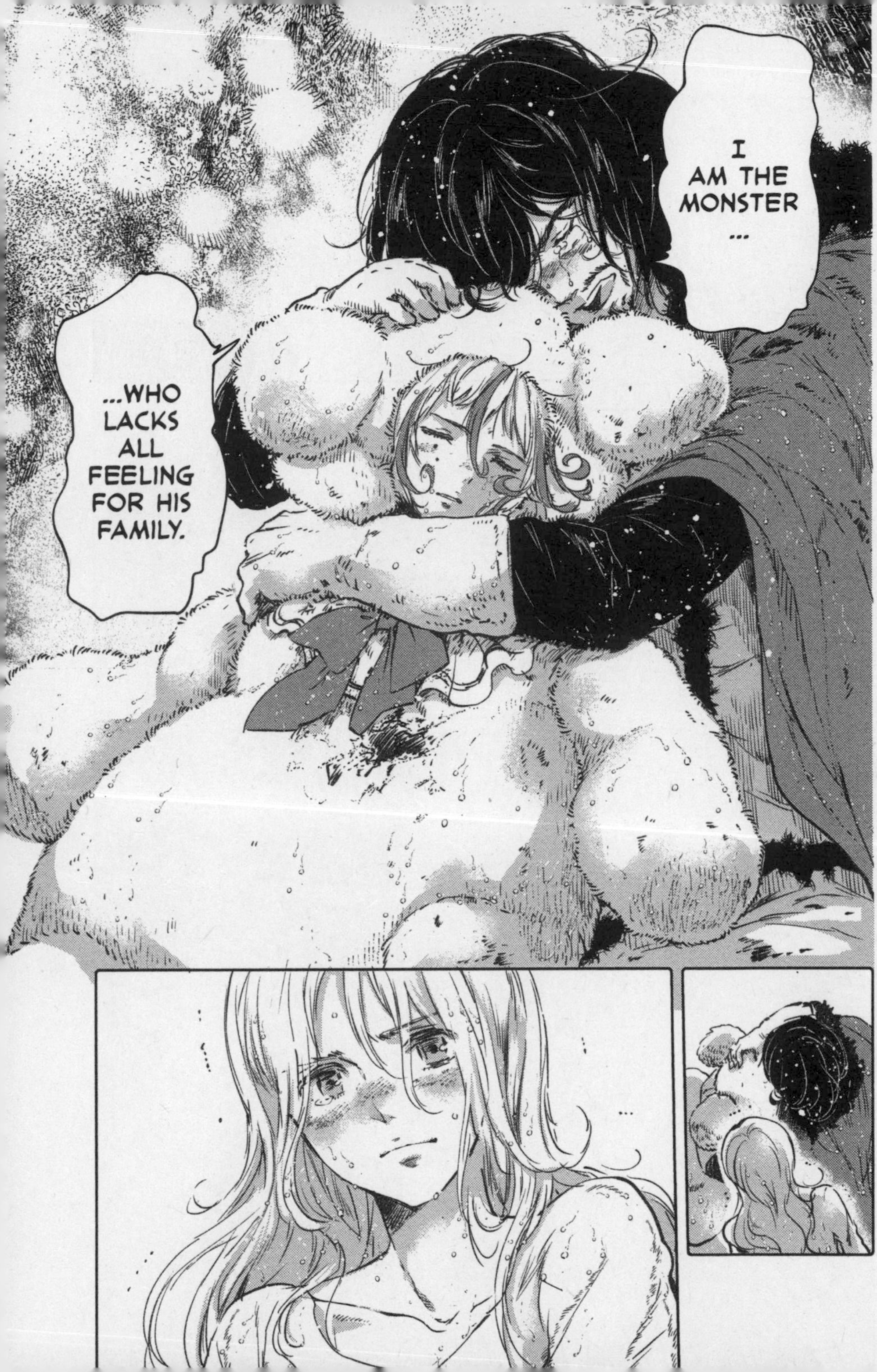
I AM THE MONSTER ...
...WHO LACKS ALL FEELING FOR HIS FAMILY.
...

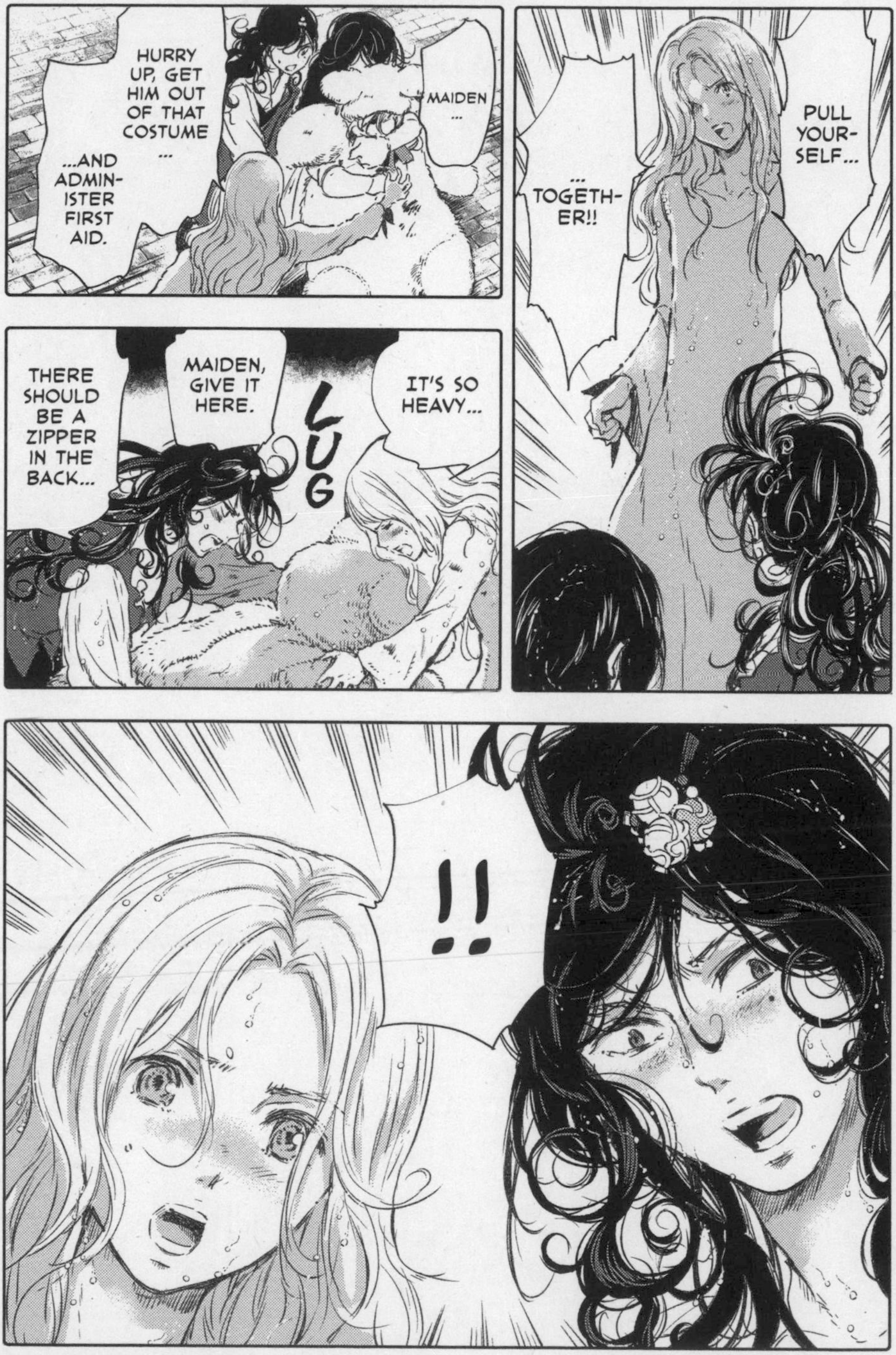
PULL YOURSELF...
...TOGETHER!!
MAIDEN...
HURRY UP, GET HIM OUT OF THAT COSTUME...
...AND ADMINISTER FIRST AID.
IT'S SO HEAVY...
LUG
MAIDEN, GIVE IT HERE.
THERE SHOULD BE A ZIPPER IN THE BACK...
!!

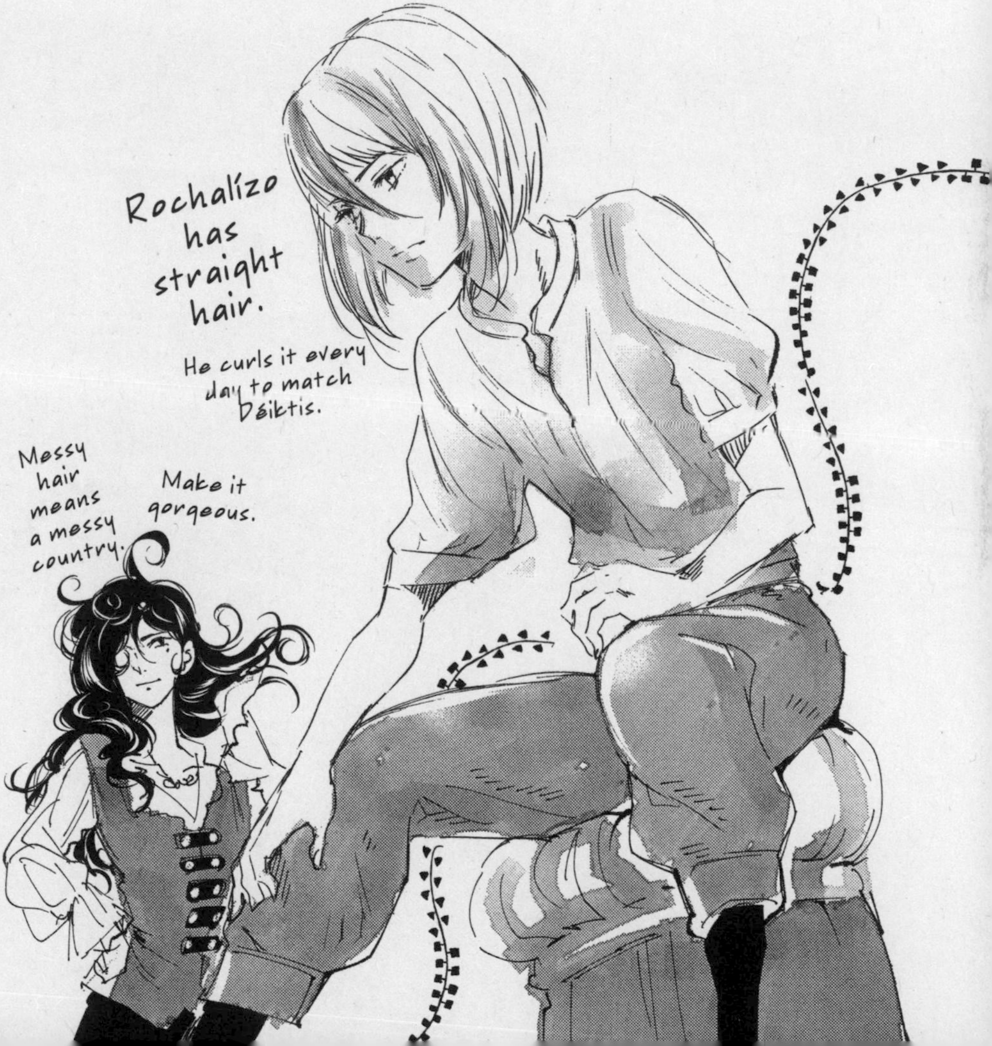
Rochalízo has straight hair.
He curls it every day to match Deiktis.
Make it gorgeous.
Messy hair means a messy country.

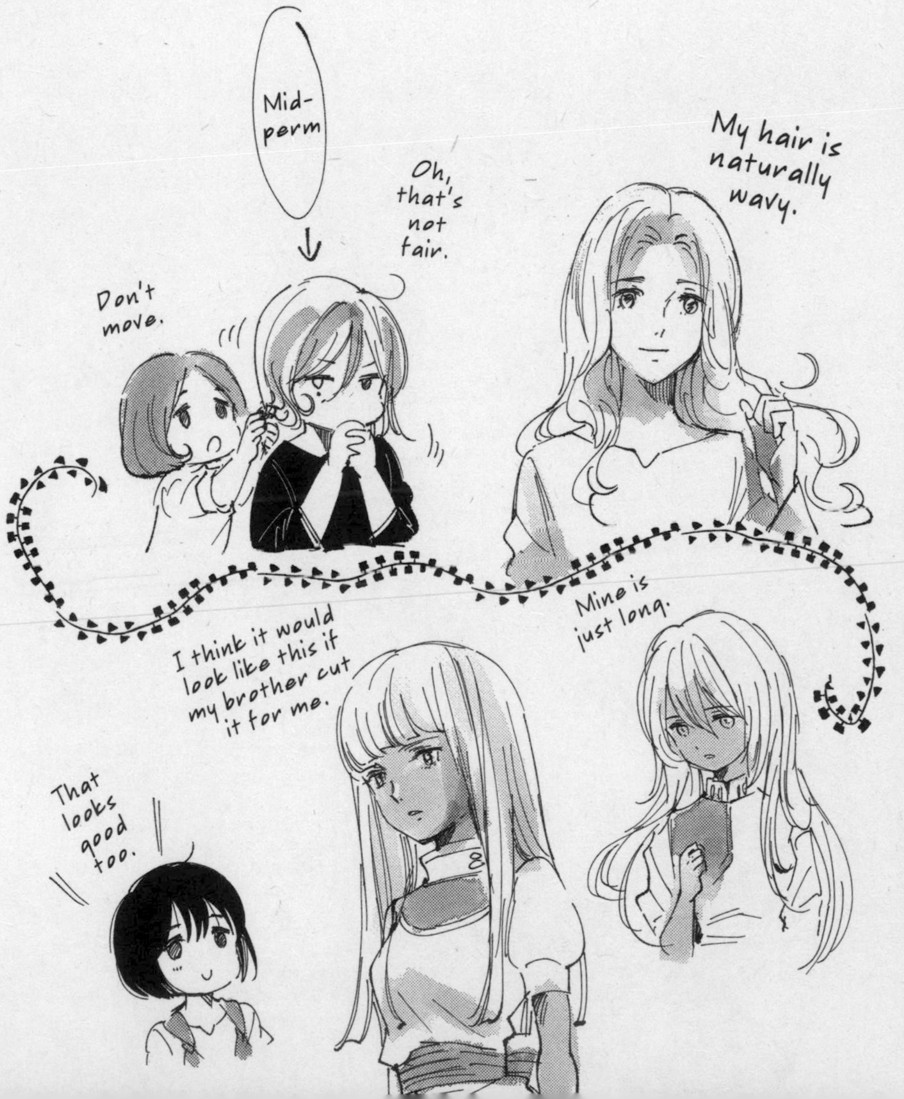
My hair is naturally wavy.
Oh, that's not fair.
Mid-perm
Don't move.
Mine is just long.
I think it would look like this if my brother cut it for me.
That looks good too.

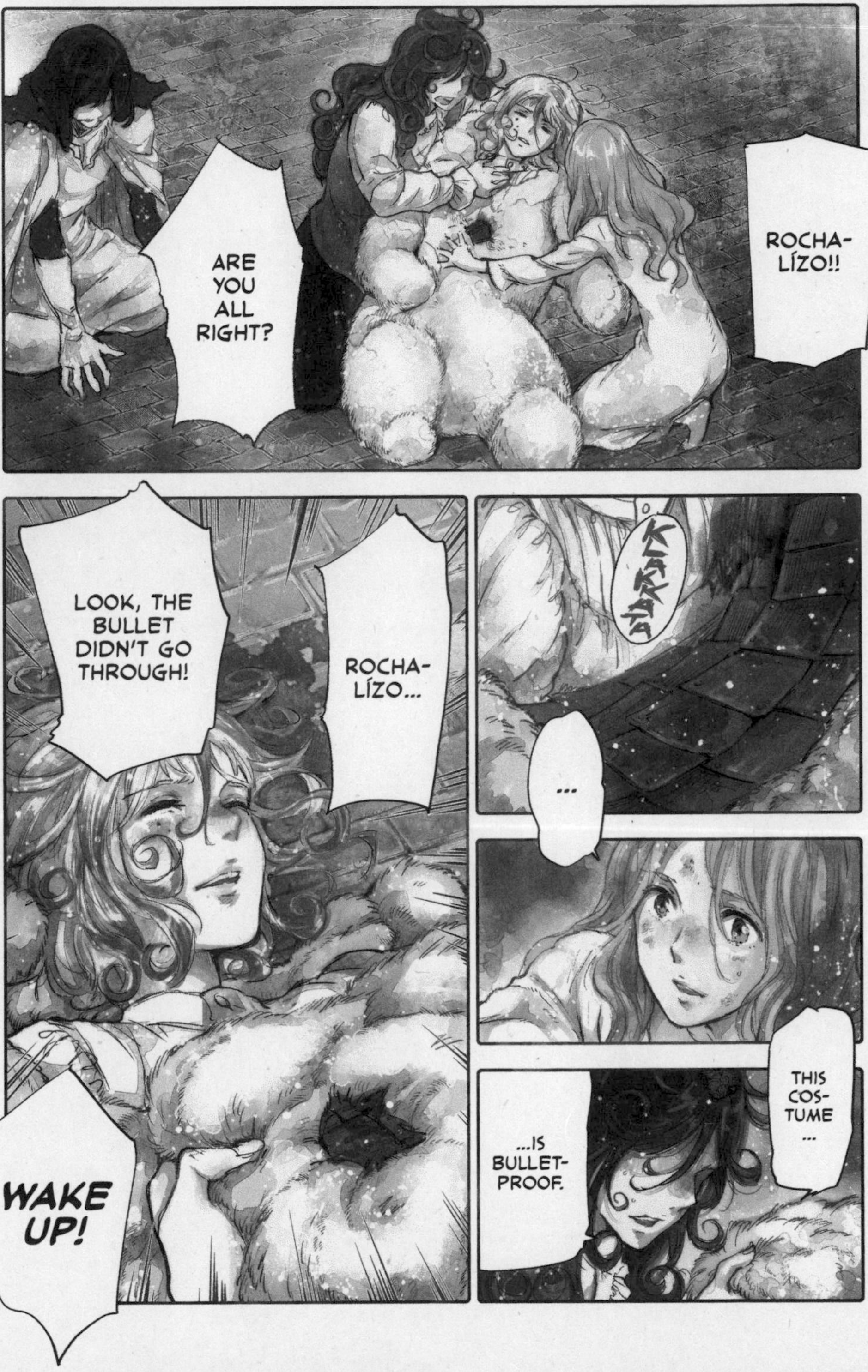
ROCHA-LÍZO!!
ARE YOU ALL RIGHT?
KLAKKATA
...
THIS COSTUME ...
...IS BULLET-PROOF.
ROCHA-LÍZO...
LOOK, THE BULLET DIDN'T GO THROUGH!
WAKE UP!

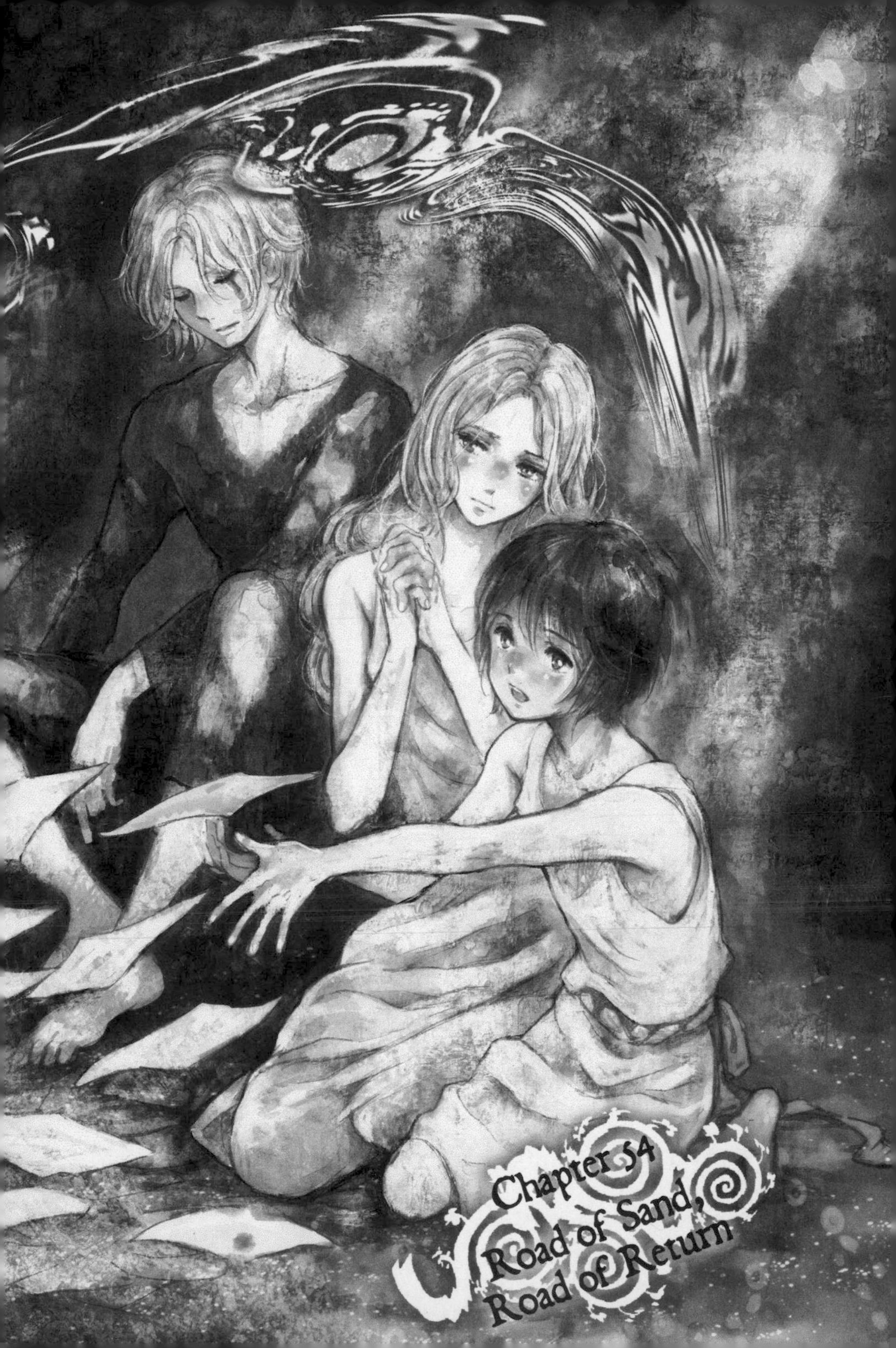
Chapter 54
Road of Sand, Road of Return

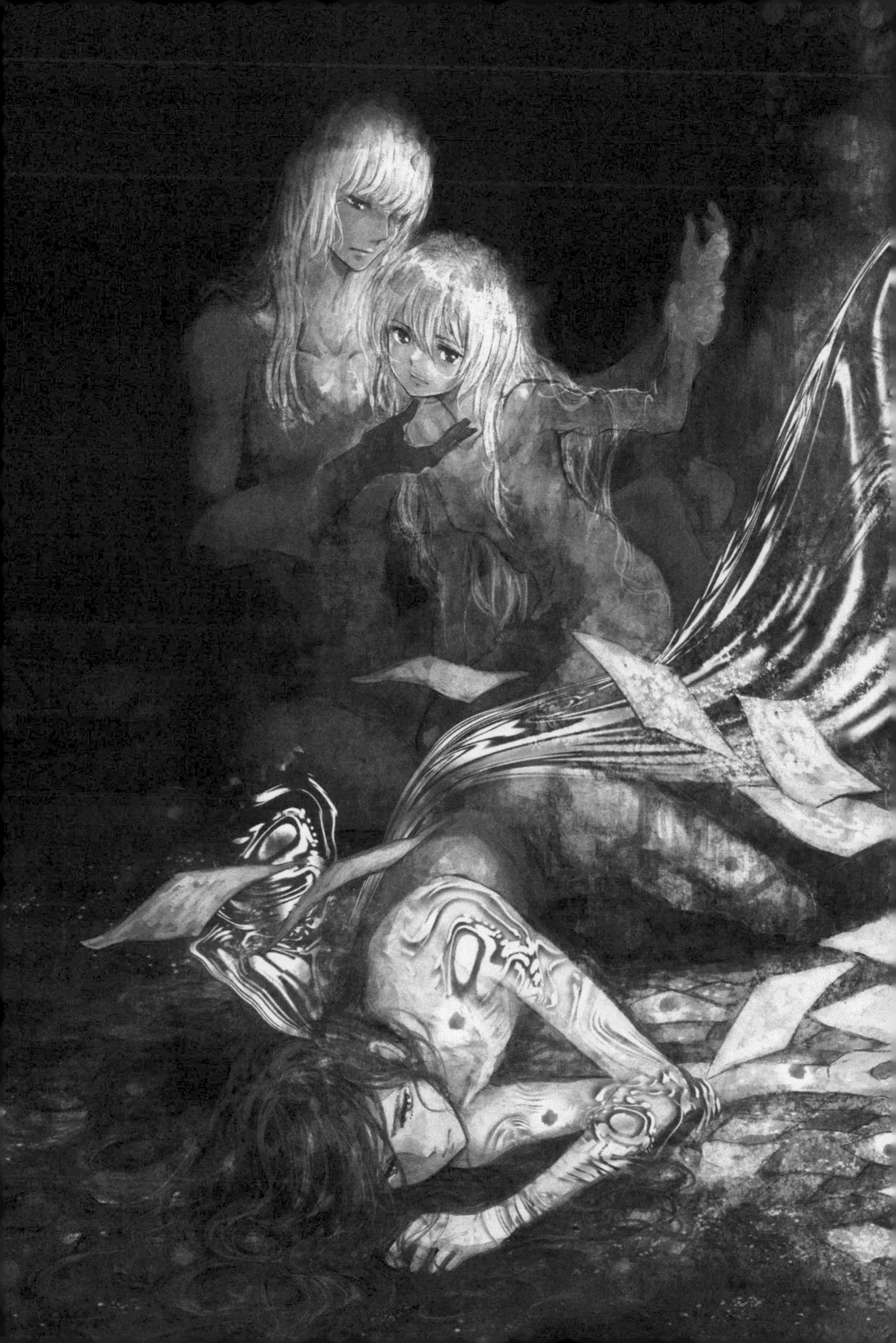

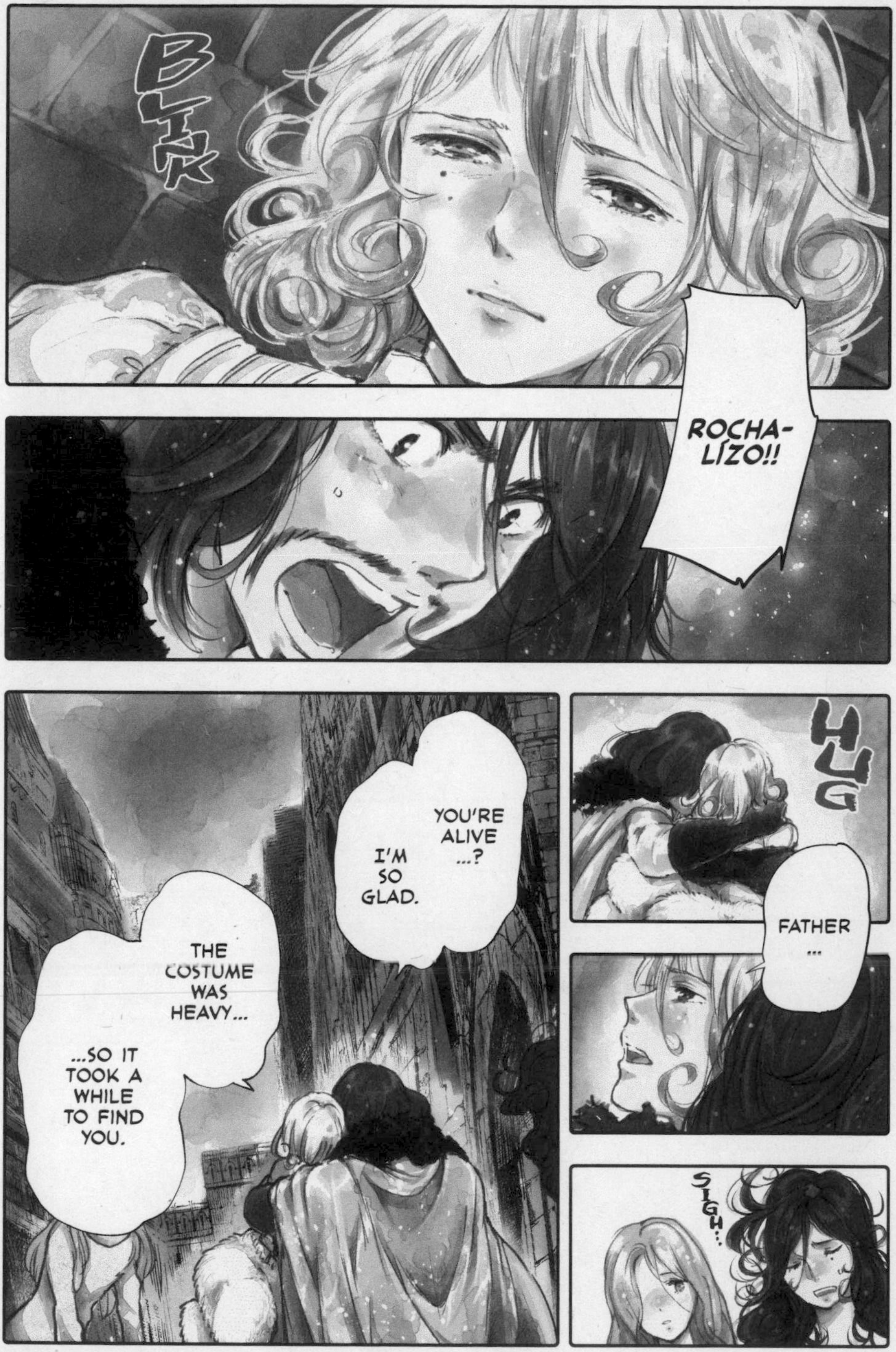

BLINK
ROCHA-
LÍZO!!
HUG
FATHER
...
SIGH...
YOU'RE ALIVE ...?
I'M SO GLAD.
THE COSTUME WAS HEAVY...
...SO IT TOOK A WHILE TO FIND YOU.

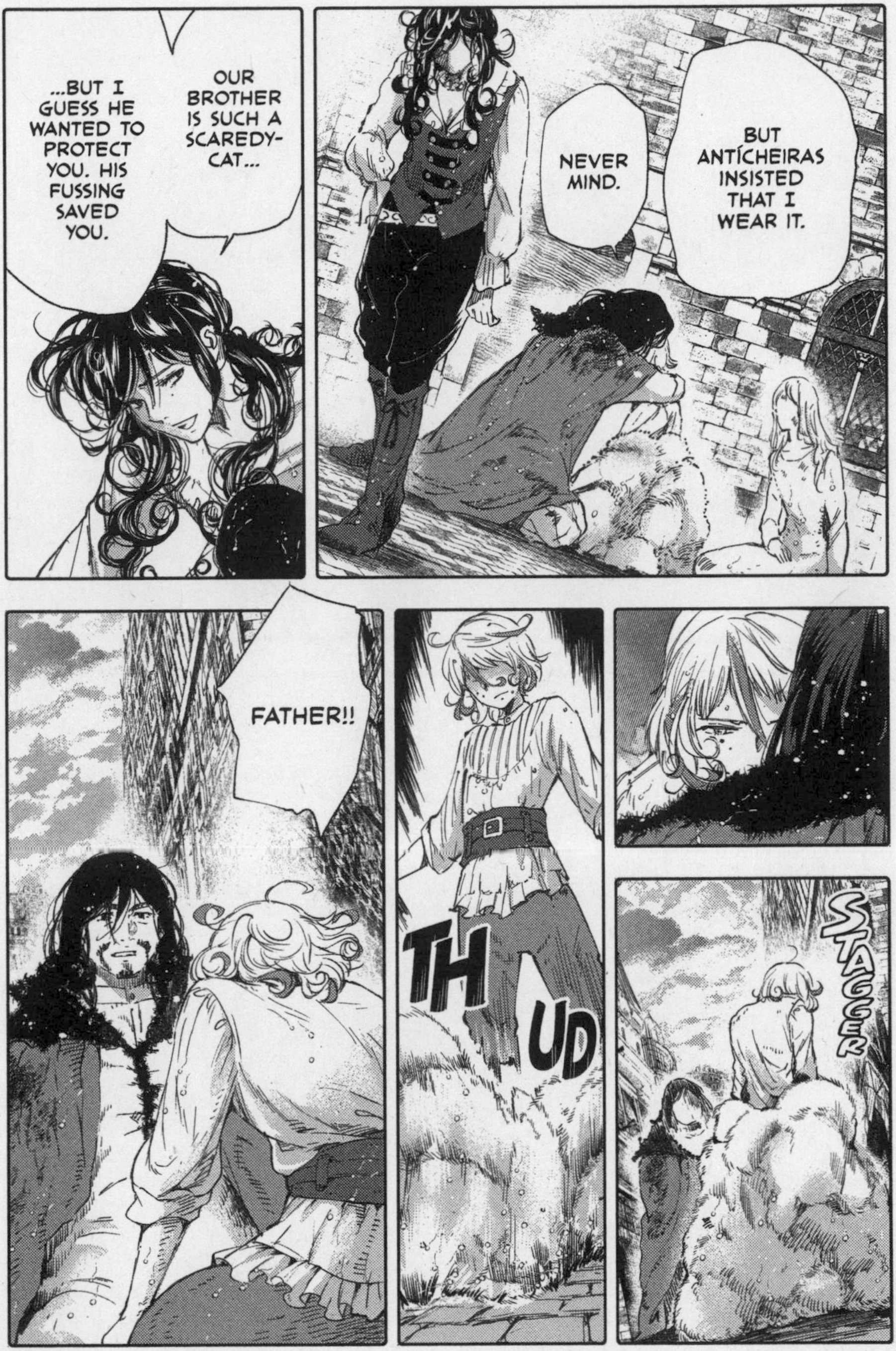
BUT ANTÍCHEIRAS INSISTED THAT I WEAR IT.
NEVER MIND.
OUR BROTHER IS SUCH A SCAREDY-CAT...
...BUT I GUESS HE WANTED TO PROTECT YOU. HIS FUSSING SAVED YOU.
STAGGER
THUD
FATHER!!

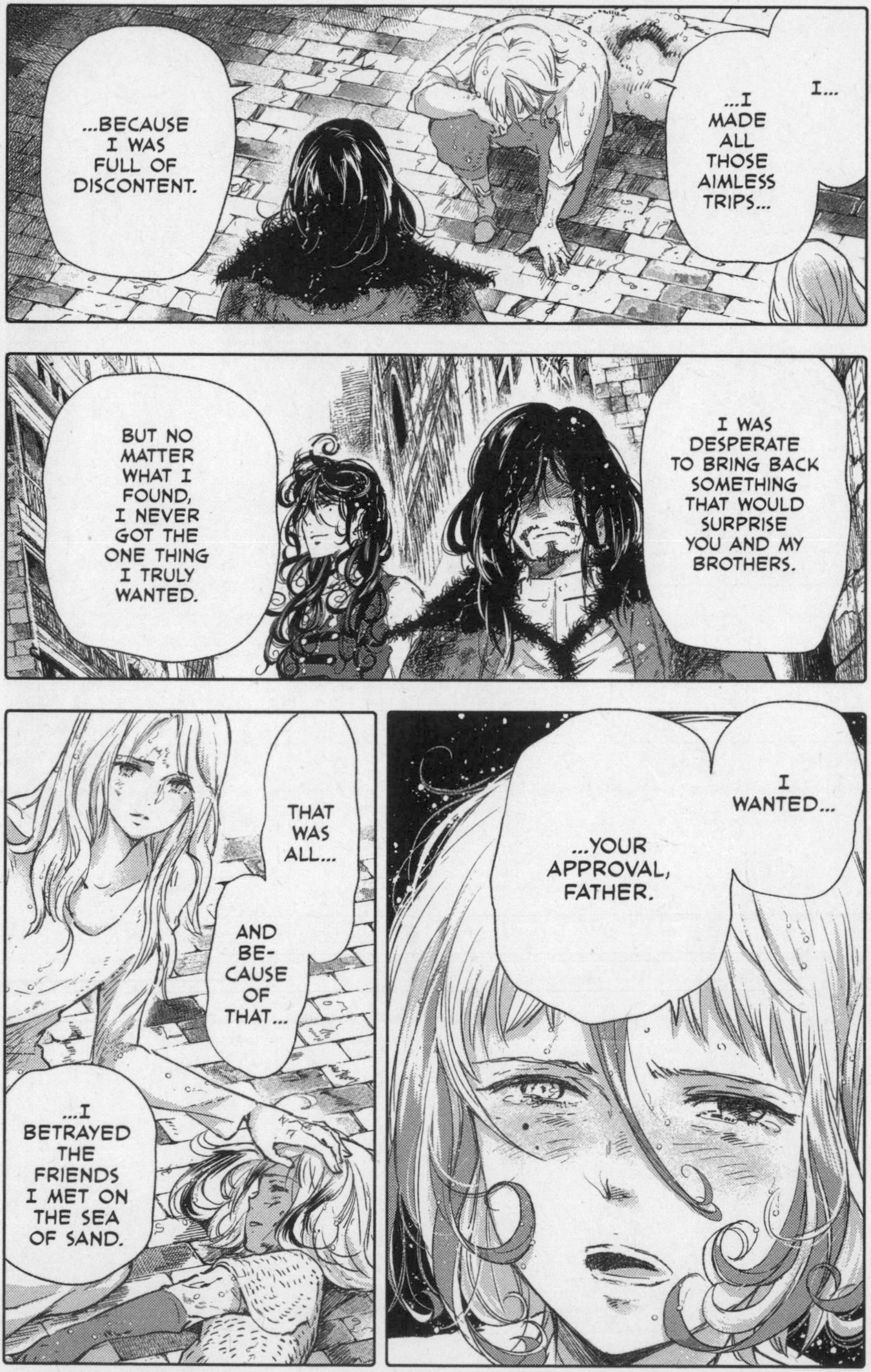
I...
...I MADE ALL THOSE AIMLESS TRIPS...
...BECAUSE I WAS FULL OF DISCONTENT.
I WAS DESPERATE TO BRING BACK SOMETHING THAT WOULD SURPRISE YOU AND MY BROTHERS.
BUT NO MATTER WHAT I FOUND, I NEVER GOT THE ONE THING I TRULY WANTED.
I WANTED...
...YOUR APPROVAL, FATHER.
THAT WAS ALL...
AND BE-CAUSE OF THAT...
...I BETRAYED THE FRIENDS I MET ON THE SEA OF SAND.

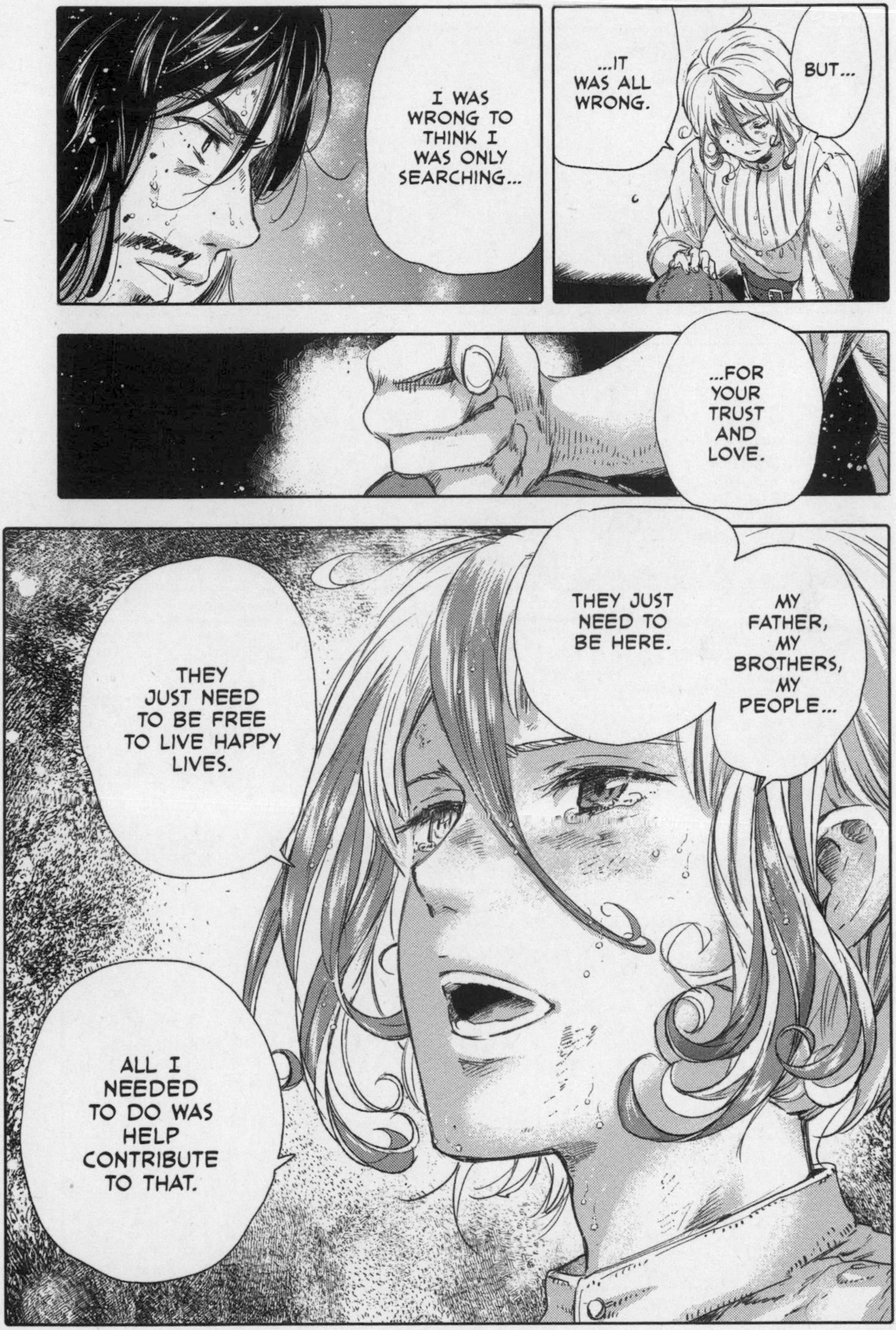
BUT...
...IT WAS ALL WRONG.
I WAS WRONG TO THINK I WAS ONLY SEARCHING...
...FOR YOUR TRUST AND LOVE.
MY FATHER, MY BROTHERS, MY PEOPLE...
THEY JUST NEED TO BE HERE.
THEY JUST NEED TO BE FREE TO LIVE HAPPY LIVES.
ALL I NEEDED TO DO WAS HELP CONTRIBUTE TO THAT.

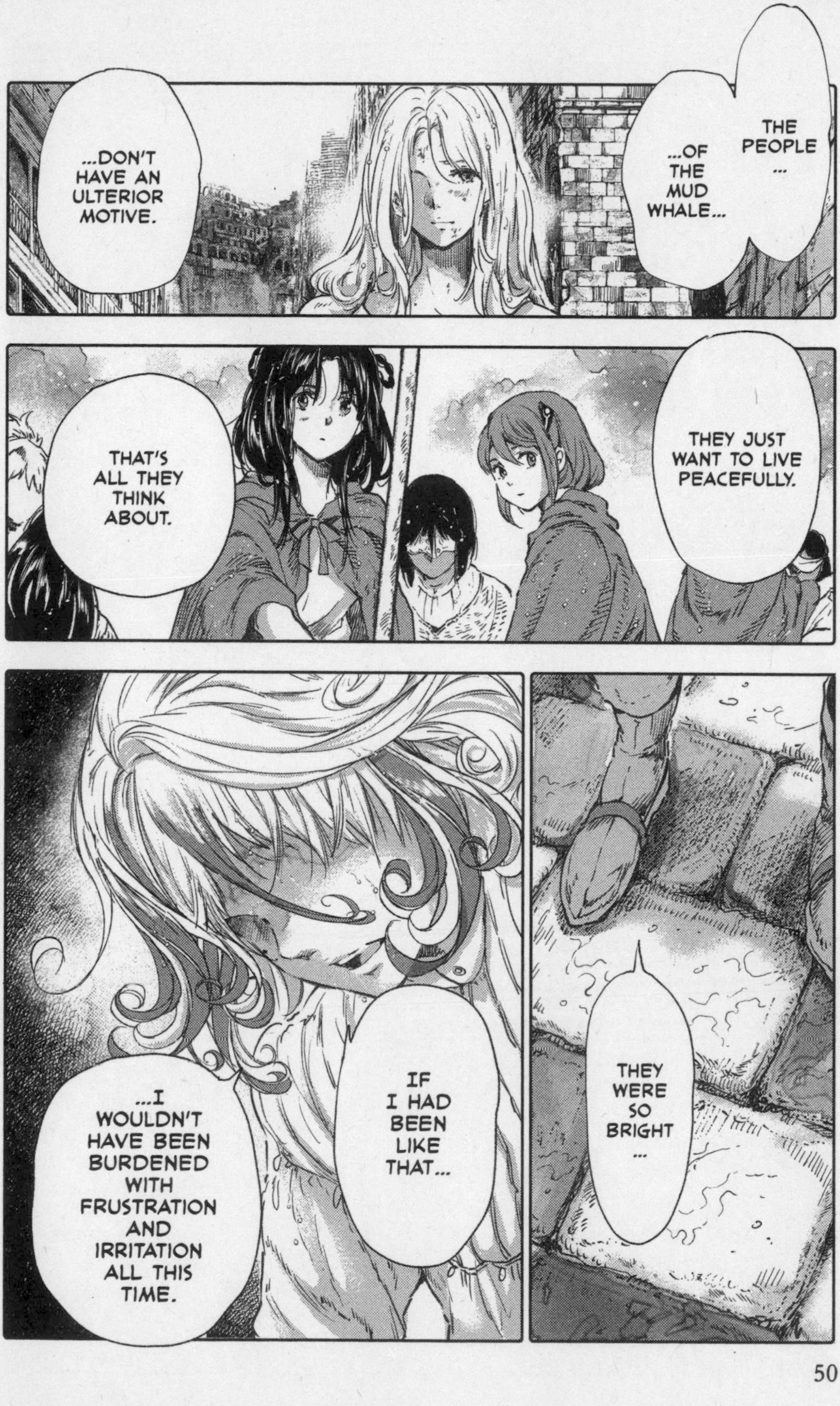
THE PEOPLE ...
...OF THE MUD WHALE...
...DON'T HAVE AN ULTERIOR MOTIVE.
THEY JUST WANT TO LIVE PEACEFULLY.
THAT'S ALL THEY THINK ABOUT.
THEY WERE SO BRIGHT ...
IF I HAD BEEN LIKE THAT...
...I WOULDN'T HAVE BEEN BURDENED WITH FRUSTRATION AND IRRITATION ALL THIS TIME.

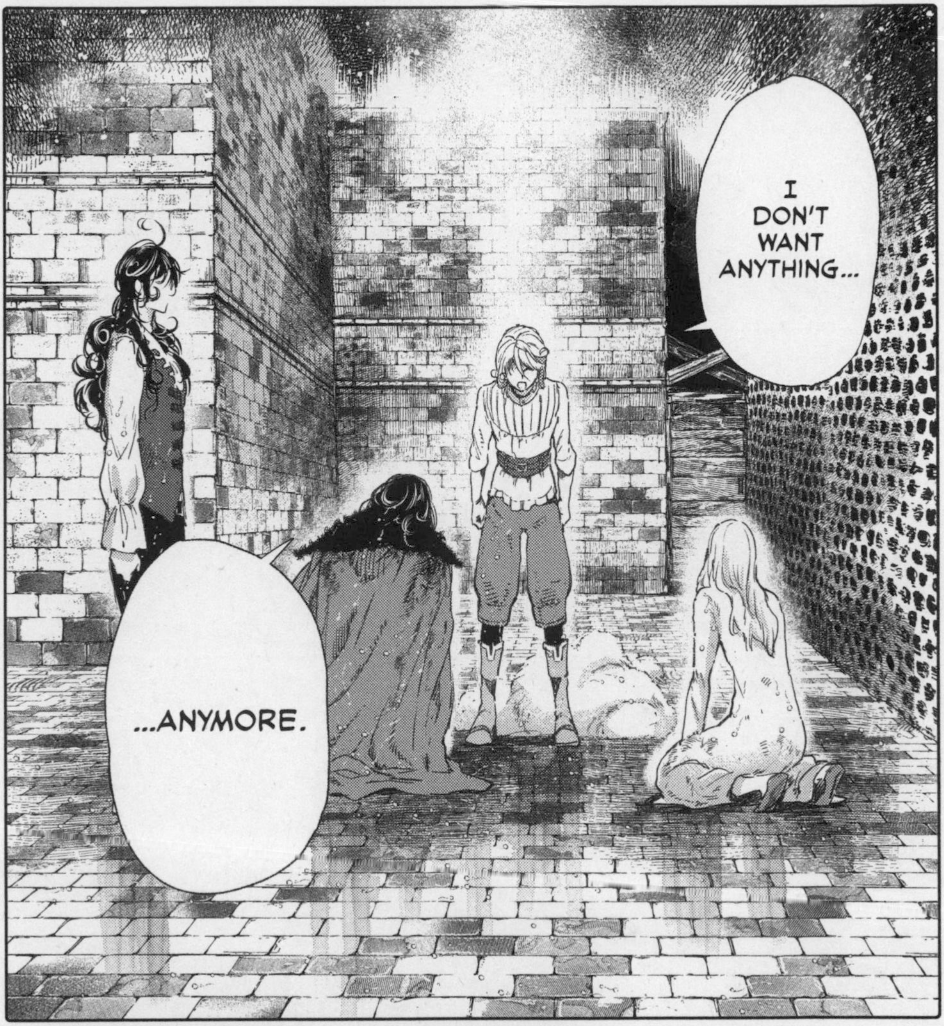
I DON'T WANT ANYTHING...
...ANYMORE.
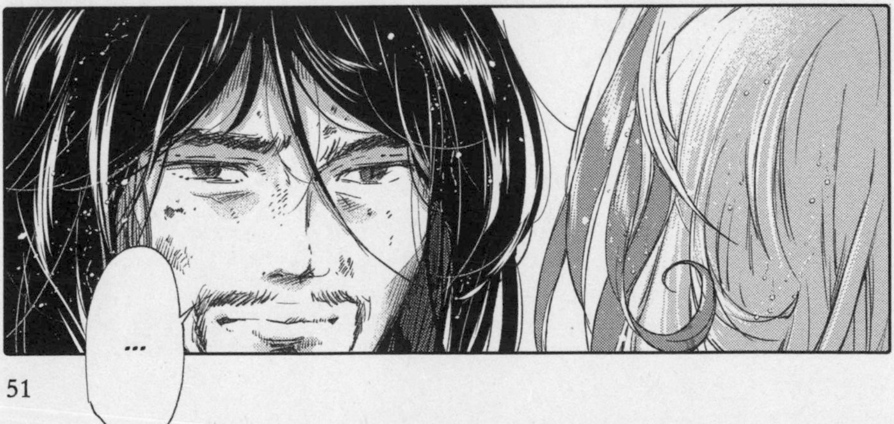
...

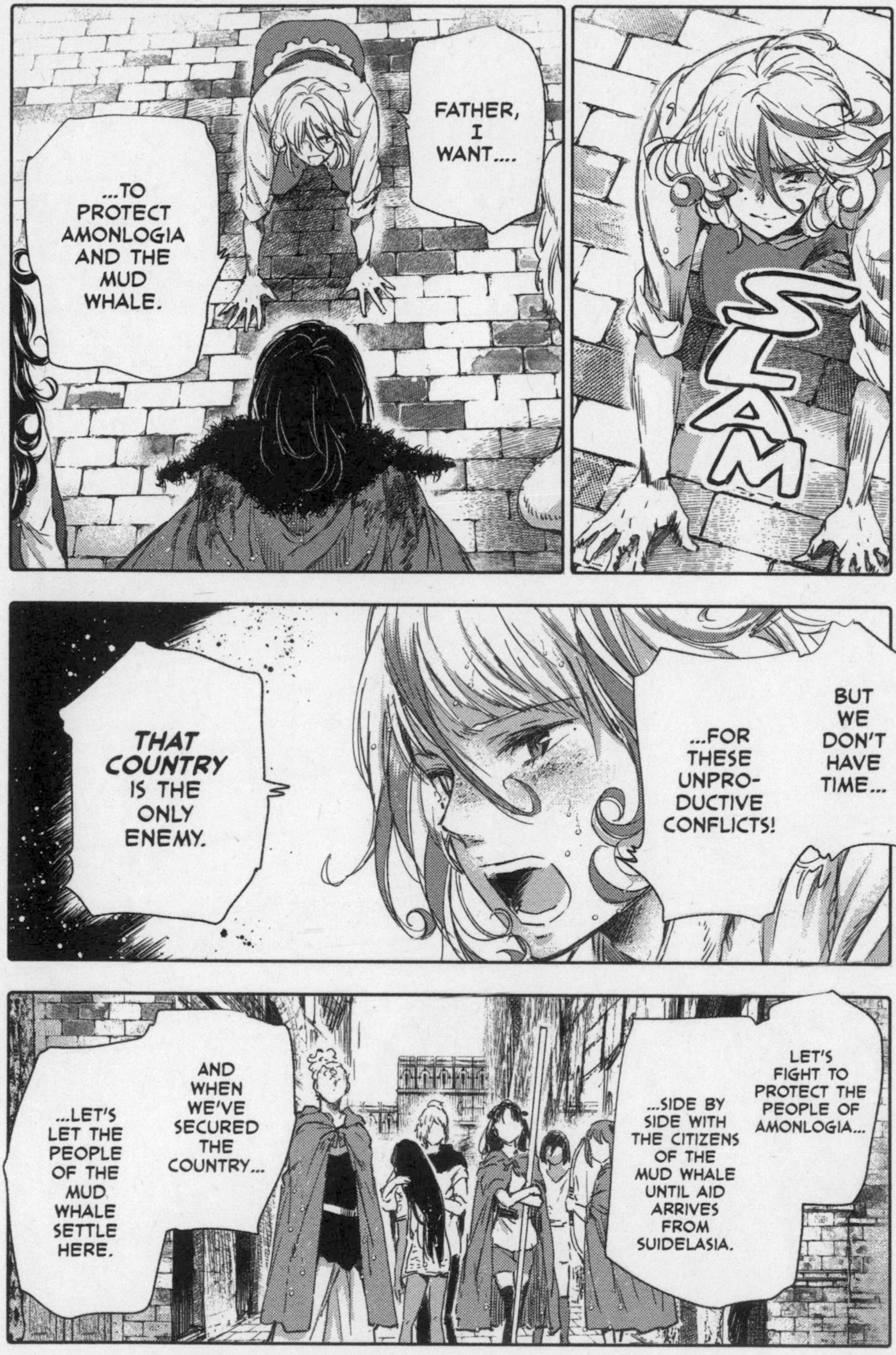
SLAM
FATHER, I WANT....
...TO PROTECT AMONLOGIA AND THE MUD WHALE.
BUT WE DON'T HAVE TIME...
...FOR THESE UNPRODUCTIVE CONFLICTS!
THAT COUNTRY IS THE ONLY ENEMY.
LET'S FIGHT TO PROTECT THE PEOPLE OF AMONLOGIA...
...SIDE BY SIDE WITH THE CITIZENS OF THE MUD WHALE UNTIL AID ARRIVES FROM SUIDELASIA.
AND WHEN WE'VE SECURED THE COUNTRY...
...LET'S LET THE PEOPLE OF THE MUD WHALE SETTLE HERE.

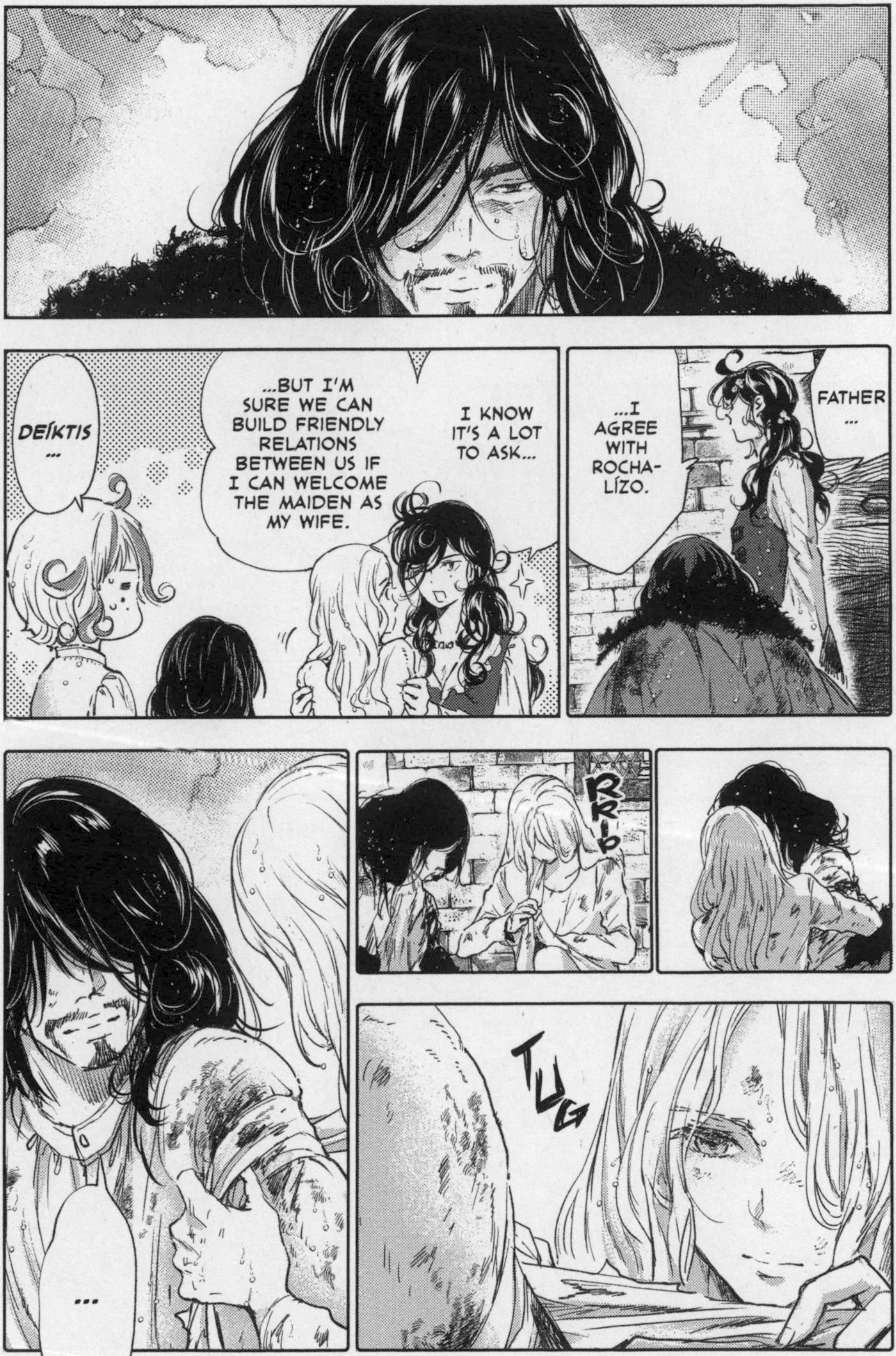
FATHER ...
...I AGREE WITH ROCHA-LÍZO.
I KNOW IT'S A LOT TO ASK...
...BUT I'M SURE WE CAN BUILD FRIENDLY RELATIONS BETWEEN US IF I CAN WELCOME THE MAIDEN AS MY WIFE.
DEÍKTIS ...
RRIP
TUG
...

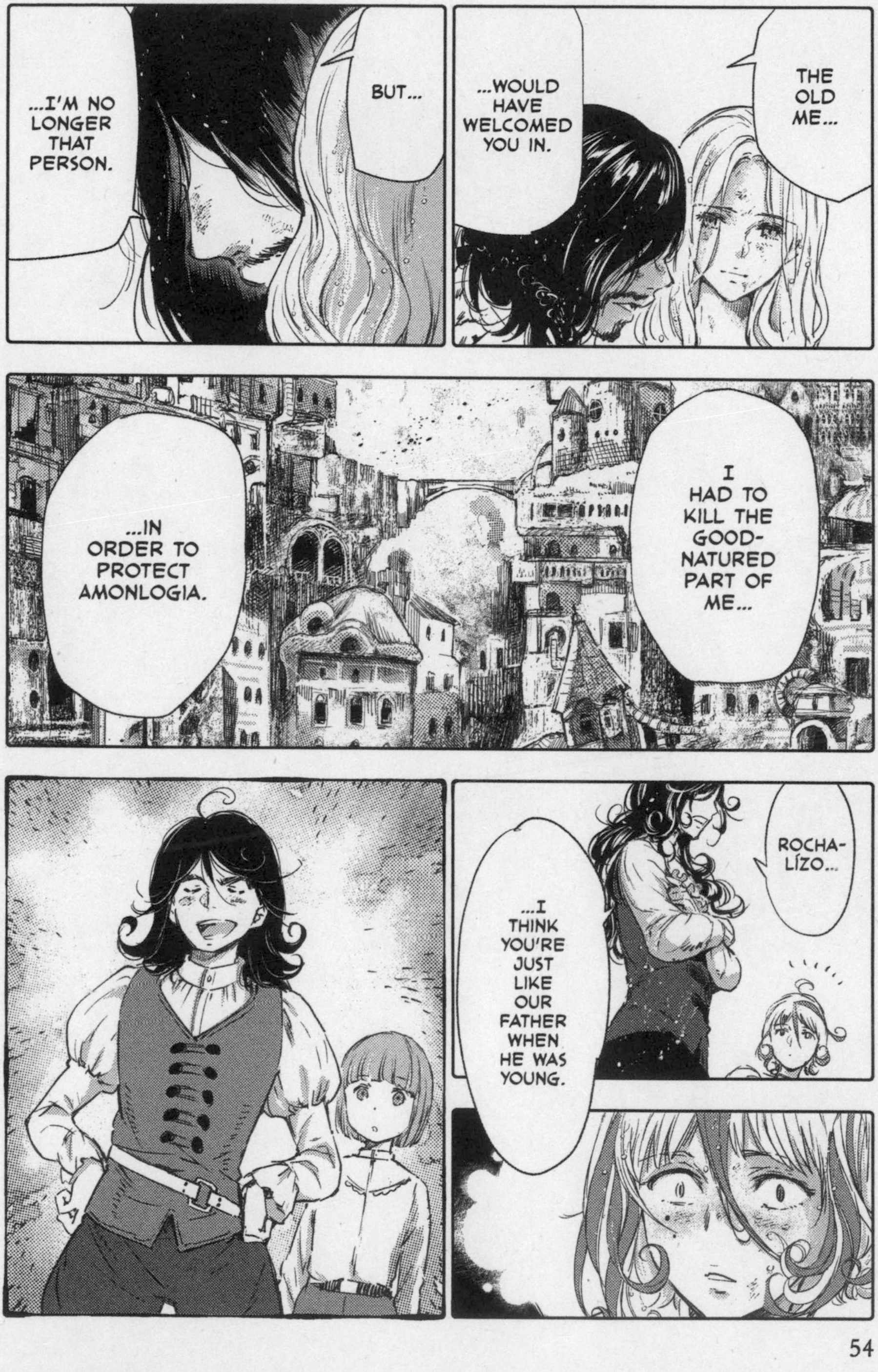
THE OLD ME...
...WOULD HAVE WELCOMED YOU IN.
BUT...
...I'M NO LONGER THAT PERSON.
I HAD TO KILL THE GOOD-NATURED PART OF ME...
...IN ORDER TO PROTECT AMONLOGIA.
ROCHA-LÍZO...
...I THINK YOU'RE JUST LIKE OUR FATHER WHEN HE WAS YOUNG.

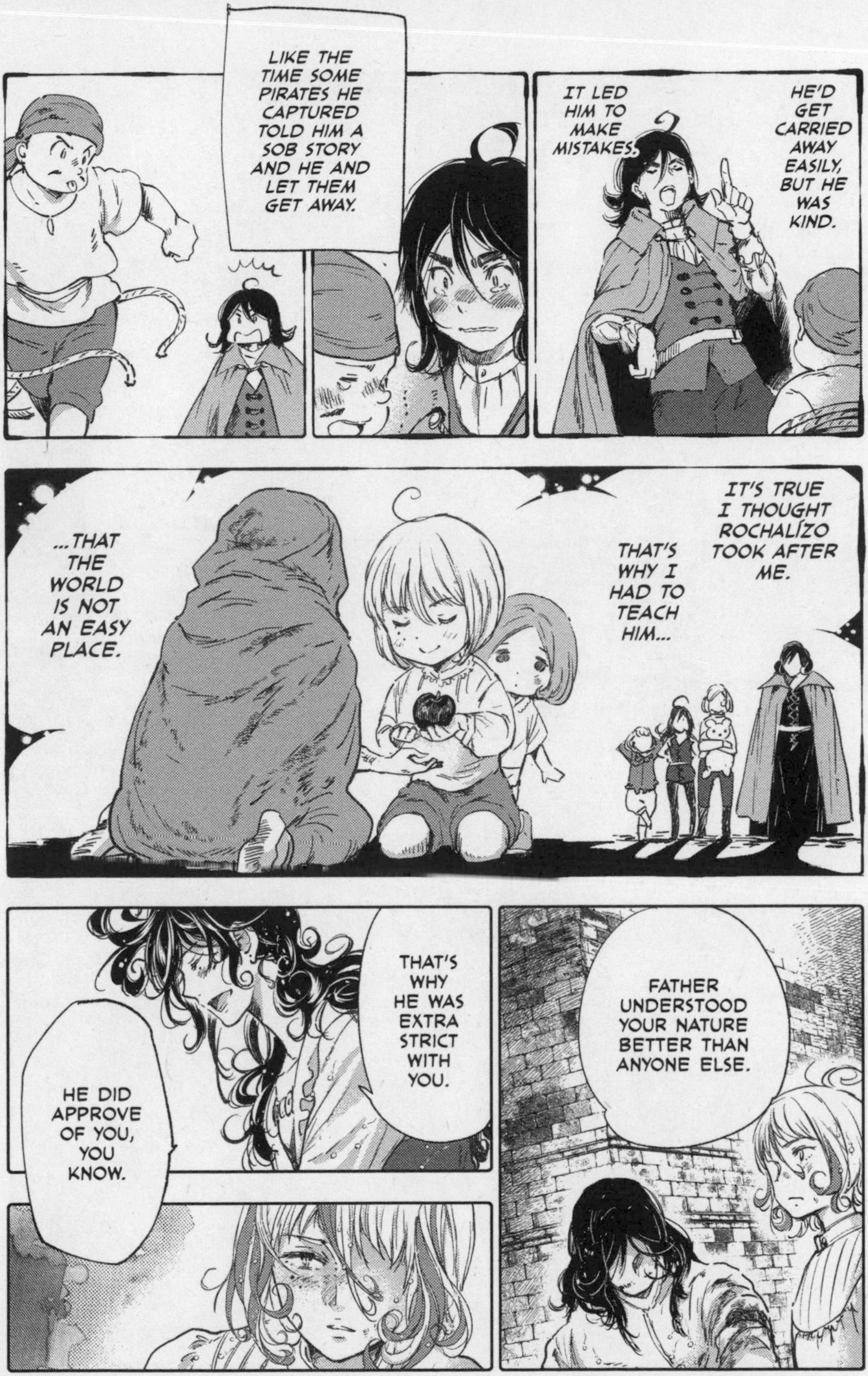
HE'D GET CARRIED AWAY EASILY, BUT HE WAS KIND.
IT LED HIM TO MAKE MISTAKES.
LIKE THE TIME SOME PIRATES HE CAPTURED TOLD HIM A SOB STORY AND HE AND LET THEM GET AWAY.
IT'S TRUE I THOUGHT ROCHALÍZO TOOK AFTER ME.
THAT'S WHY I HAD TO TEACH HIM...
...THAT THE WORLD IS NOT AN EASY PLACE.
FATHER UNDERSTOOD YOUR NATURE BETTER THAN ANYONE ELSE.
THAT'S WHY HE WAS EXTRA STRICT WITH YOU.
HE DID APPROVE OF YOU, YOU KNOW.

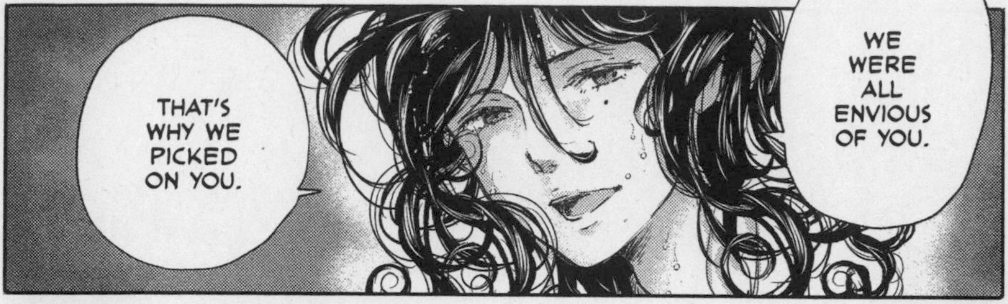
WE WERE ALL ENVIOUS OF YOU.
THAT'S WHY WE PICKED ON YOU.

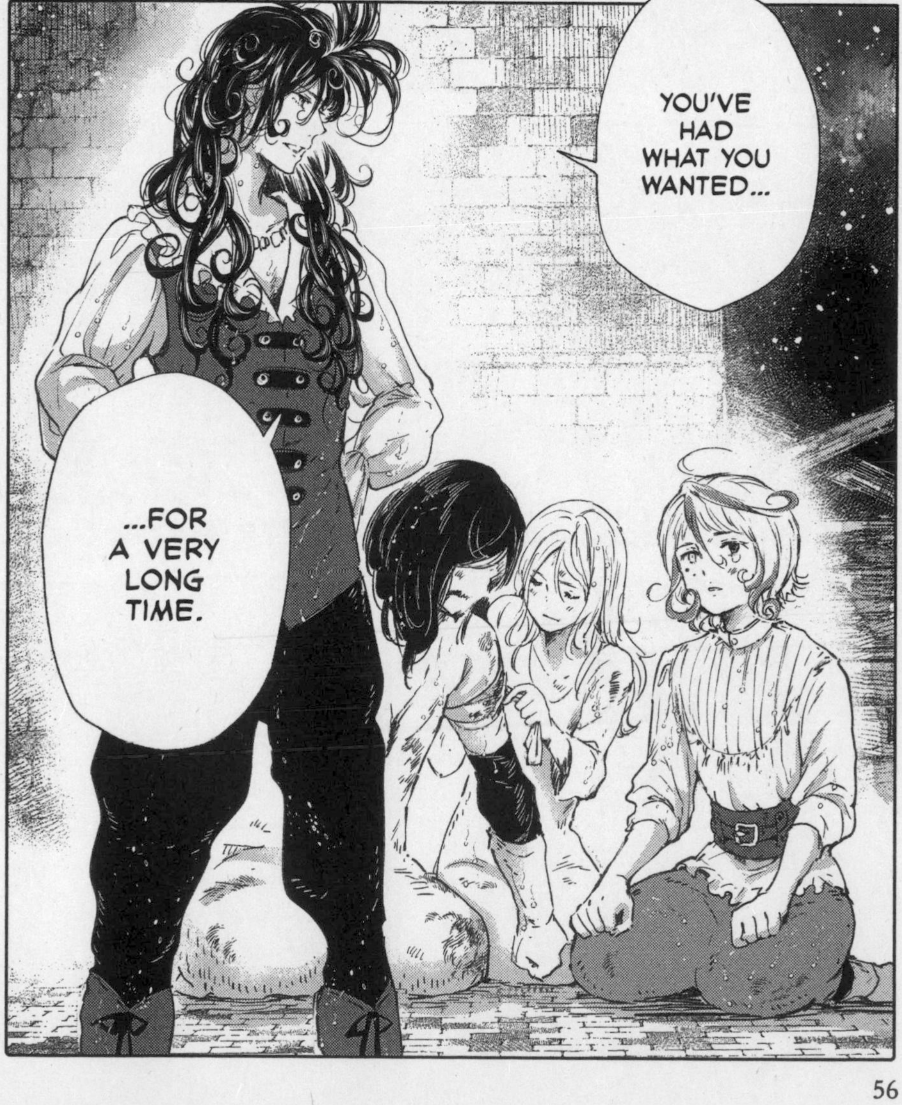
YOU'VE HAD WHAT YOU WANTED...
...FOR A VERY LONG TIME.

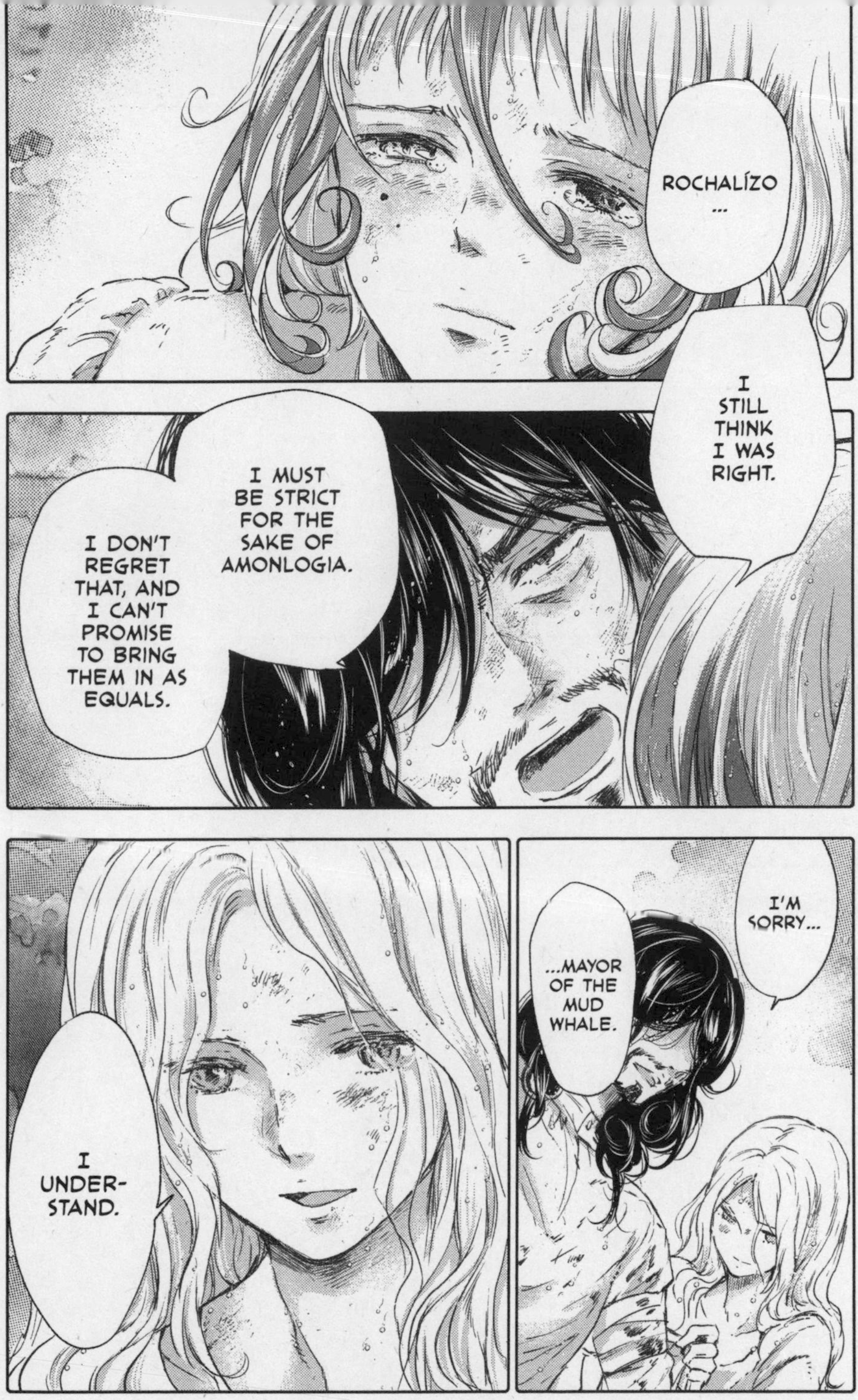
ROCHALÍZO ...
I STILL THINK I WAS RIGHT.
I MUST BE STRICT FOR THE SAKE OF AMONLOGIA.
I DON'T REGRET THAT, AND I CAN'T PROMISE TO BRING THEM IN AS EQUALS.
I'M SORRY...
...MAYOR OF THE MUD WHALE.
I UNDER-STAND.

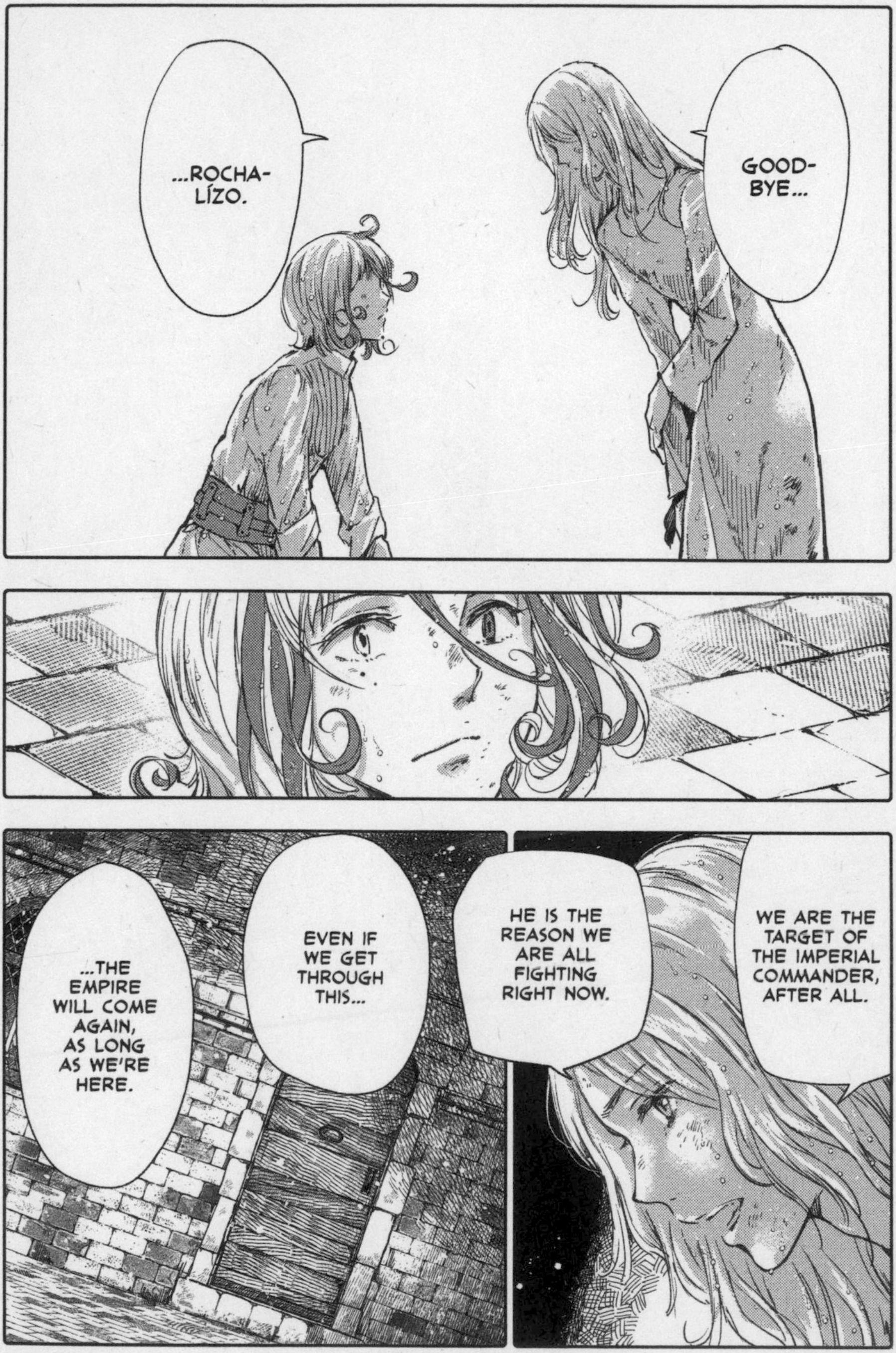
GOOD-BYE...
...ROCHALÍZO.
WE ARE THE TARGET OF THE IMPERIAL COMMANDER, AFTER ALL.
HE IS THE REASON WE ARE ALL FIGHTING RIGHT NOW.
EVEN IF WE GET THROUGH THIS...
...THE EMPIRE WILL COME AGAIN, AS LONG AS WE'RE HERE.

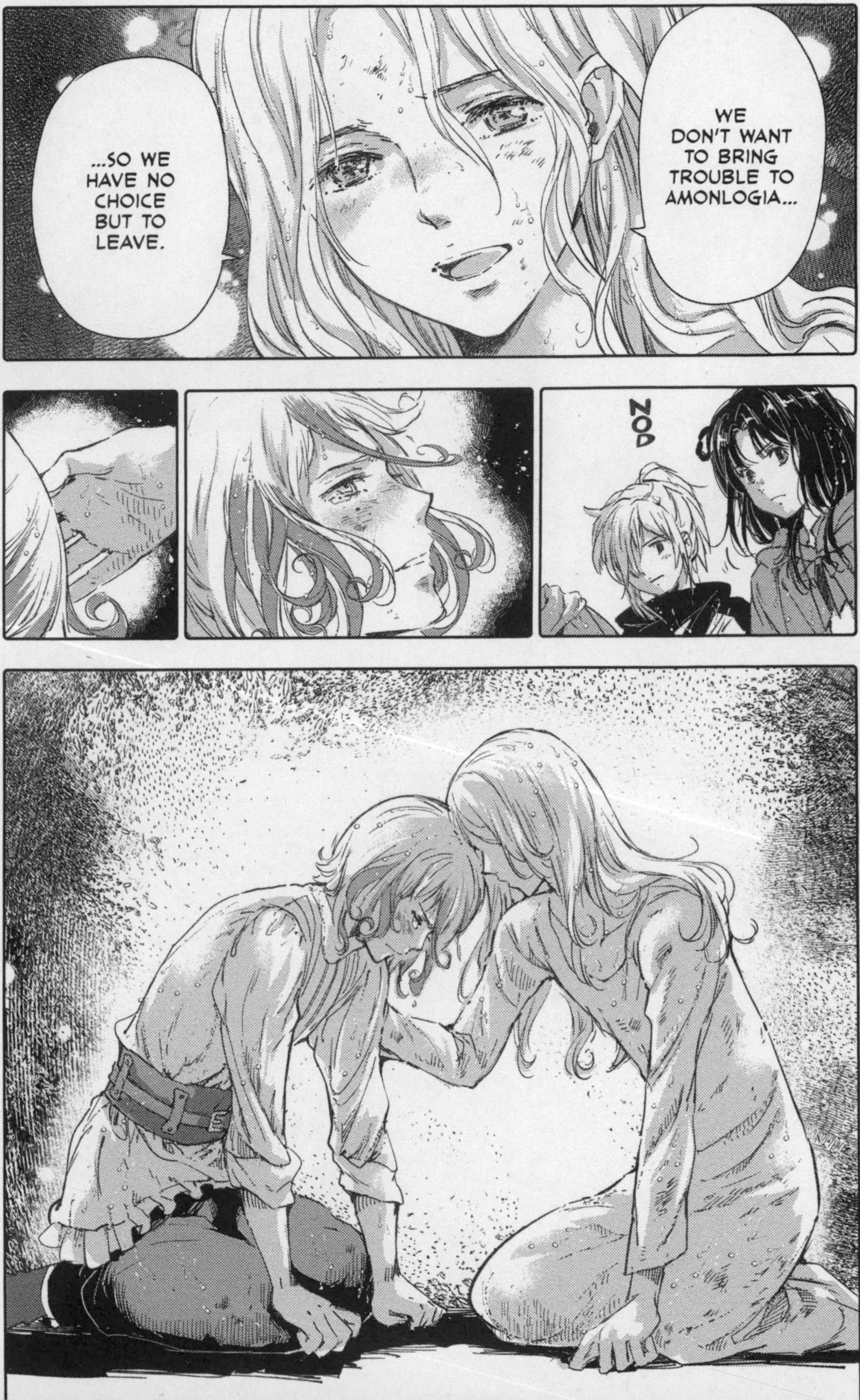
WE DON'T WANT TO BRING TROUBLE TO AMONLOGIA...
...SO WE HAVE NO CHOICE BUT TO LEAVE.
NOD

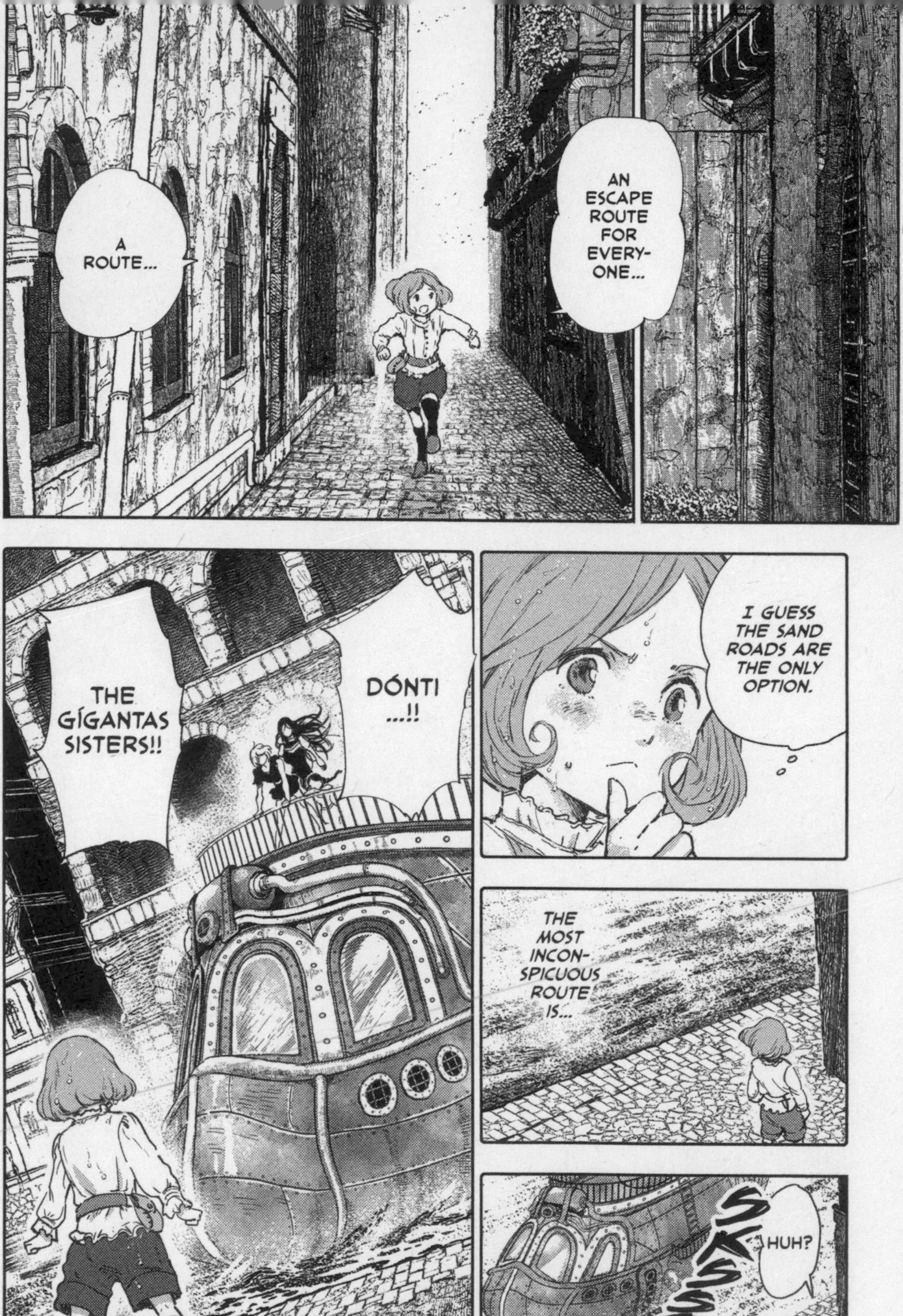
AN ESCAPE ROUTE FOR EVERY-ONE...
A ROUTE...
I GUESS THE SAND ROADS ARE THE ONLY OPTION.
THE MOST INCON-SPICUOUS ROUTE IS...
HUH?
SKSSSH
DÓNTI ...!!
THE GÍGANTAS SISTERS!!

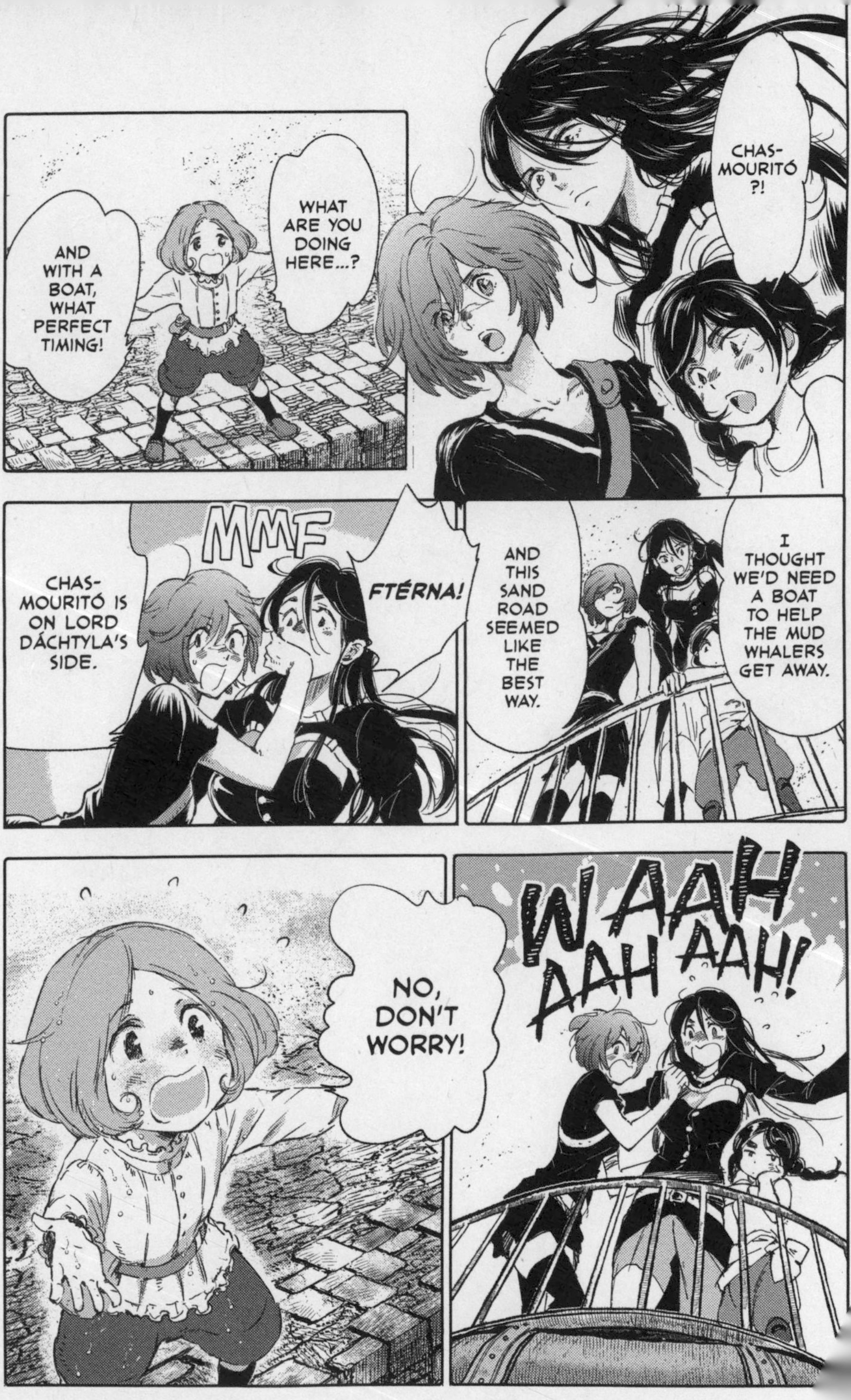
CHAS-MOURITÓ ?!
WHAT ARE YOU DOING HERE...?
AND WITH A BOAT, WHAT PERFECT TIMING!
I THOUGHT WE'D NEED A BOAT TO HELP THE MUD WHALERS GET AWAY.
AND THIS SAND ROAD SEEMED LIKE THE BEST WAY.
MMF
FTÉRNA!
CHAS-MOURITÓ IS ON LORD DÁCHTYLA'S SIDE.
WAAH AAH AAH!
NO, DON'T WORRY!

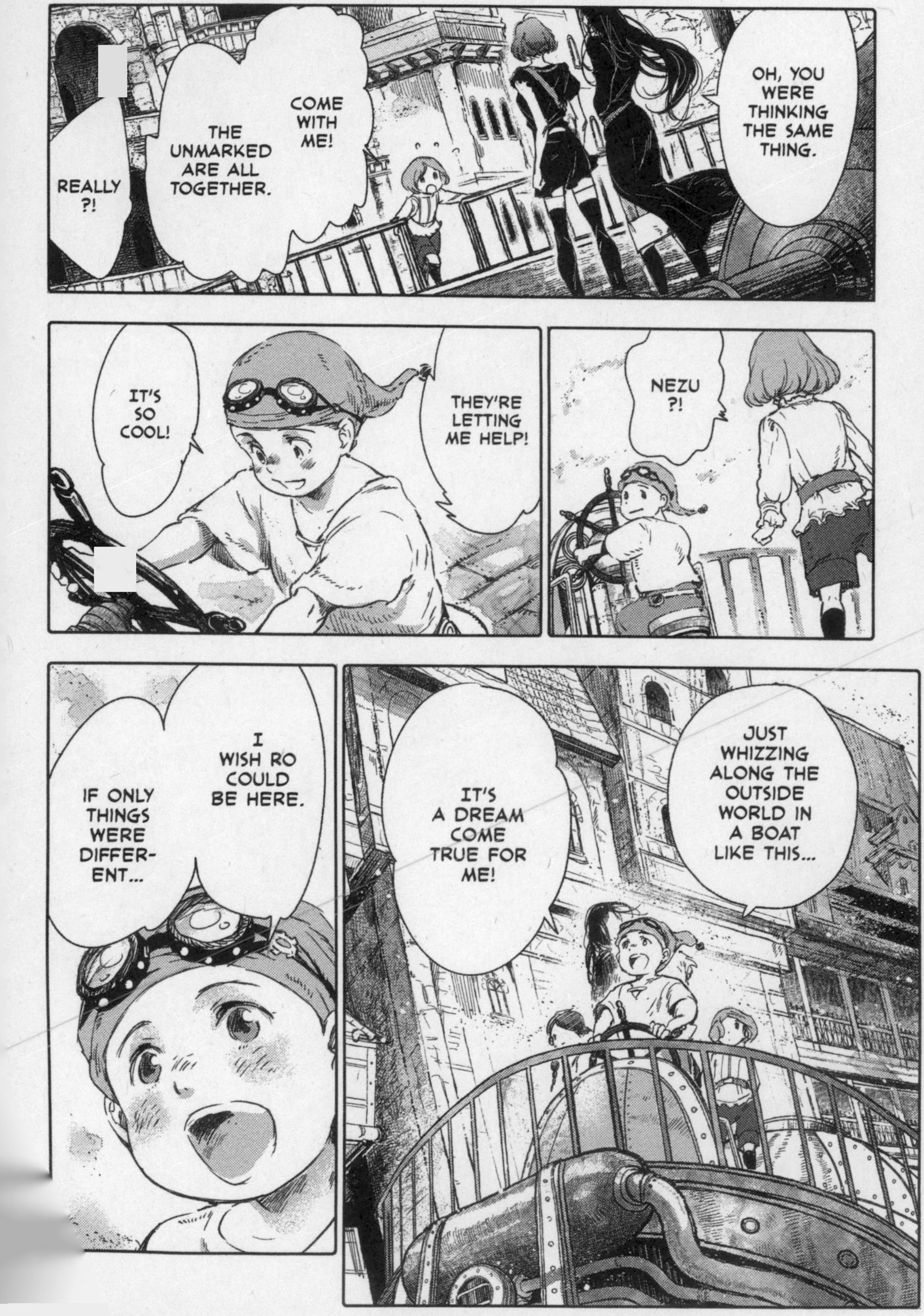
OH, YOU WERE THINKING THE SAME THING.
COME WITH ME!
THE UNMARKED ARE ALL TOGETHER.
REALLY?!
NEZU?!
THEY'RE LETTING ME HELP!
IT'S SO COOL!
JUST WHIZZING ALONG THE OUTSIDE WORLD IN A BOAT LIKE THIS...
IT'S A DREAM COME TRUE FOR ME!
I WISH RO COULD BE HERE.
IF ONLY THINGS WERE DIFFERENT...

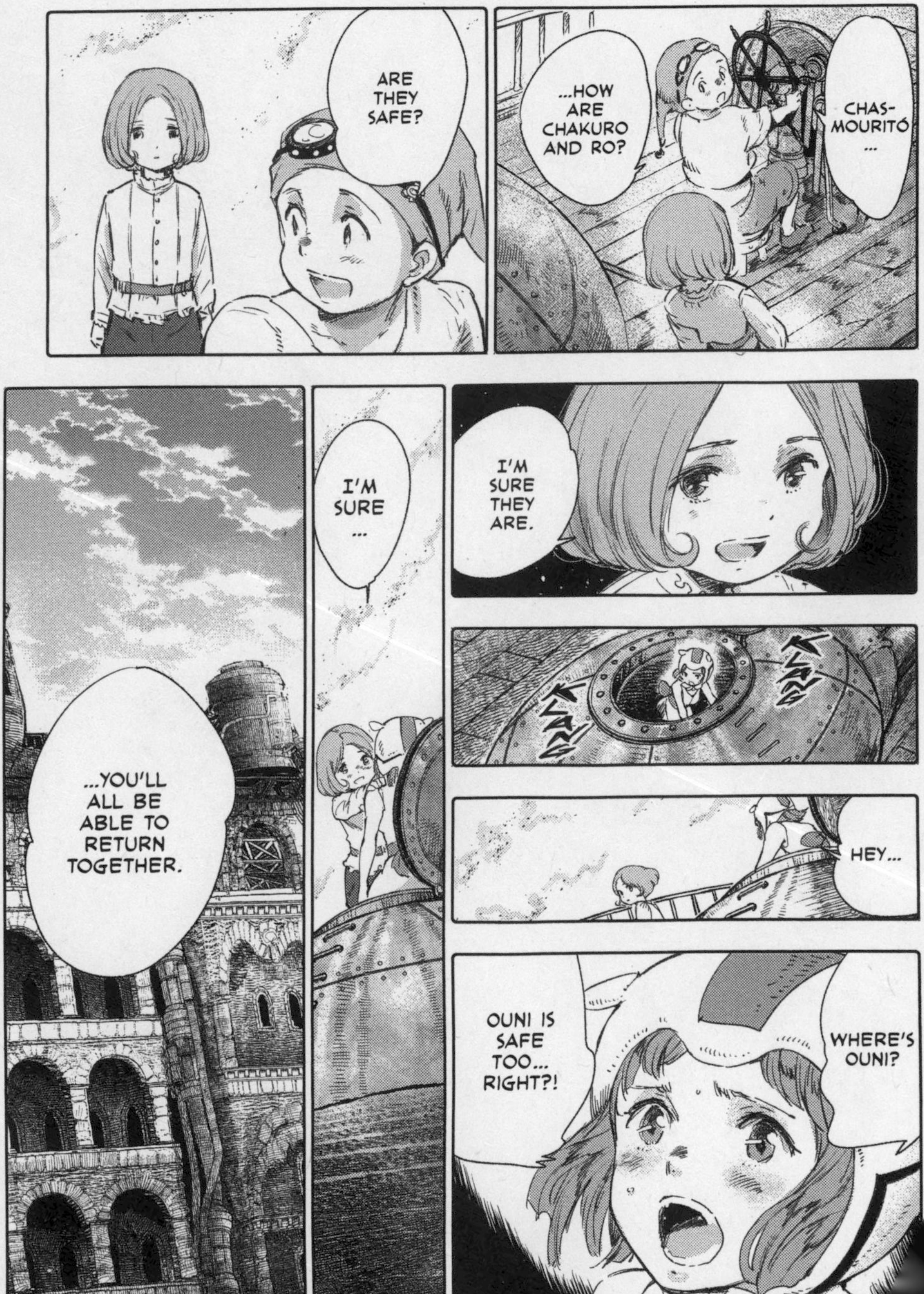
CHAS-MOURITÓ...
...HOW ARE CHAKURO AND RO?
ARE THEY SAFE?
I'M SURE THEY ARE.
KLANG
KLANG
HEY...
WHERE'S OUNI?
OUNI IS SAFE TOO... RIGHT?!
I'M SURE...
...YOU'LL ALL BE ABLE TO RETURN TOGETHER.

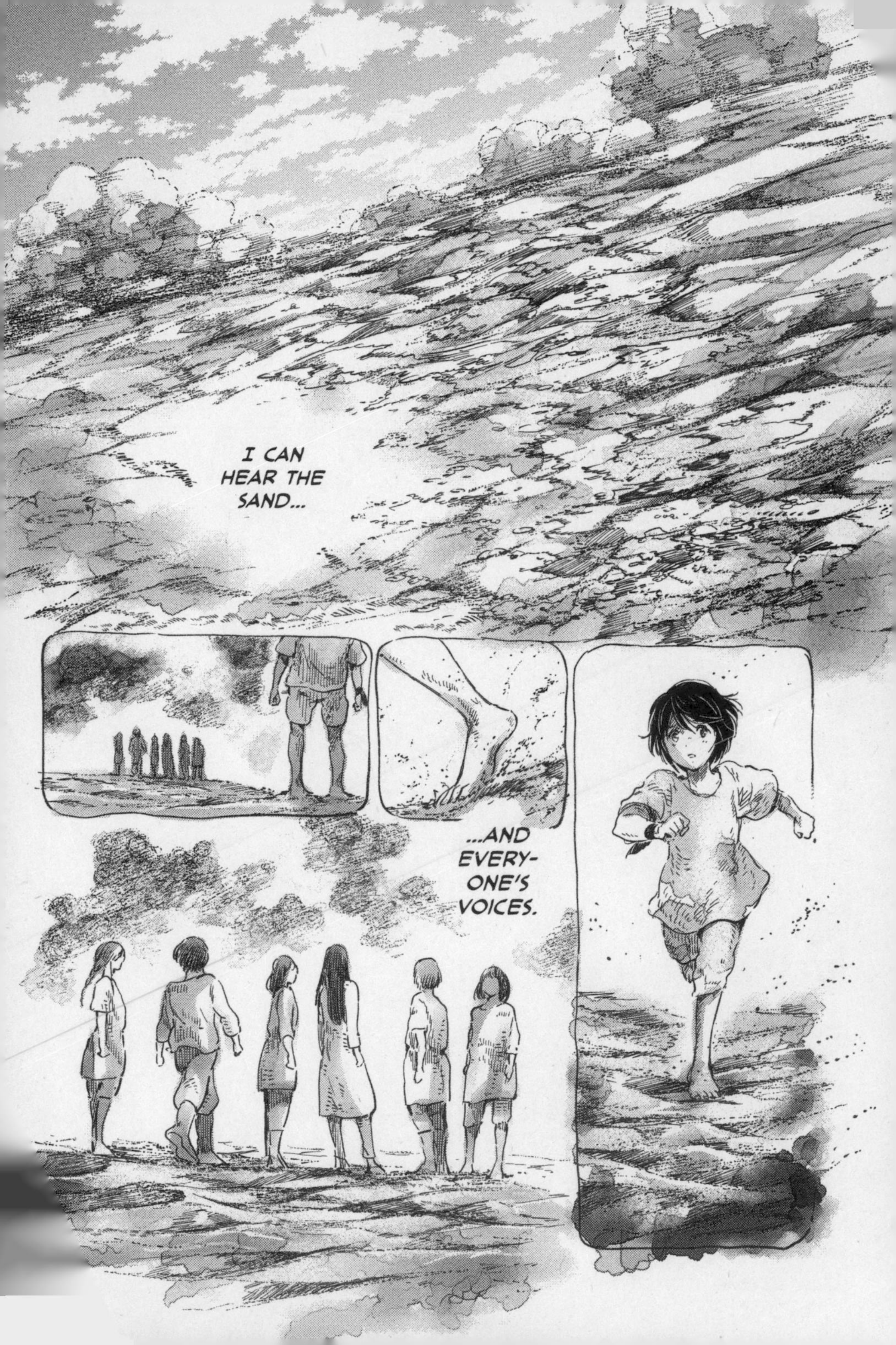
I CAN HEAR THE SAND...
...AND EVERY-ONE'S VOICES.

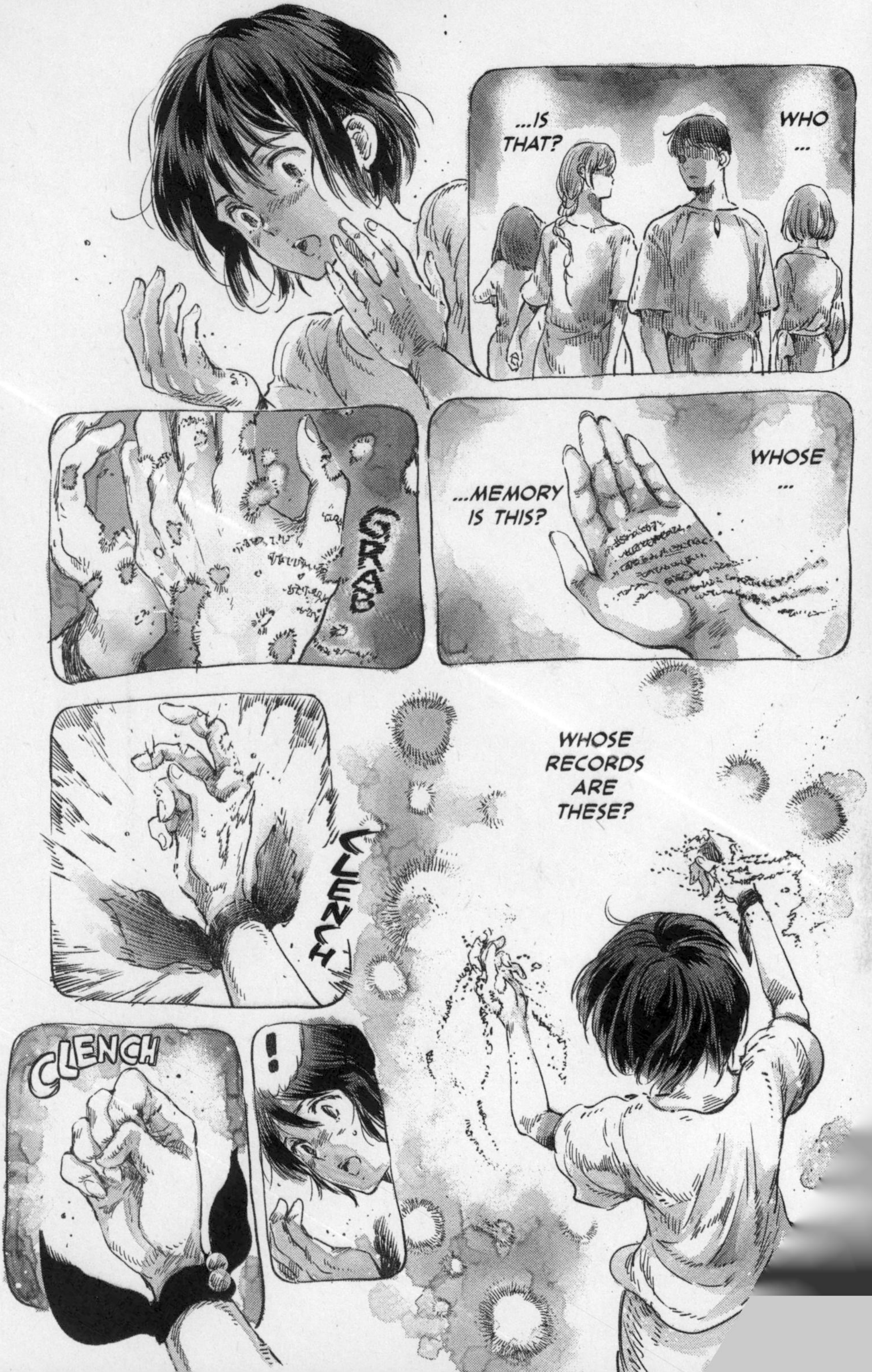
WHO ...
...IS THAT?
WHOSE ...
...MEMORY IS THIS?
GRAB
WHOSE RECORDS ARE THESE?
CLENCH
!
CLENCH

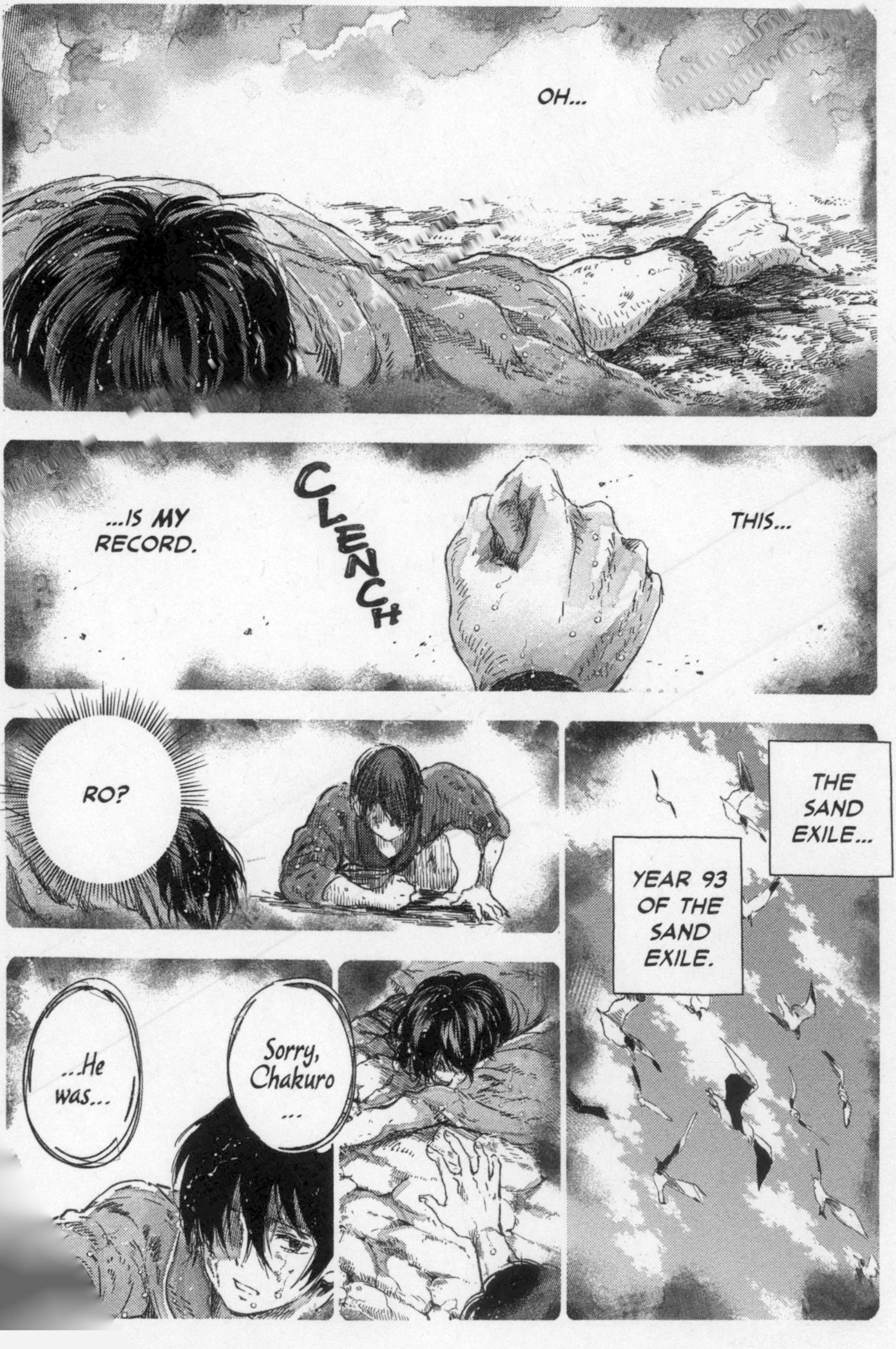
OH...
THIS...
CLENCH
...IS MY RECORD.
THE SAND EXILE...
YEAR 93 OF THE SAND EXILE.
RO?
Sorry, Chakuro...
...He was...

COM-MANDER?
IT'S OKAY...
...I CAN WALK BY MYSELF.

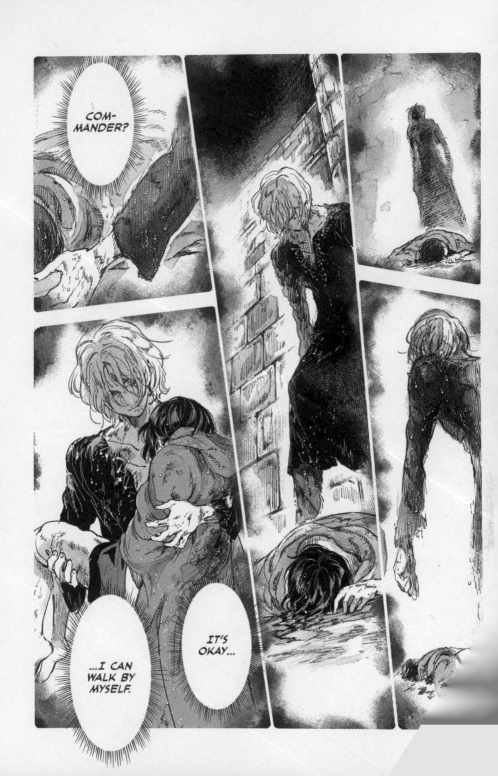

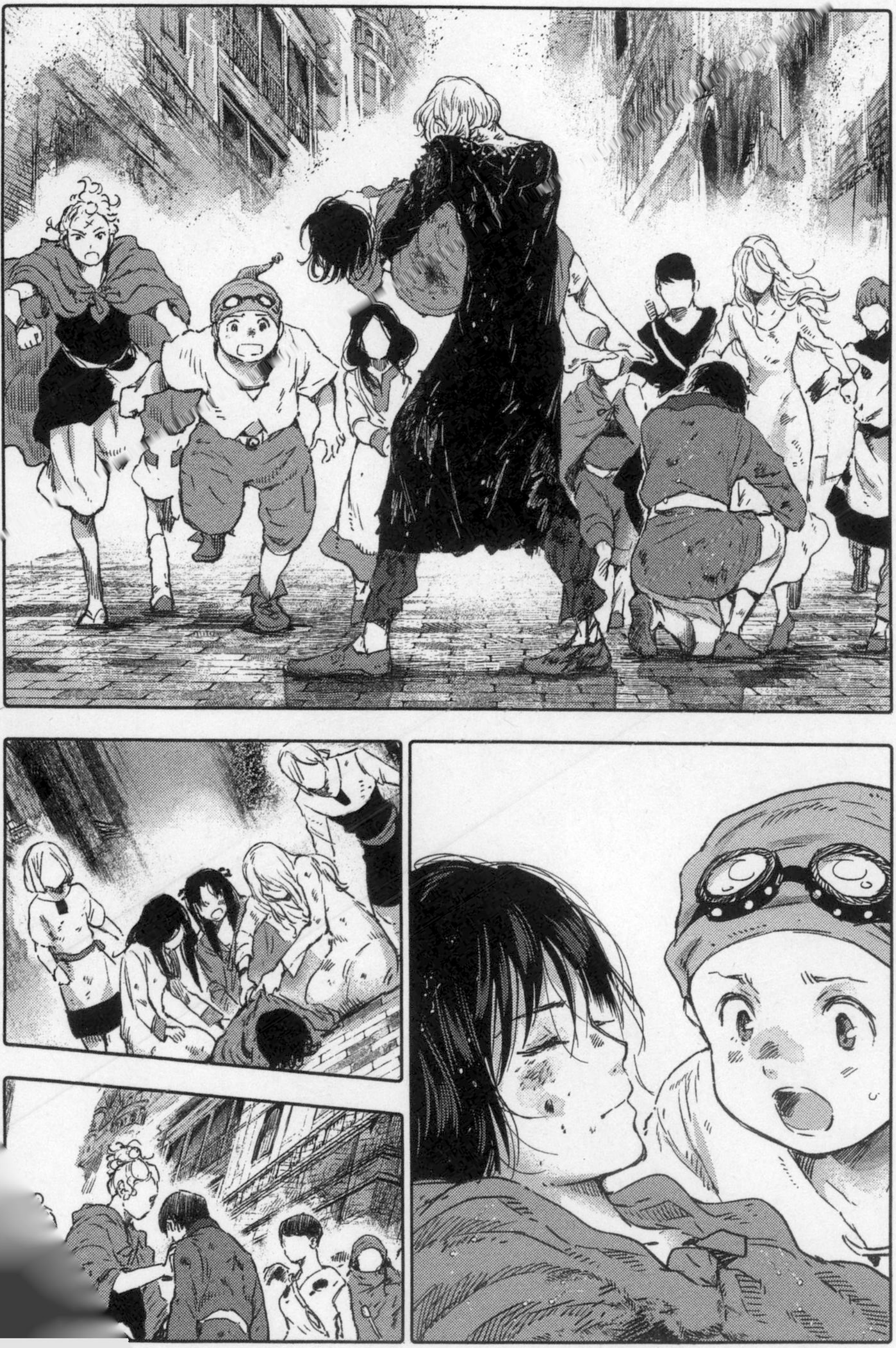

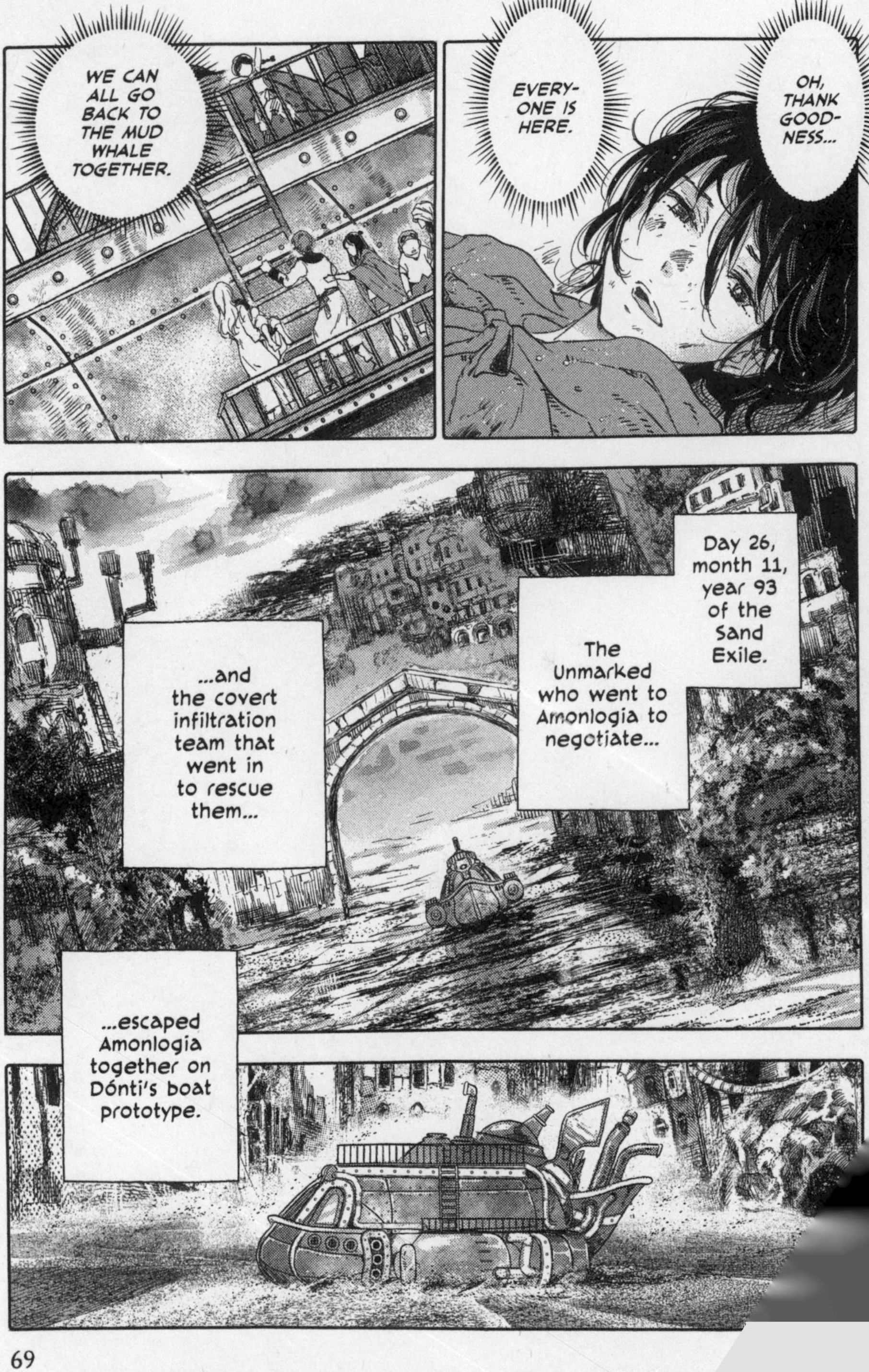
OH, THANK GOOD-NESS...
EVERY-ONE IS HERE.
WE CAN ALL GO BACK TO THE MUD WHALE TOGETHER.
Day 26, month 11, year 93 of the Sand Exile.
The Unmarked who went to Amonlogia to negotiate...
...and the covert infiltration team that went in to rescue them...
...escaped Amonlogia together on Dónti's boat prototype.

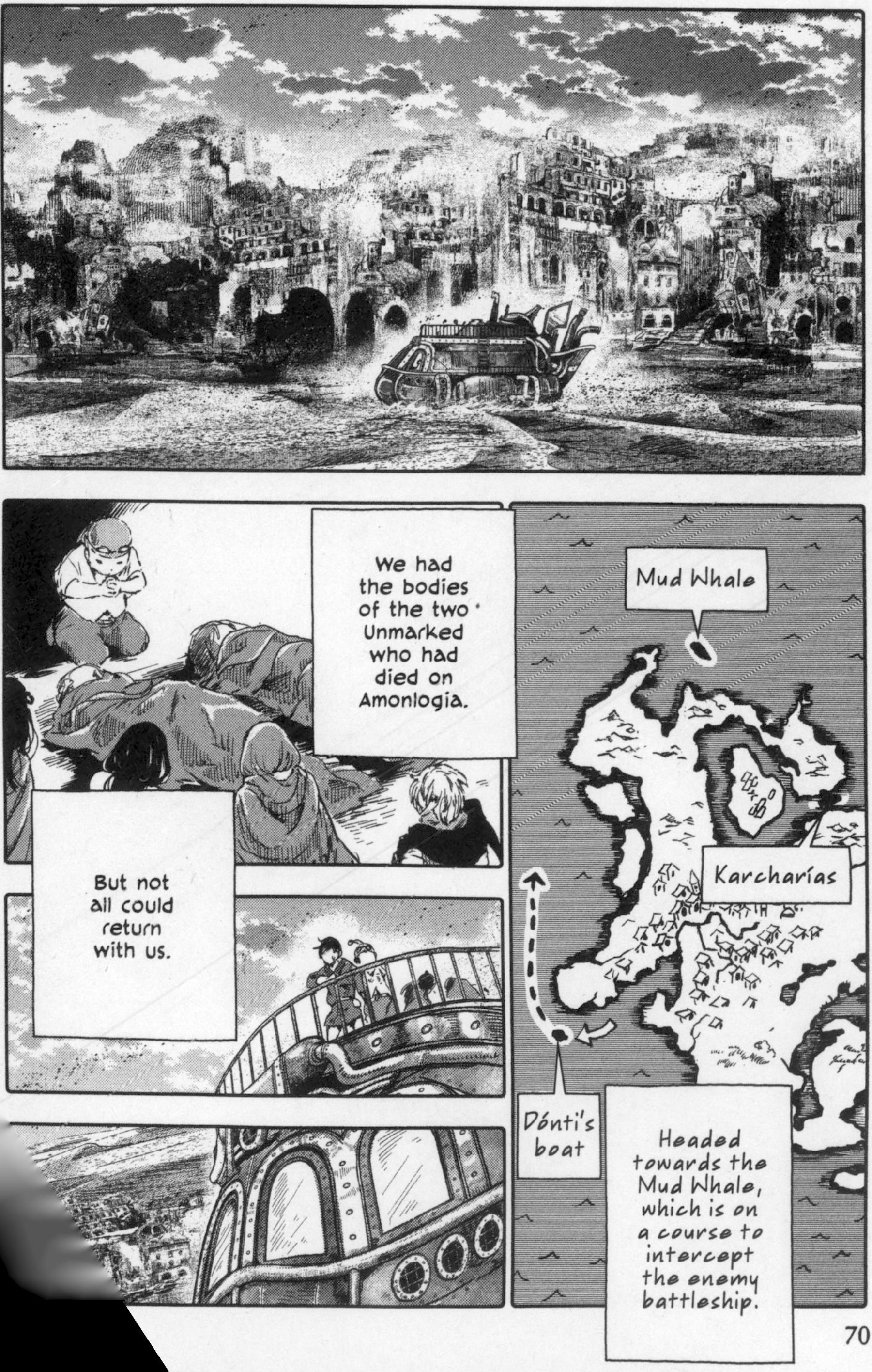
Mud Whale
Karcharías
Dónti's boat
Headed towards the Mud Whale, which is on a course to intercept the enemy battleship.
We had the bodies of the two Unmarked who had died on Amonlogia.
But not all could return with us.

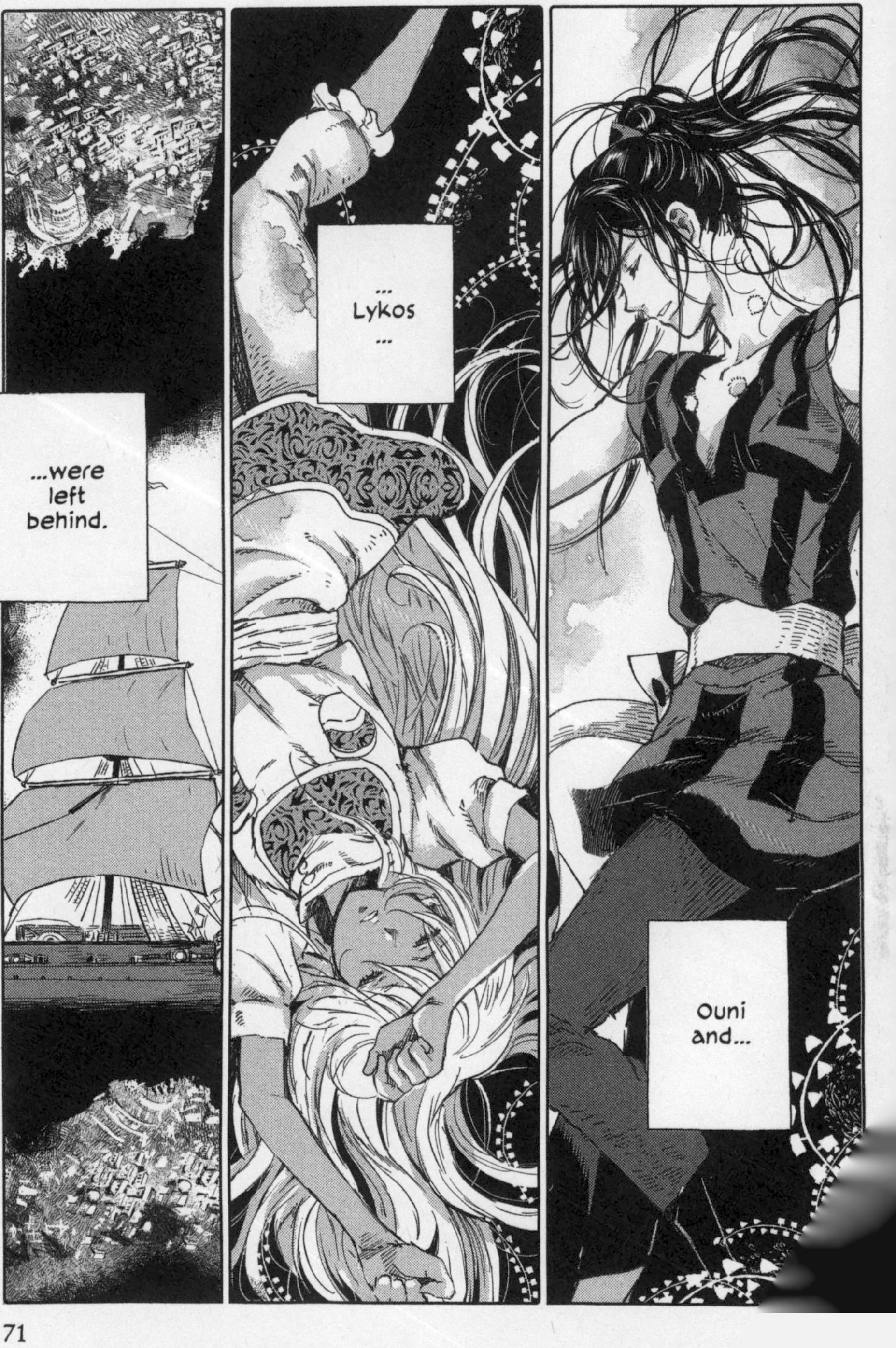
Ouni and...
... Lykos ...
...were left behind.

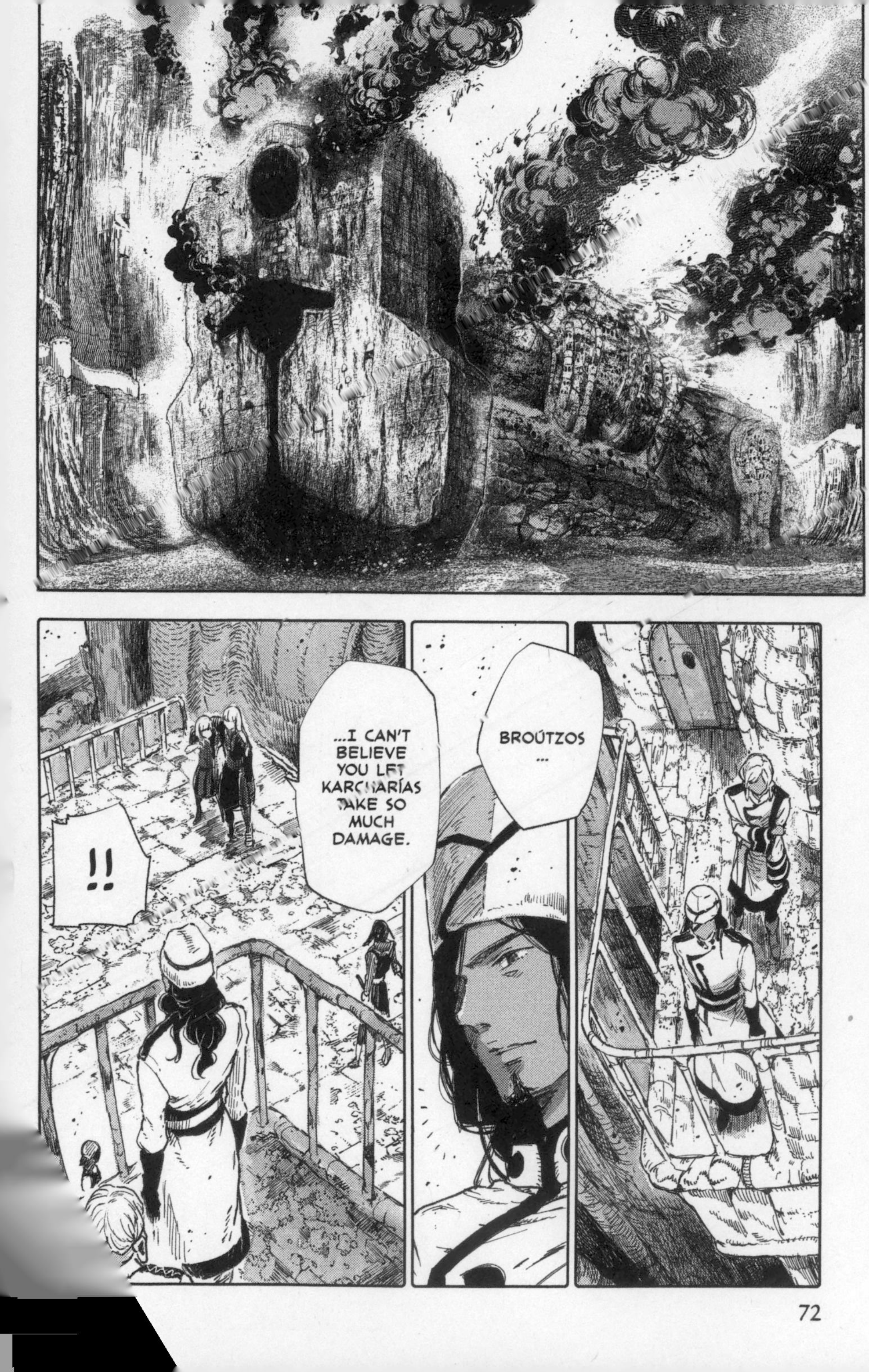

BROÚTZOS ...
...I CAN'T BELIEVE YOU LET KARCHARÍAS TAKE SO MUCH DAMAGE.
!!

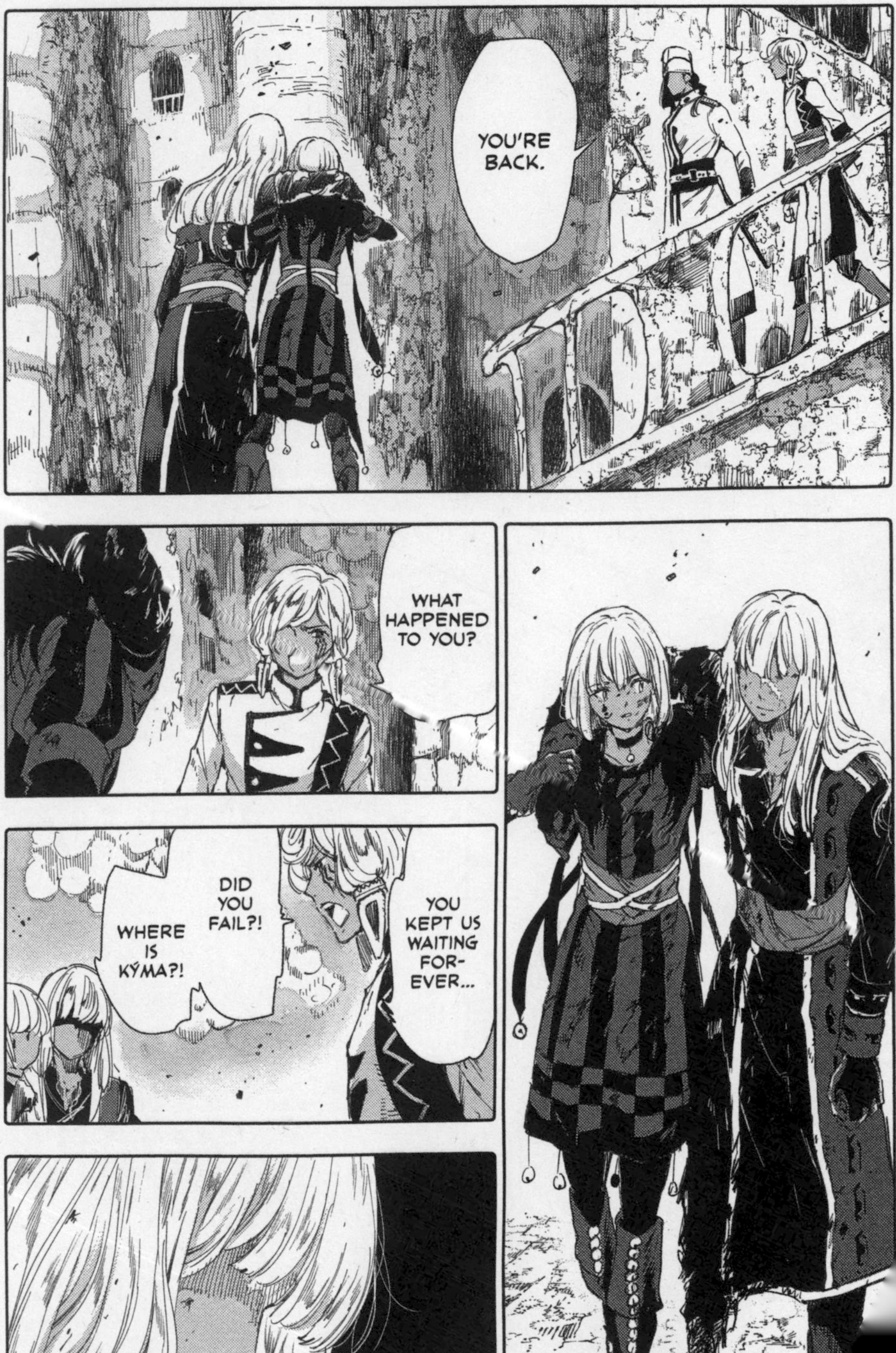
YOU'RE BACK.
WHAT HAPPENED TO YOU?
YOU KEPT US WAITING FOR-EVER...
DID YOU FAIL?!
WHERE IS KÝMA?!

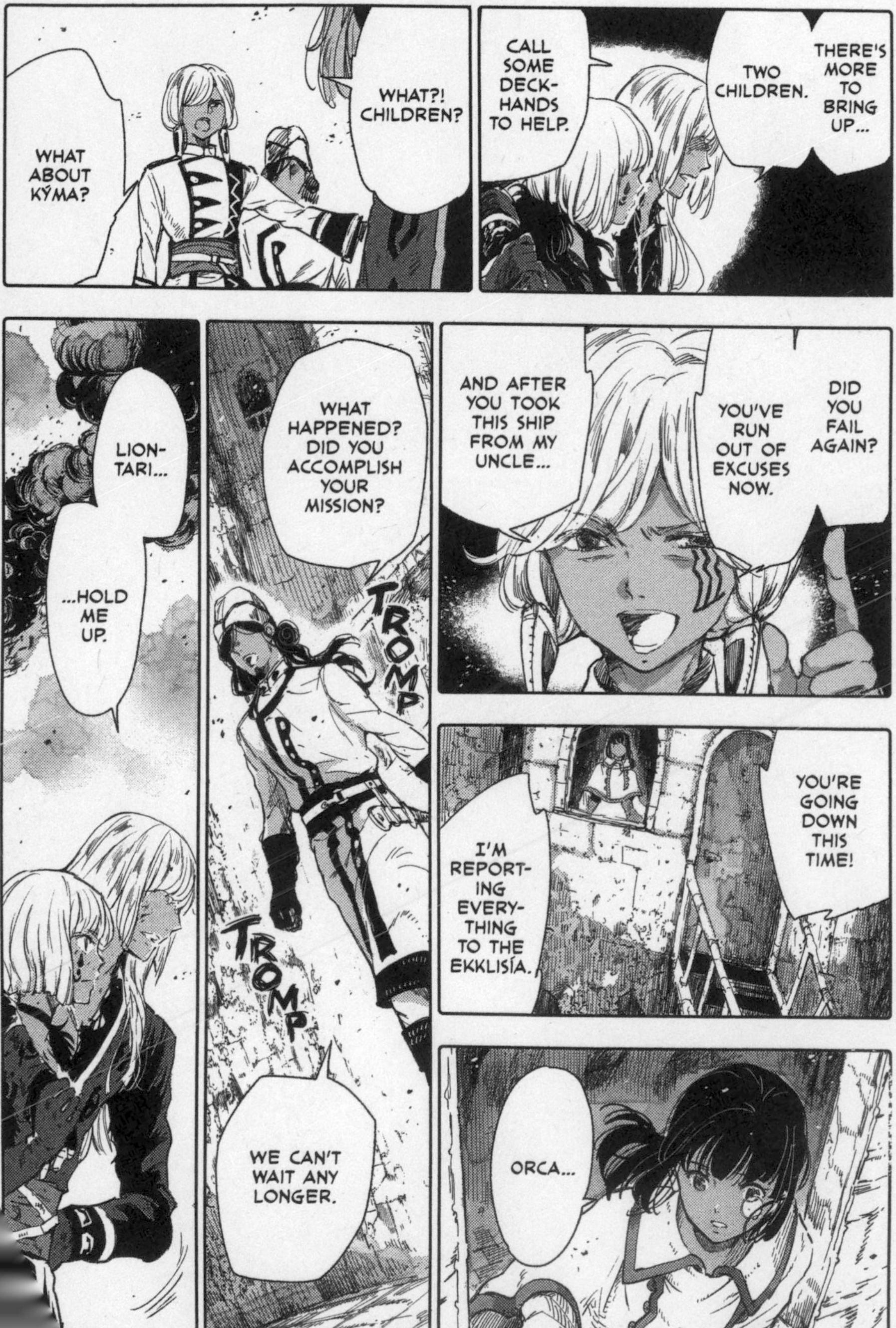
THERE'S MORE TO BRING UP...
TWO CHILDREN.
CALL SOME DECK-HANDS TO HELP.
WHAT?! CHILDREN?
WHAT ABOUT KÝMA?
DID YOU FAIL AGAIN?
YOU'VE RUN OUT OF EXCUSES NOW.
AND AFTER YOU TOOK THIS SHIP FROM MY UNCLE...
YOU'RE GOING DOWN THIS TIME!
I'M REPORTING EVERYTHING TO THE EKKLISÍA.
ORCA...
WHAT HAPPENED? DID YOU ACCOMPLISH YOUR MISSION?
TROMP
TROMP
WE CAN'T WAIT ANY LONGER.
LION-TARI...
...HOLD ME UP.

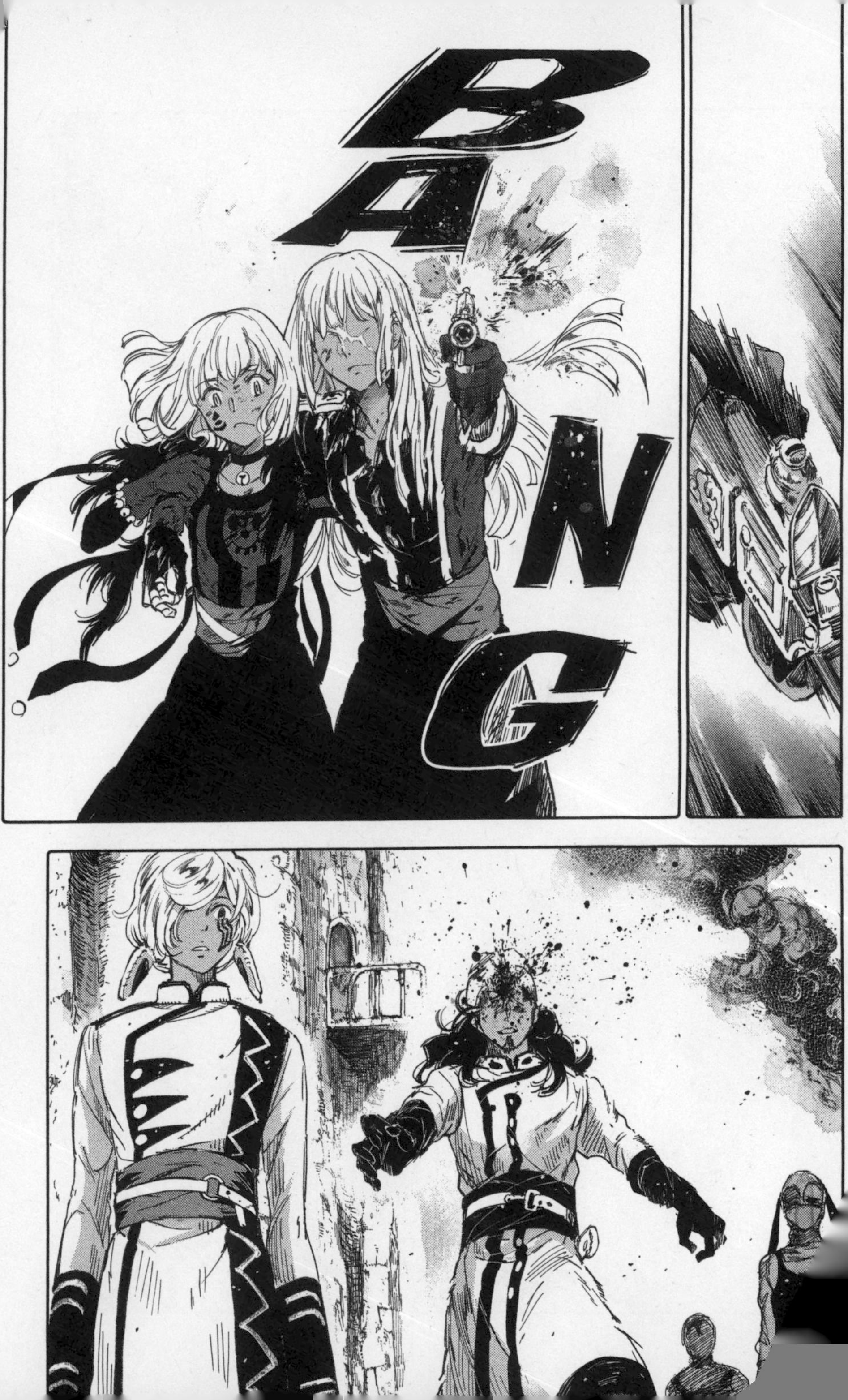
BANG

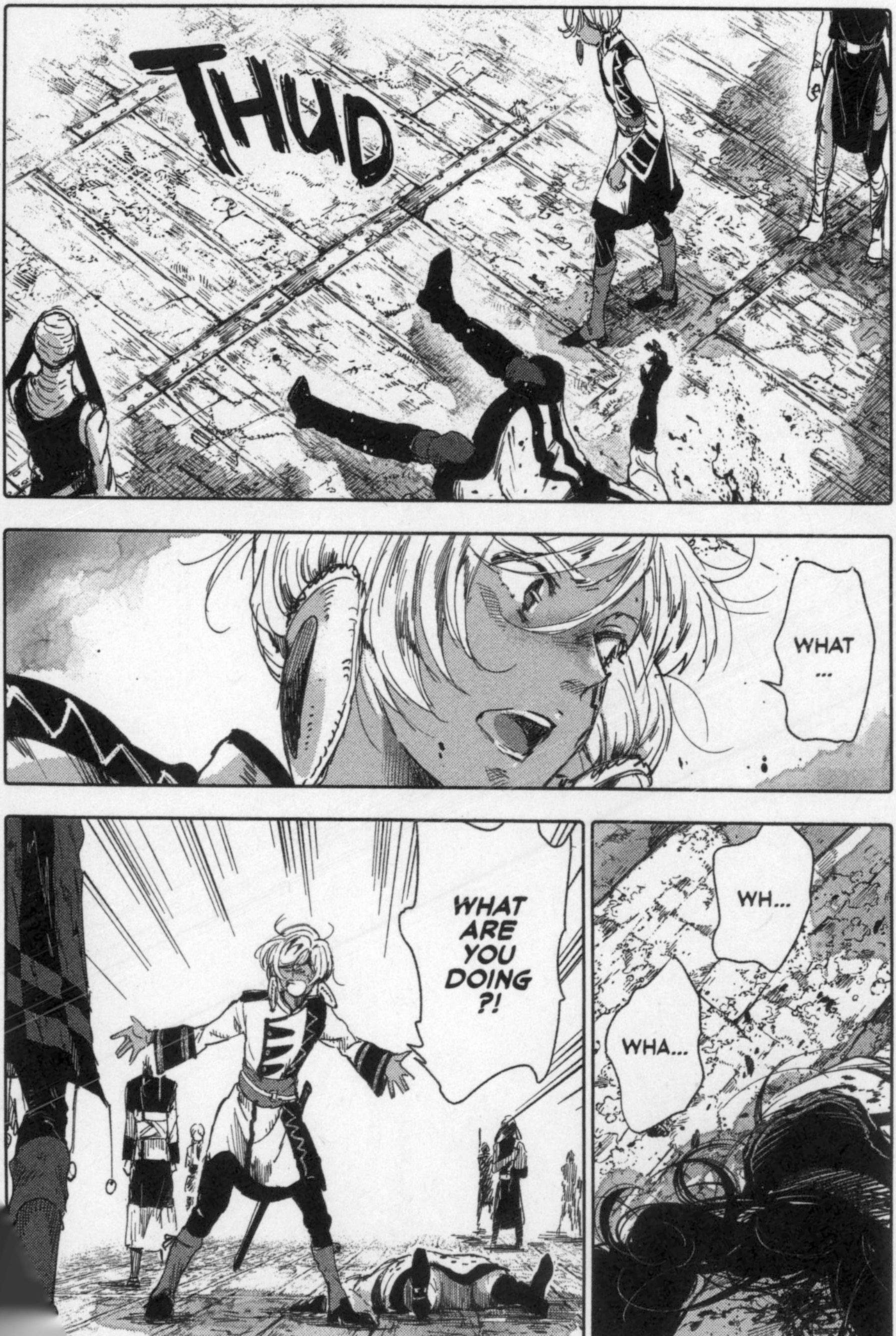
THUD
WHAT...
WH...
WHA...
WHAT ARE YOU DOING?!

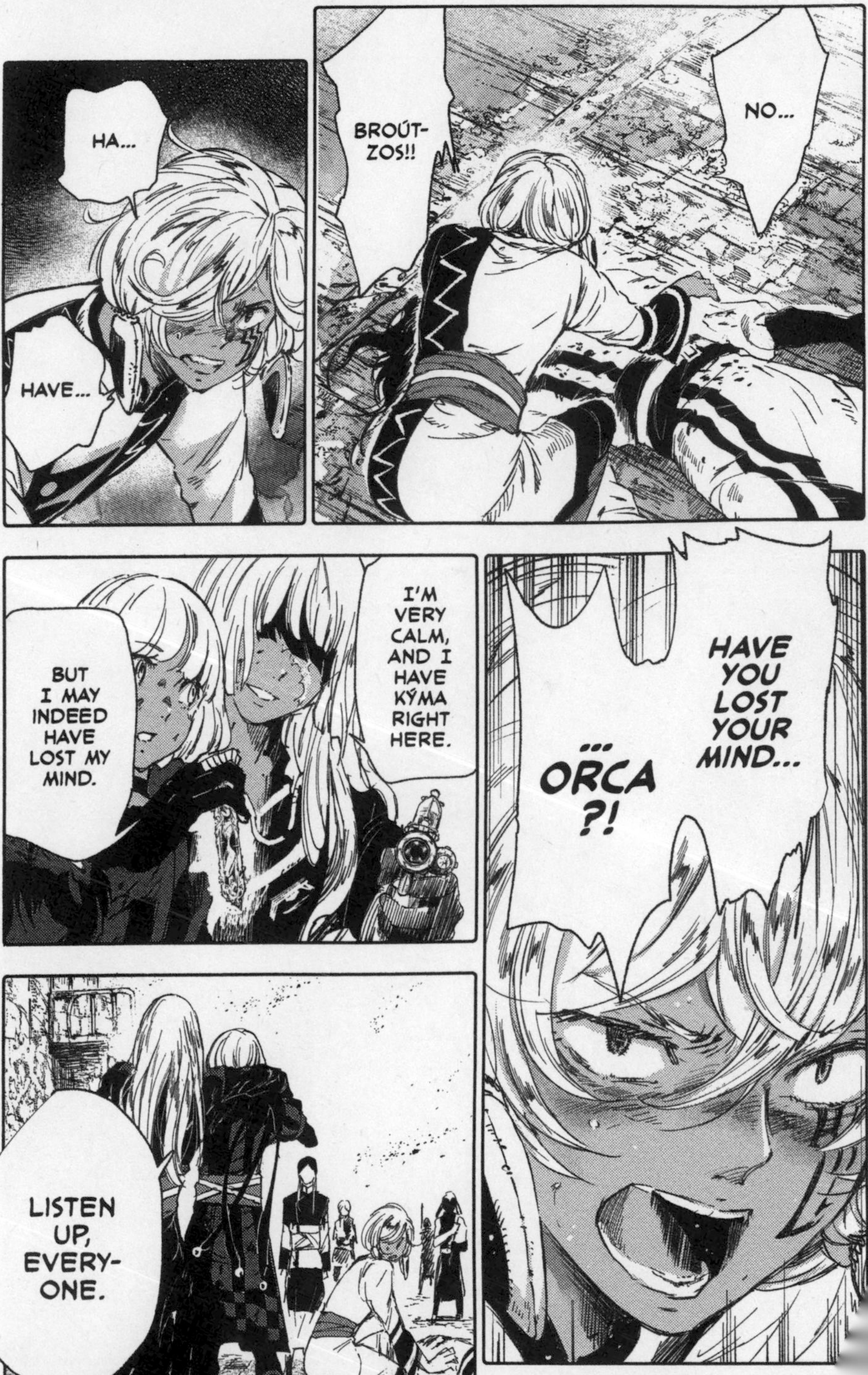
NO...
BROÚT-ZOS!!
HA...
HAVE...
HAVE YOU LOST YOUR MIND...
...ORCA?!
I'M VERY CALM, AND I HAVE KÝMA RIGHT HERE.
BUT I MAY INDEED HAVE LOST MY MIND.
LISTEN UP, EVERY-ONE.

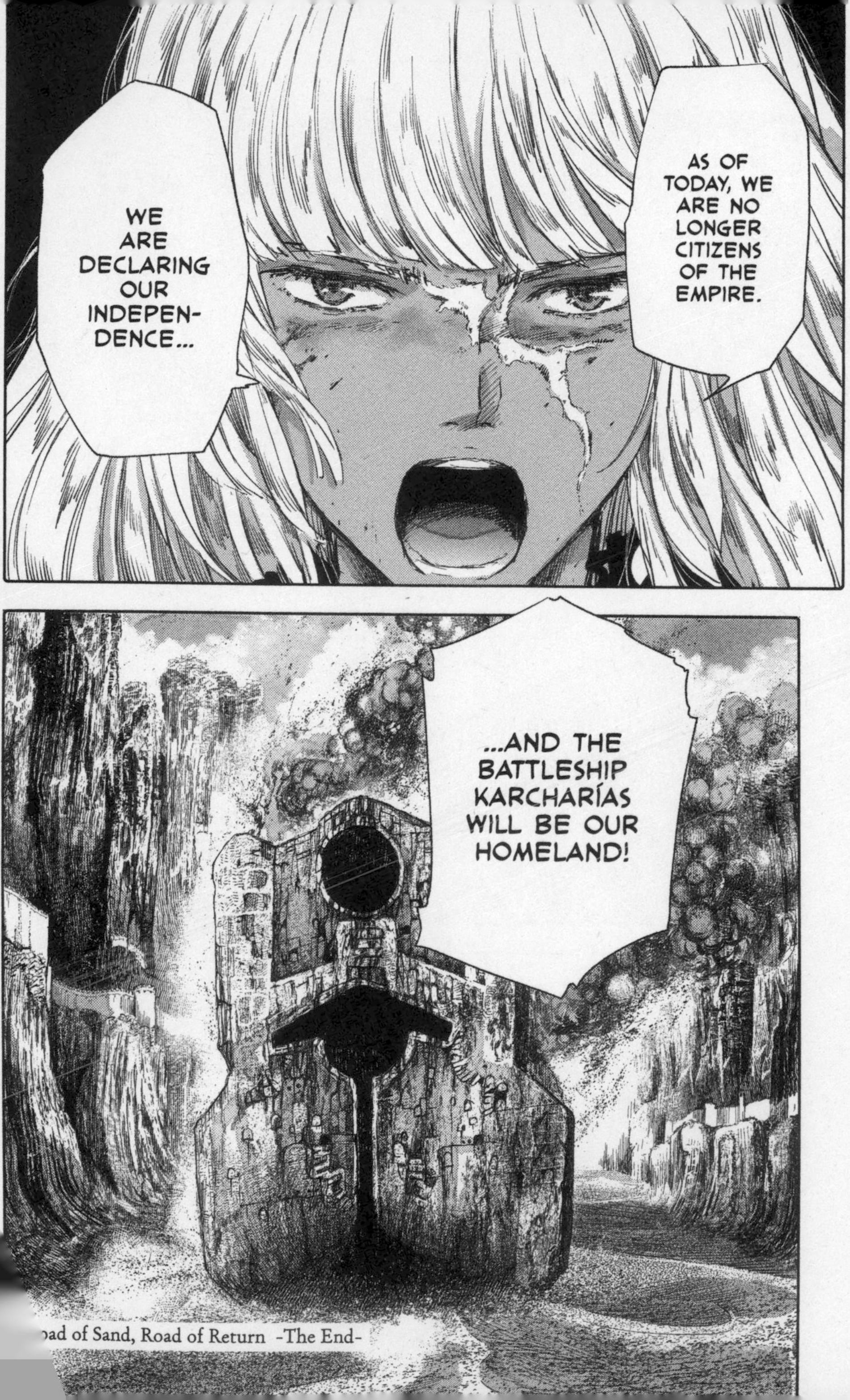
AS OF TODAY, WE ARE NO LONGER CITIZENS OF THE EMPIRE.
WE ARE DECLARING OUR INDEPEN-DENCE...
...AND THE BATTLESHIP KARCHARÍAS WILL BE OUR HOMELAND!

oad of Sand, Road of Return -The End-

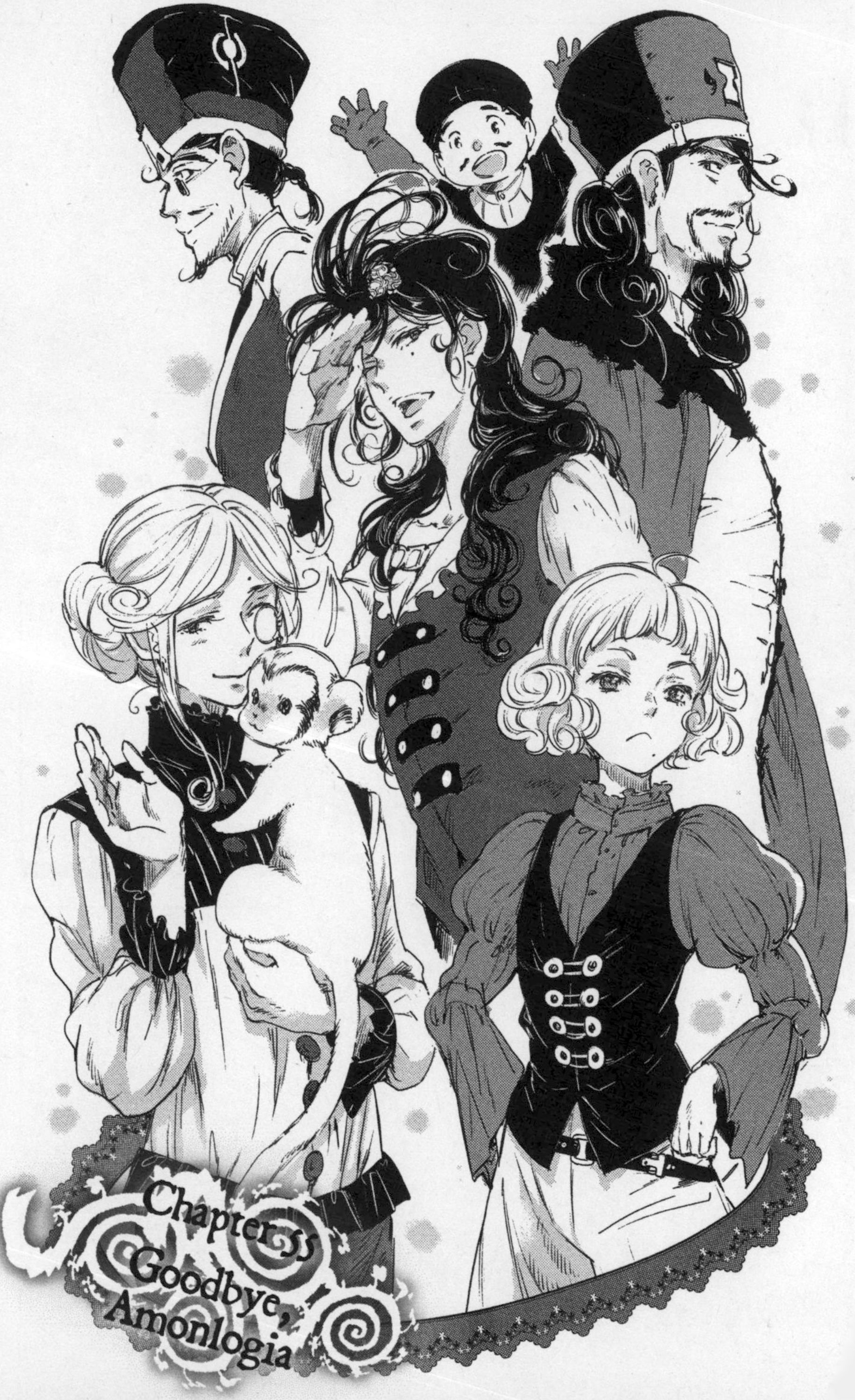
Chapter 55
Goodbye, Amonlogia

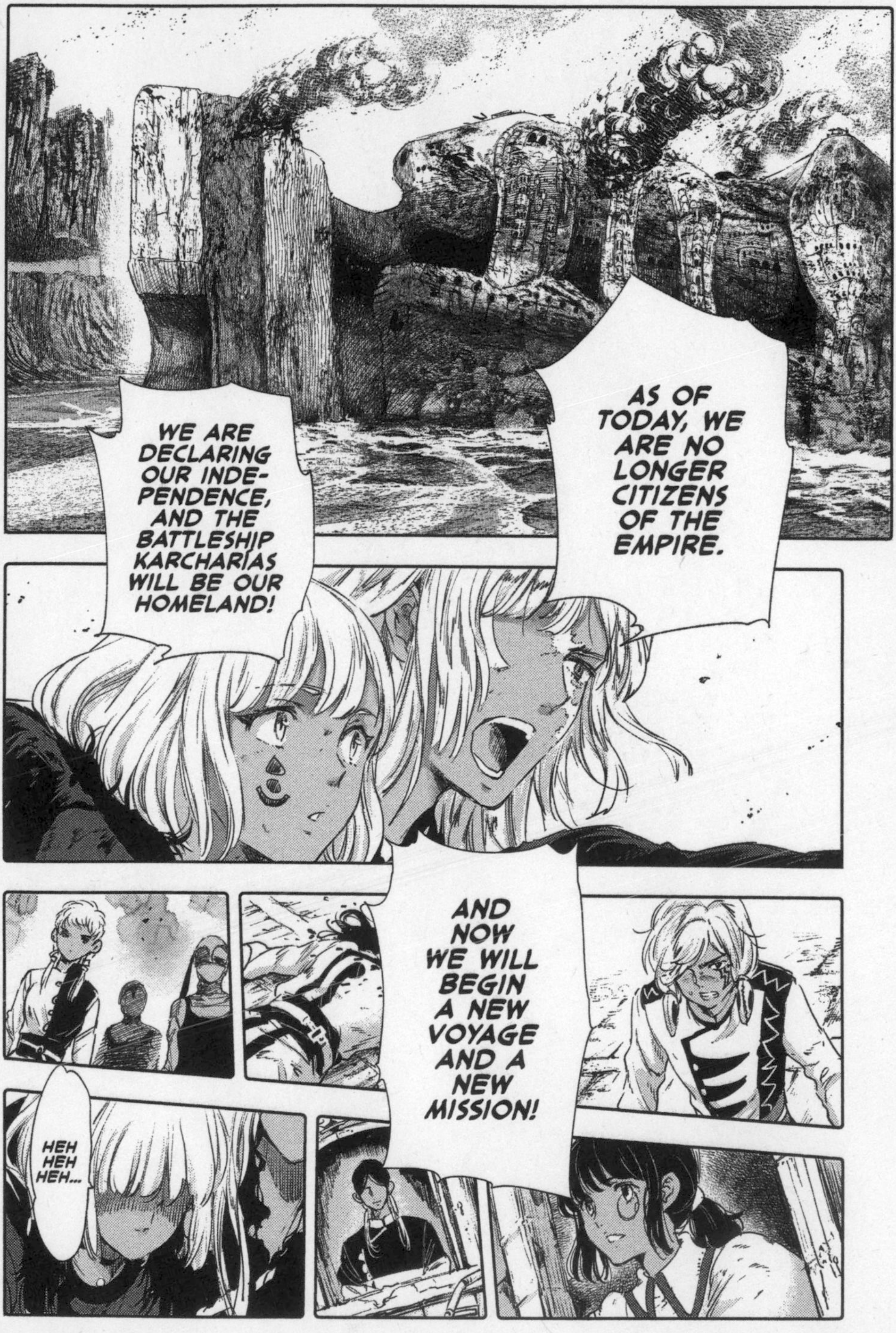
AS OF TODAY, WE ARE NO LONGER CITIZENS OF THE EMPIRE.
WE ARE DECLARING OUR INDE-PENDENCE, AND THE BATTLESHIP KARCHARIAS WILL BE OUR HOMELAND!
AND NOW WE WILL BEGIN A NEW VOYAGE AND A NEW MISSION!
HEH HEH HEH...

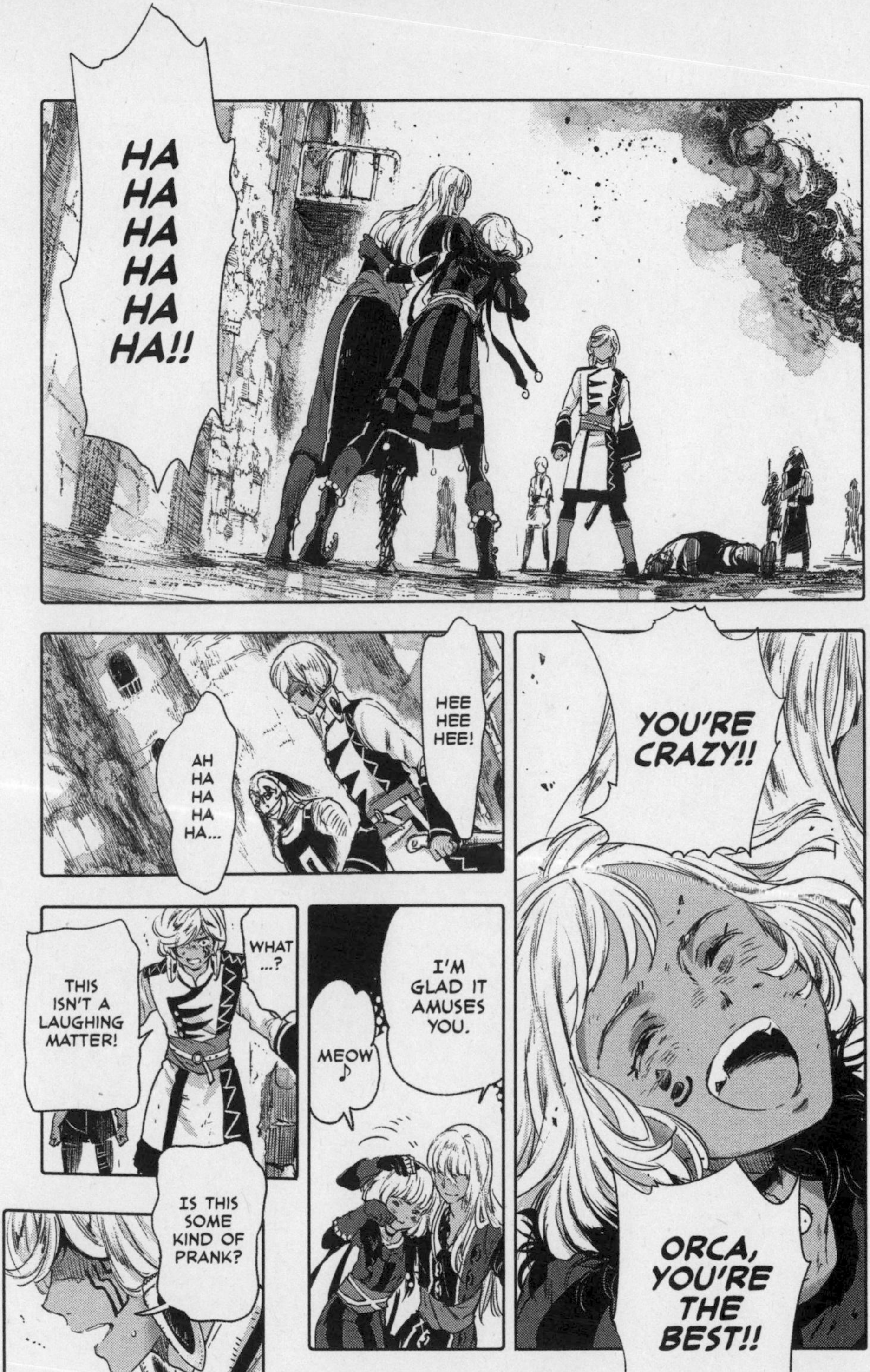
HA HA HA HA HA HA!!
YOU'RE CRAZY!!
ORCA, YOU'RE THE BEST!!
HEE HEE HEE!
AH HA HA HA HA...
I'M GLAD IT AMUSES YOU.
MEOW ♪
WHAT ...?
THIS ISN'T A LAUGHING MATTER!
IS THIS SOME KIND OF PRANK?
...

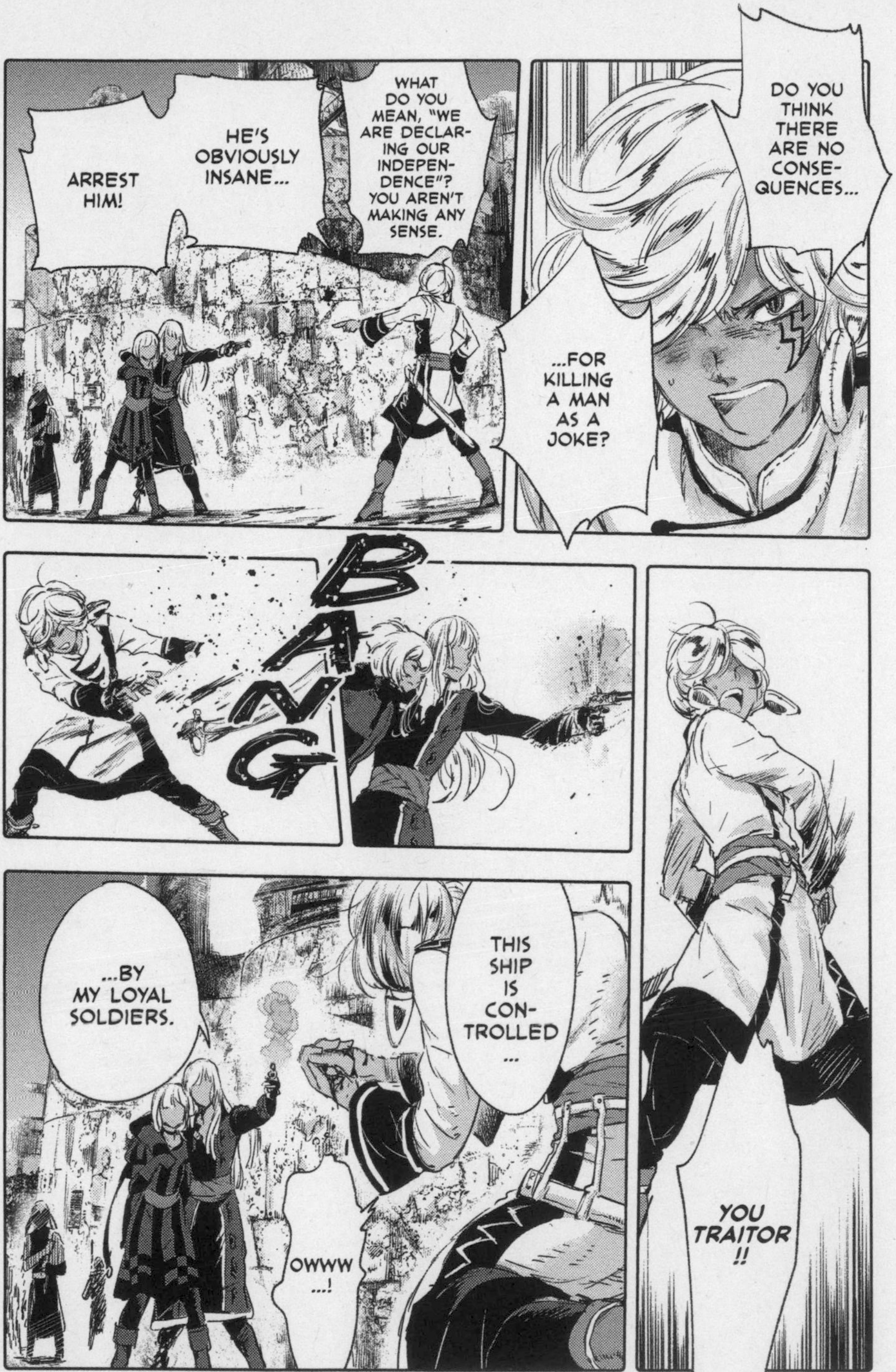
DO YOU THINK THERE ARE NO CONSEQUENCES...
...FOR KILLING A MAN AS A JOKE?
WHAT DO YOU MEAN, "WE ARE DECLARING OUR INDEPENDENCE"? YOU AREN'T MAKING ANY SENSE.
HE'S OBVIOUSLY INSANE...
ARREST HIM!
YOU TRAITOR!!
BANG
THIS SHIP IS CONTROLLED...
...BY MY LOYAL SOLDIERS.
OWWW...!

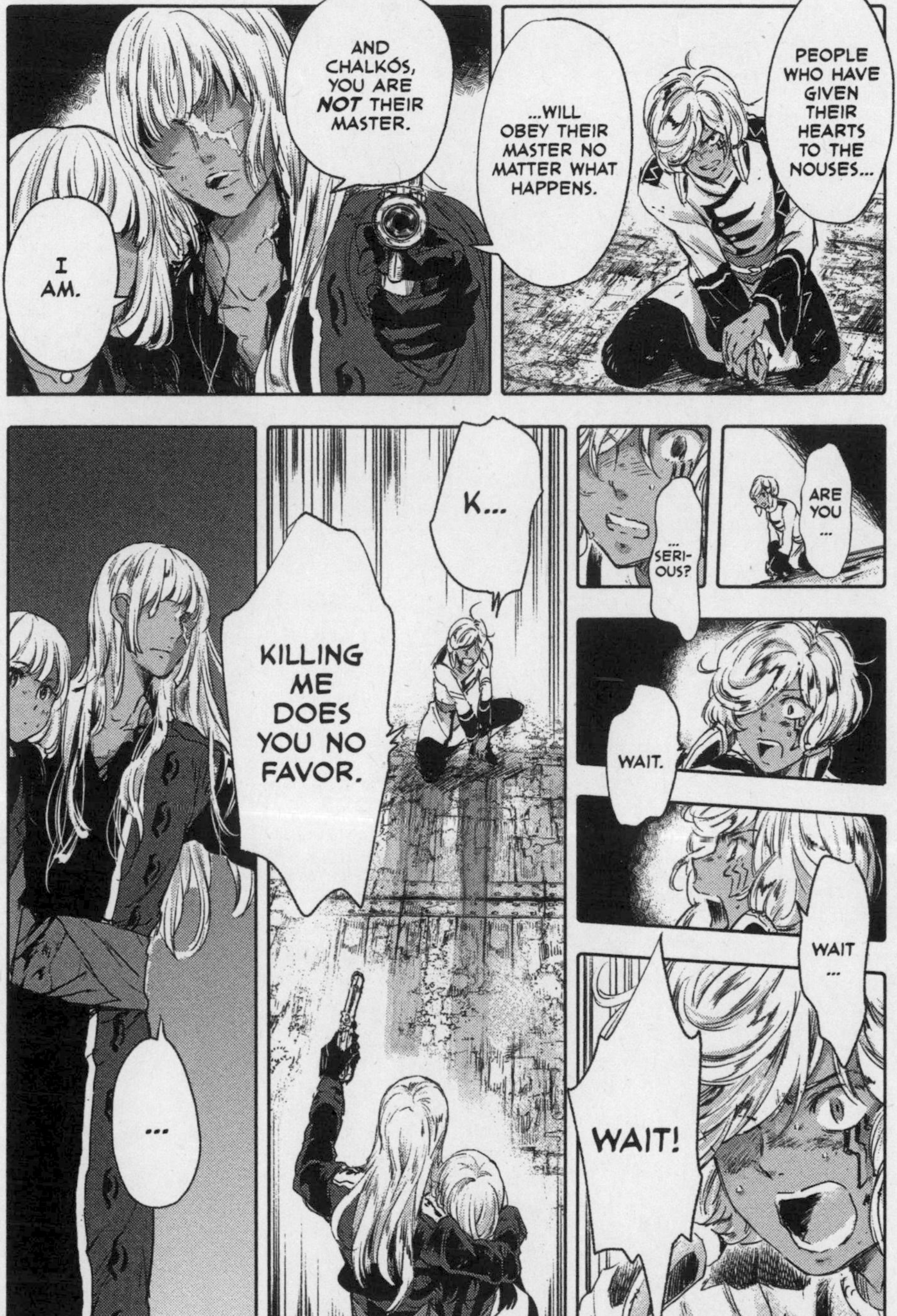

PEOPLE WHO HAVE GIVEN THEIR HEARTS TO THE NOUSES...
...WILL OBEY THEIR MASTER NO MATTER WHAT HAPPENS.
AND CHALKÓS, YOU ARE *NOT* THEIR MASTER.
I AM.
ARE YOU ...
... SERI-OUS?
WAIT.
WAIT ...
WAIT!
K...
KILLING ME DOES YOU NO FAVOR.
...

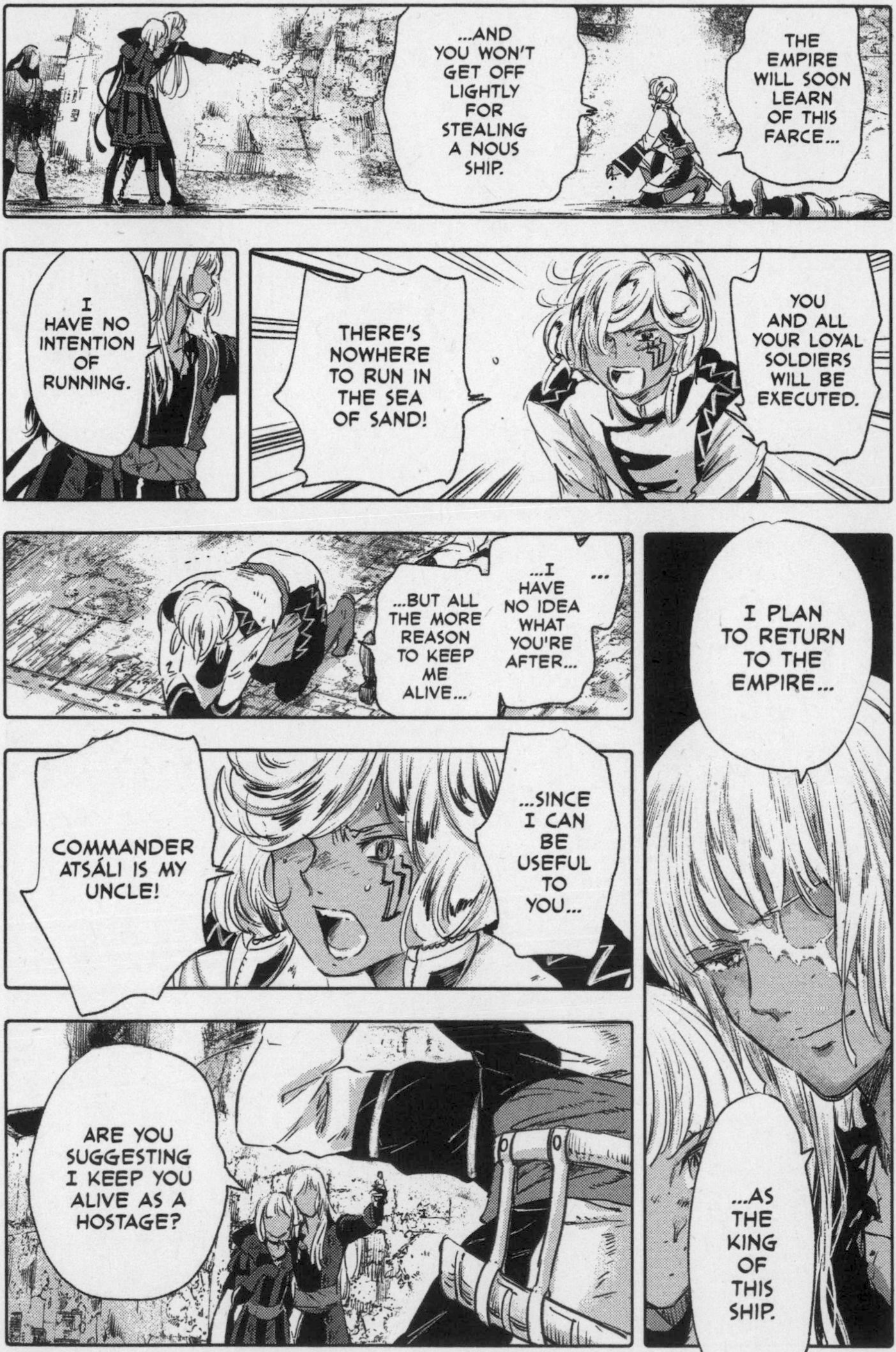
THE EMPIRE WILL SOON LEARN OF THIS FARCE...
...AND YOU WON'T GET OFF LIGHTLY FOR STEALING A NOUS SHIP.
YOU AND ALL YOUR LOYAL SOLDIERS WILL BE EXECUTED.
THERE'S NOWHERE TO RUN IN THE SEA OF SAND!
I HAVE NO INTENTION OF RUNNING.
I PLAN TO RETURN TO THE EMPIRE...
...AS THE KING OF THIS SHIP.
...
...I HAVE NO IDEA WHAT YOU'RE AFTER...
...BUT ALL THE MORE REASON TO KEEP ME ALIVE...
...SINCE I CAN BE USEFUL TO YOU...
COMMANDER ATSÁLI IS MY UNCLE!
ARE YOU SUGGESTING I KEEP YOU ALIVE AS A HOSTAGE?

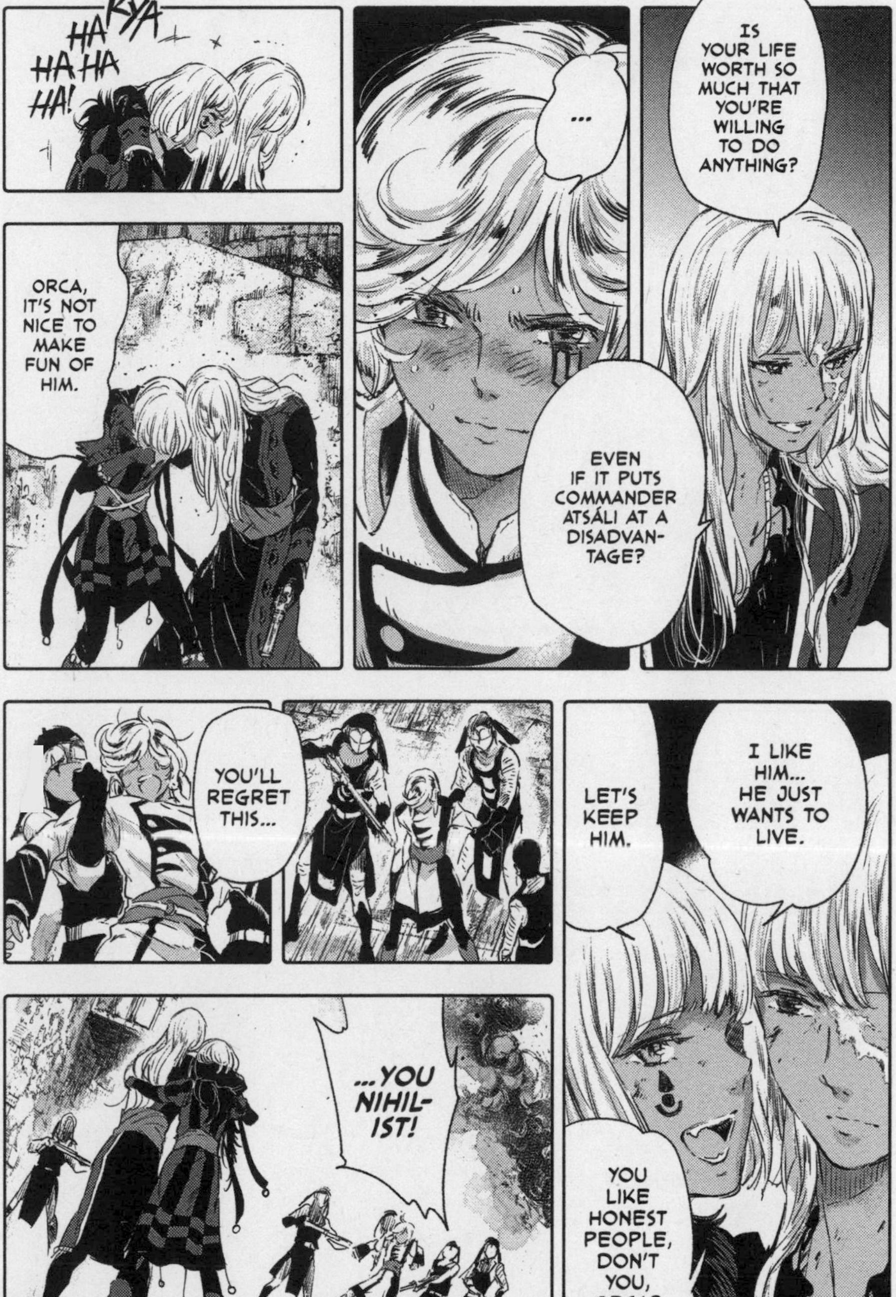
IS YOUR LIFE WORTH SO MUCH THAT YOU'RE WILLING TO DO ANYTHING?
EVEN IF IT PUTS COMMANDER ATSÁLI AT A DISADVAN-TAGE?
...
HA HA HA HA! KYA
ORCA, IT'S NOT NICE TO MAKE FUN OF HIM.
I LIKE HIM... HE JUST WANTS TO LIVE.
LET'S KEEP HIM.
YOU LIKE HONEST PEOPLE, DON'T YOU, ORCA?
YOU'LL REGRET THIS...
...YOU NIHIL-IST!

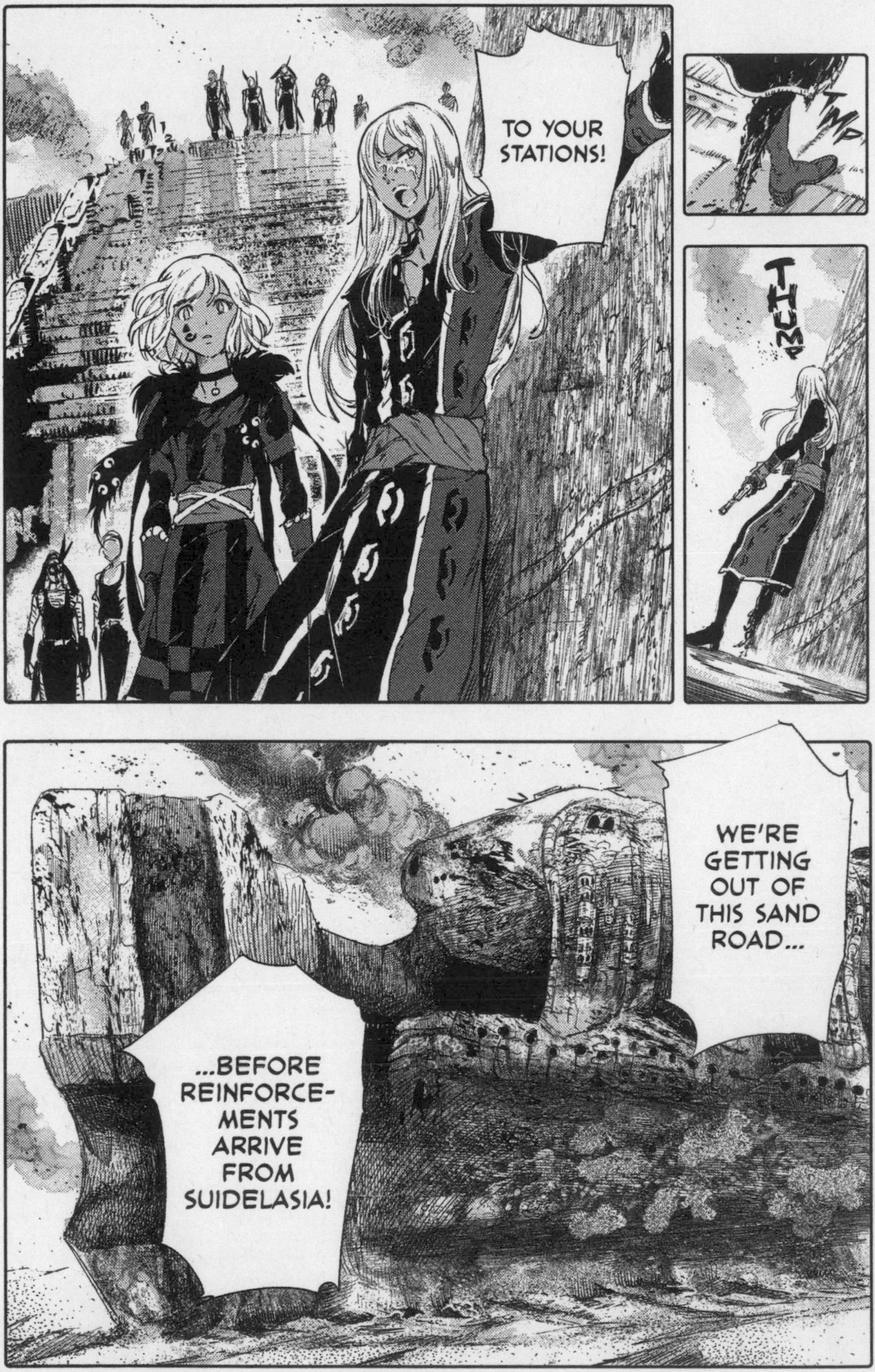
TMP
THUMP
TO YOUR STATIONS!
WE'RE GETTING OUT OF THIS SAND ROAD...
...BEFORE REINFORCEMENTS ARRIVE FROM SUIDELASIA!

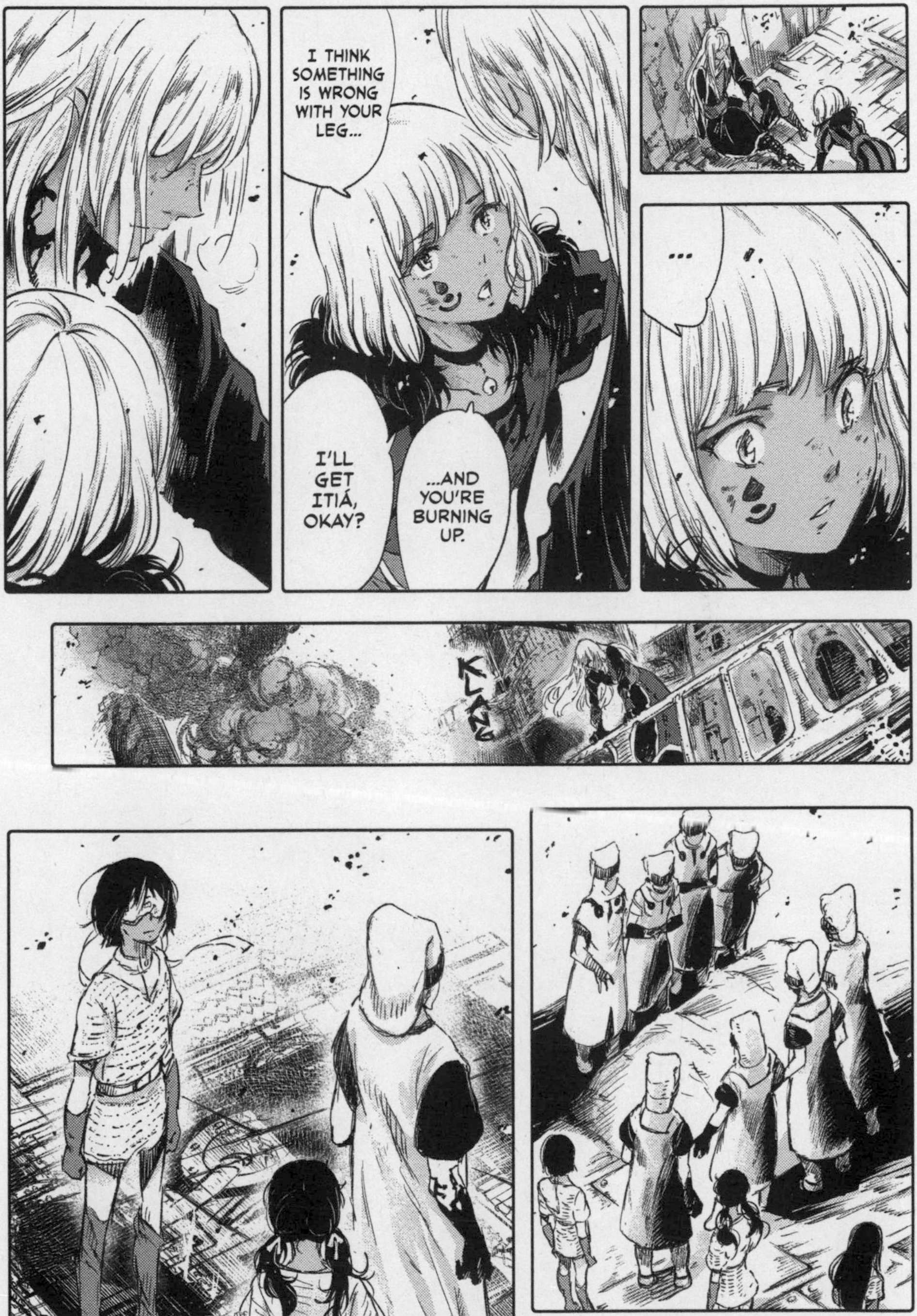
...
I THINK SOMETHING IS WRONG WITH YOUR LEG...
...AND YOU'RE BURNING UP.
I'LL GET ITIÁ, OKAY?
KLANG

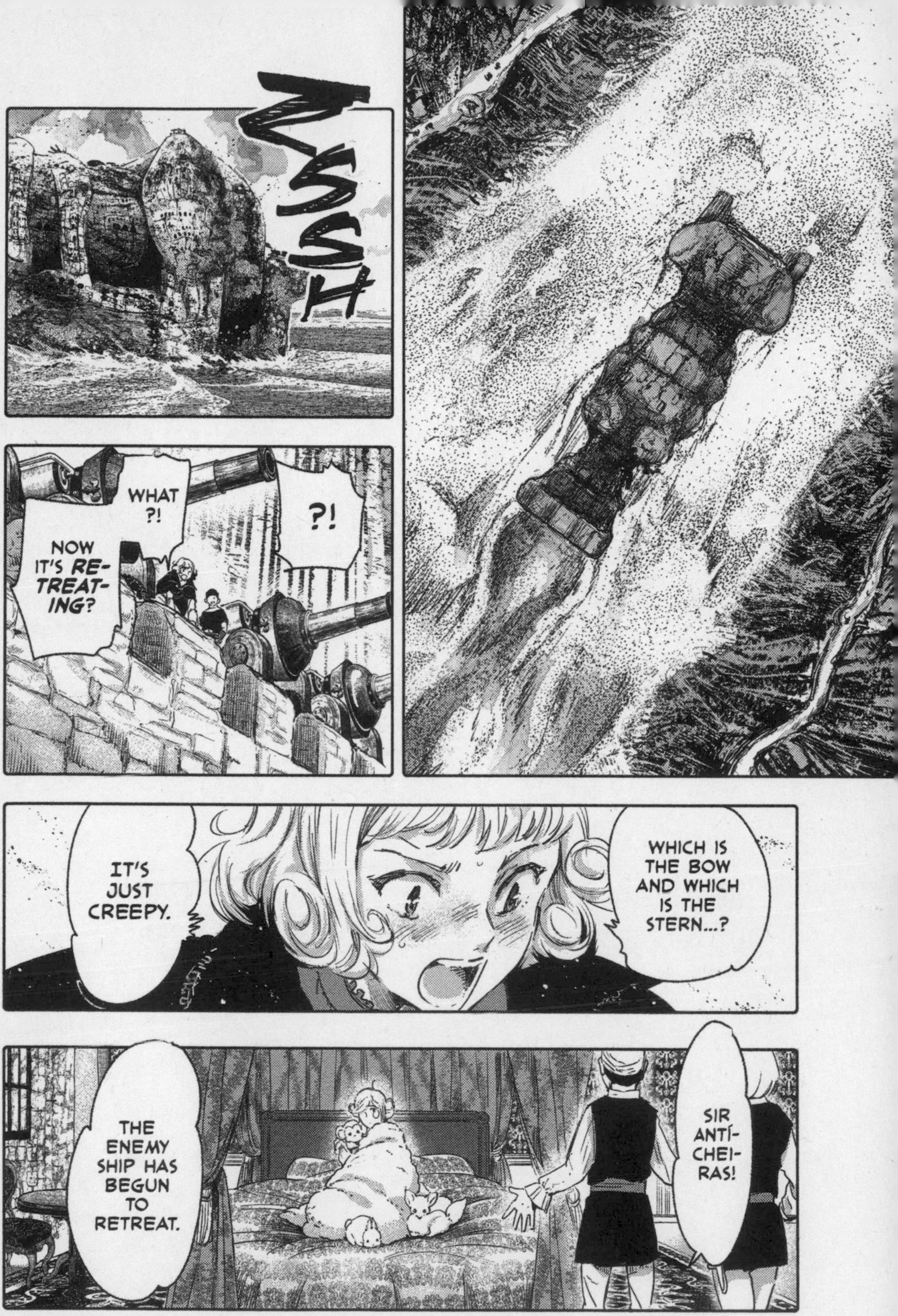
ZSSH
?!
WHAT ?!
NOW IT'S RE-TREAT-ING?
WHICH IS THE BOW AND WHICH IS THE STERN...?
IT'S JUST CREEPY.
SIR ANTÍCHEIRAS!
THE ENEMY SHIP HAS BEGUN TO RETREAT.

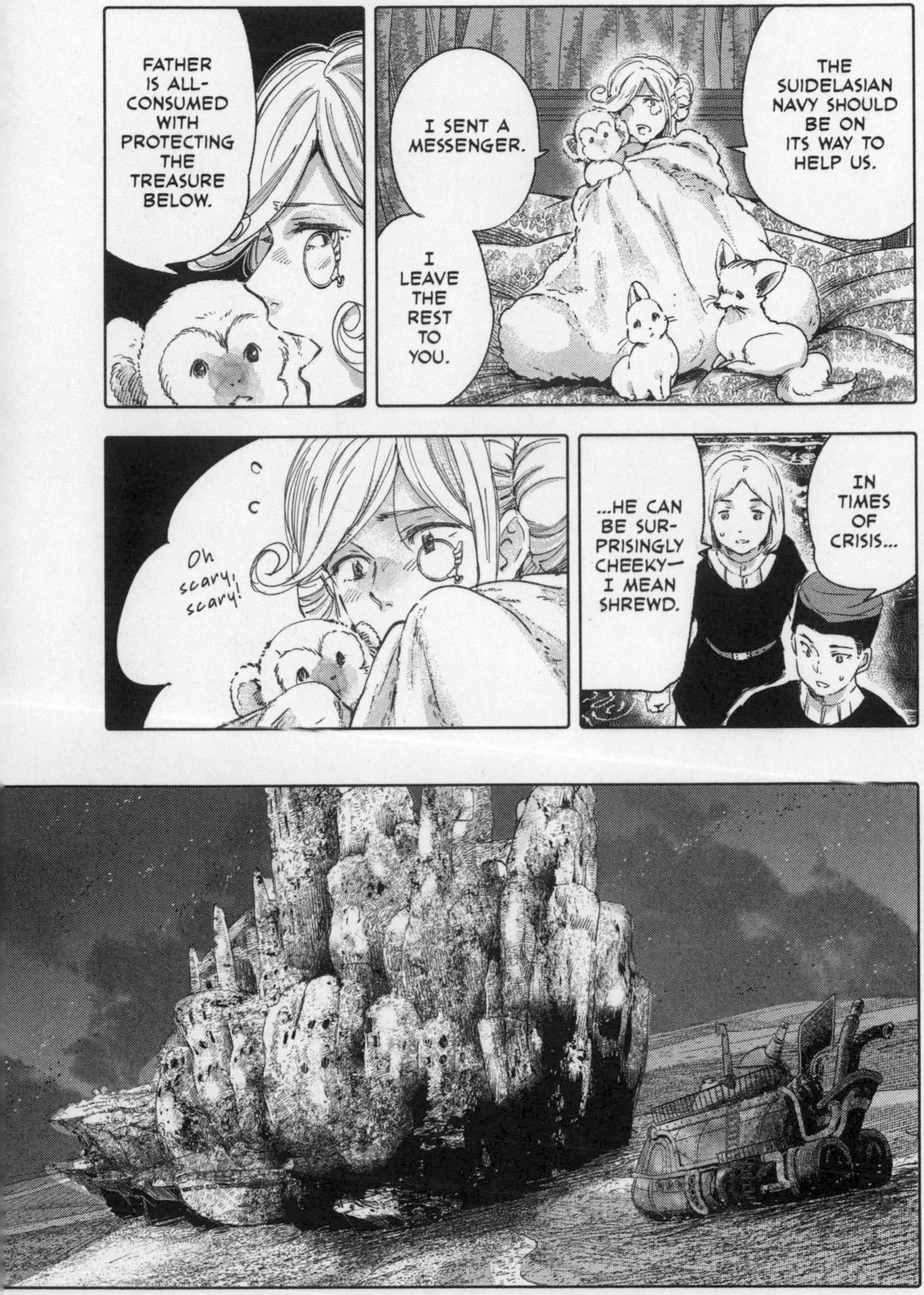
THE SUIDELASIAN NAVY SHOULD BE ON ITS WAY TO HELP US.
I SENT A MESSENGER.
I LEAVE THE REST TO YOU.
FATHER IS ALL-CONSUMED WITH PROTECTING THE TREASURE BELOW.
IN TIMES OF CRISIS...
...HE CAN BE SURPRISINGLY CHEEKY— I MEAN SHREWD.
Oh scary, scary!

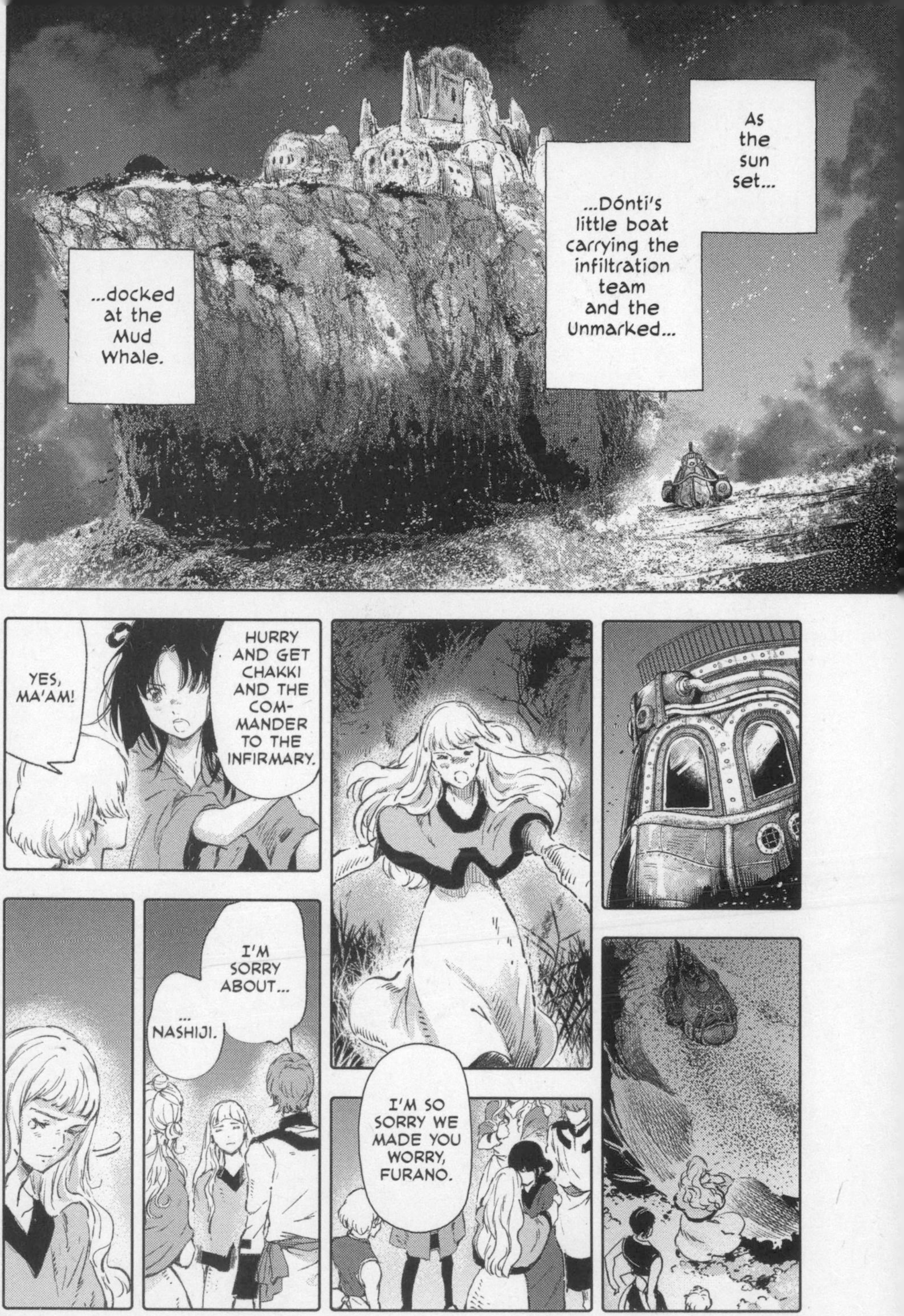
As the sun set...
...Dónti's little boat carrying the infiltration team and the Unmarked...
...docked at the Mud Whale.
HURRY AND GET CHAKKI AND THE COM-MANDER TO THE INFIRMARY.
YES, MA'AM!
I'M SO SORRY WE MADE YOU WORRY, FURANO.
I'M SORRY ABOUT...
...NASHIJI.

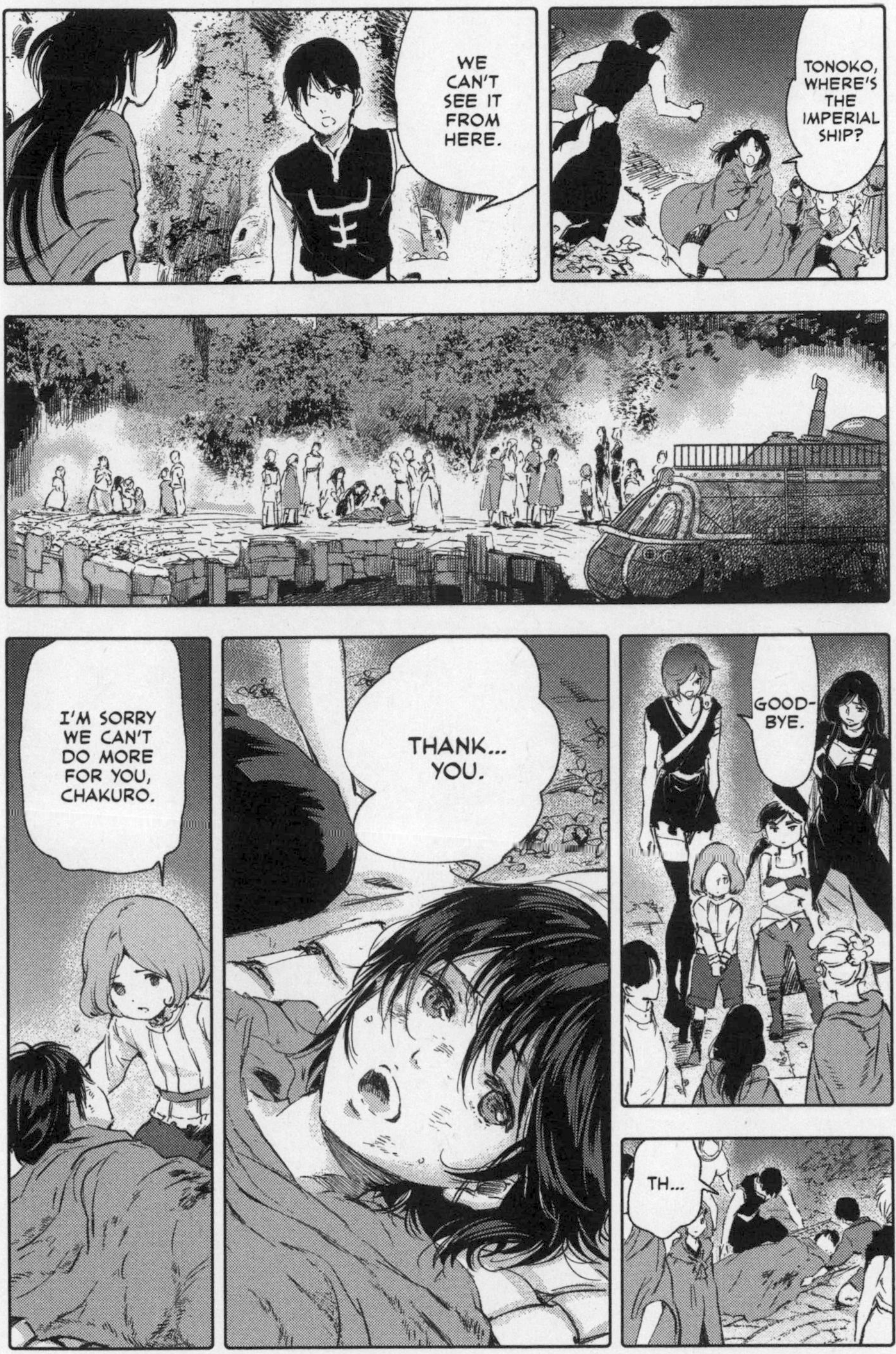
TONOKO, WHERE'S THE IMPERIAL SHIP?
WE CAN'T SEE IT FROM HERE.
GOOD-BYE.
TH...
THANK... YOU.
I'M SORRY WE CAN'T DO MORE FOR YOU, CHAKURO.

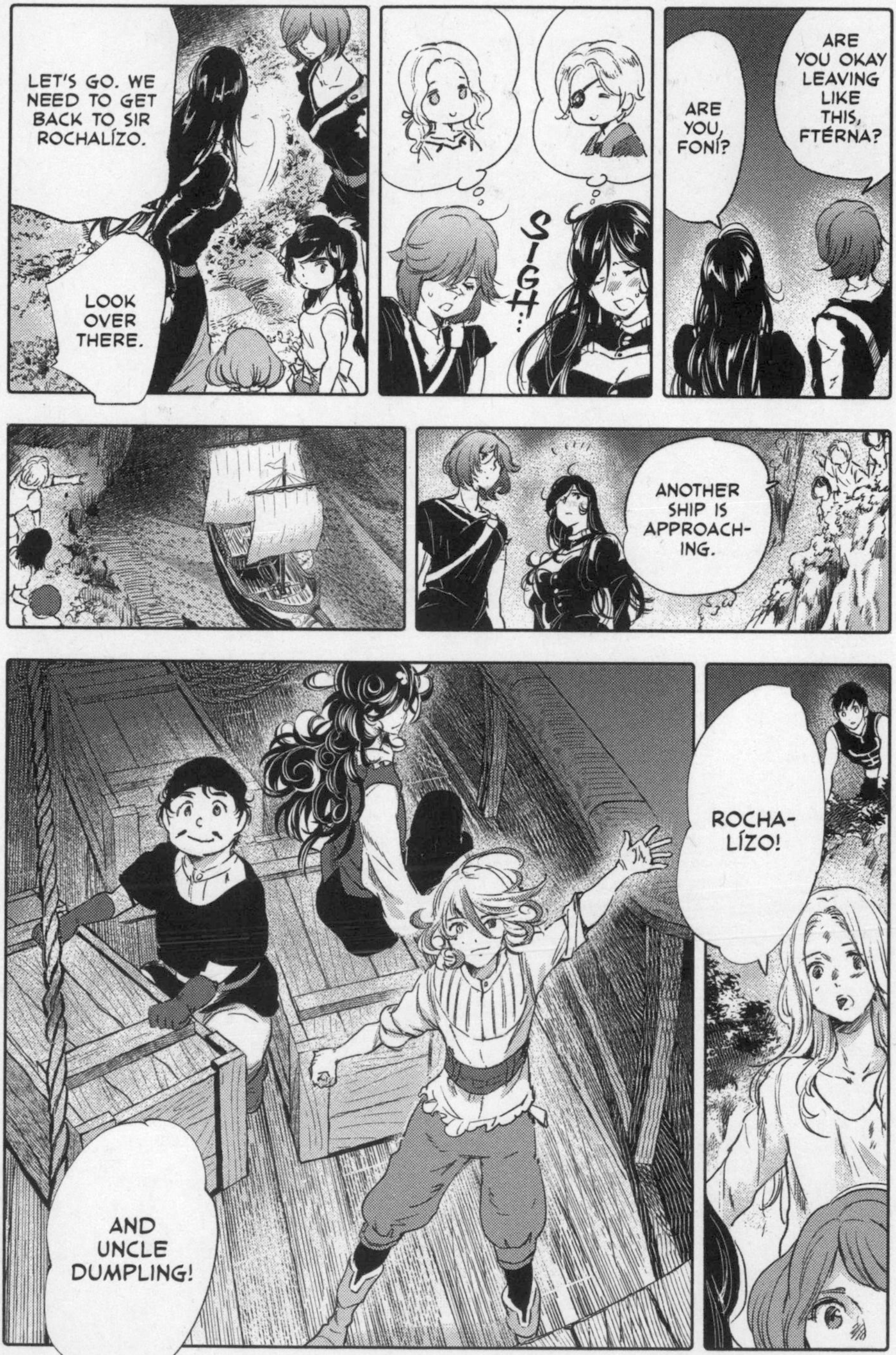
ARE YOU OKAY LEAVING LIKE THIS, FTÉRNA?
ARE YOU, FONÍ?
SIGH...
LET'S GO. WE NEED TO GET BACK TO SIR ROCHALÍZO.
LOOK OVER THERE.
ANOTHER SHIP IS APPROACH-ING.
ROCHA-LÍZO!
AND UNCLE DUMPLING!

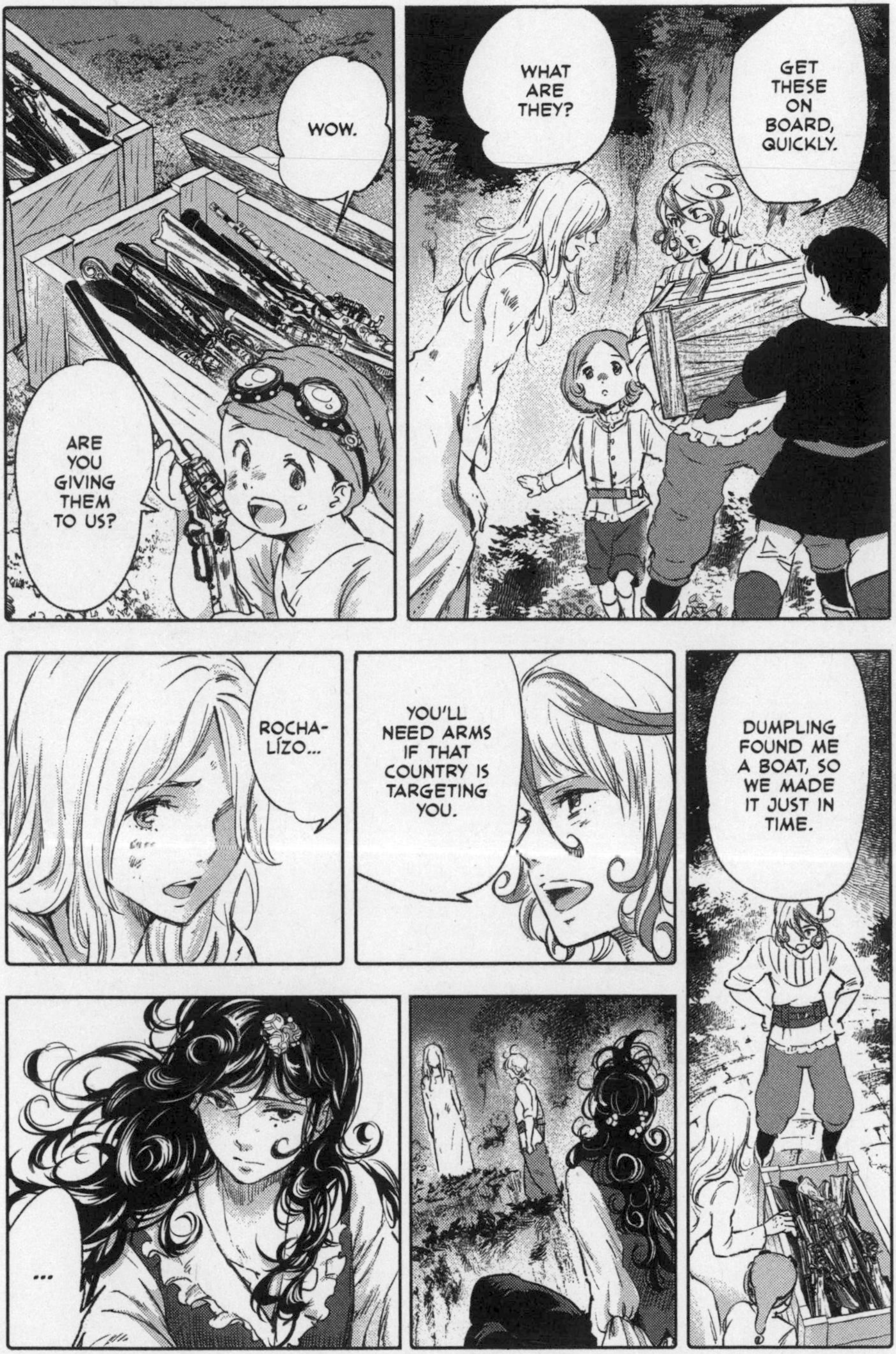
GET THESE ON BOARD, QUICKLY.
WHAT ARE THEY?
WOW.
ARE YOU GIVING THEM TO US?
DUMPLING FOUND ME A BOAT, SO WE MADE IT JUST IN TIME.
YOU'LL NEED ARMS IF THAT COUNTRY IS TARGETING YOU.
ROCHA-LÍZO...
...

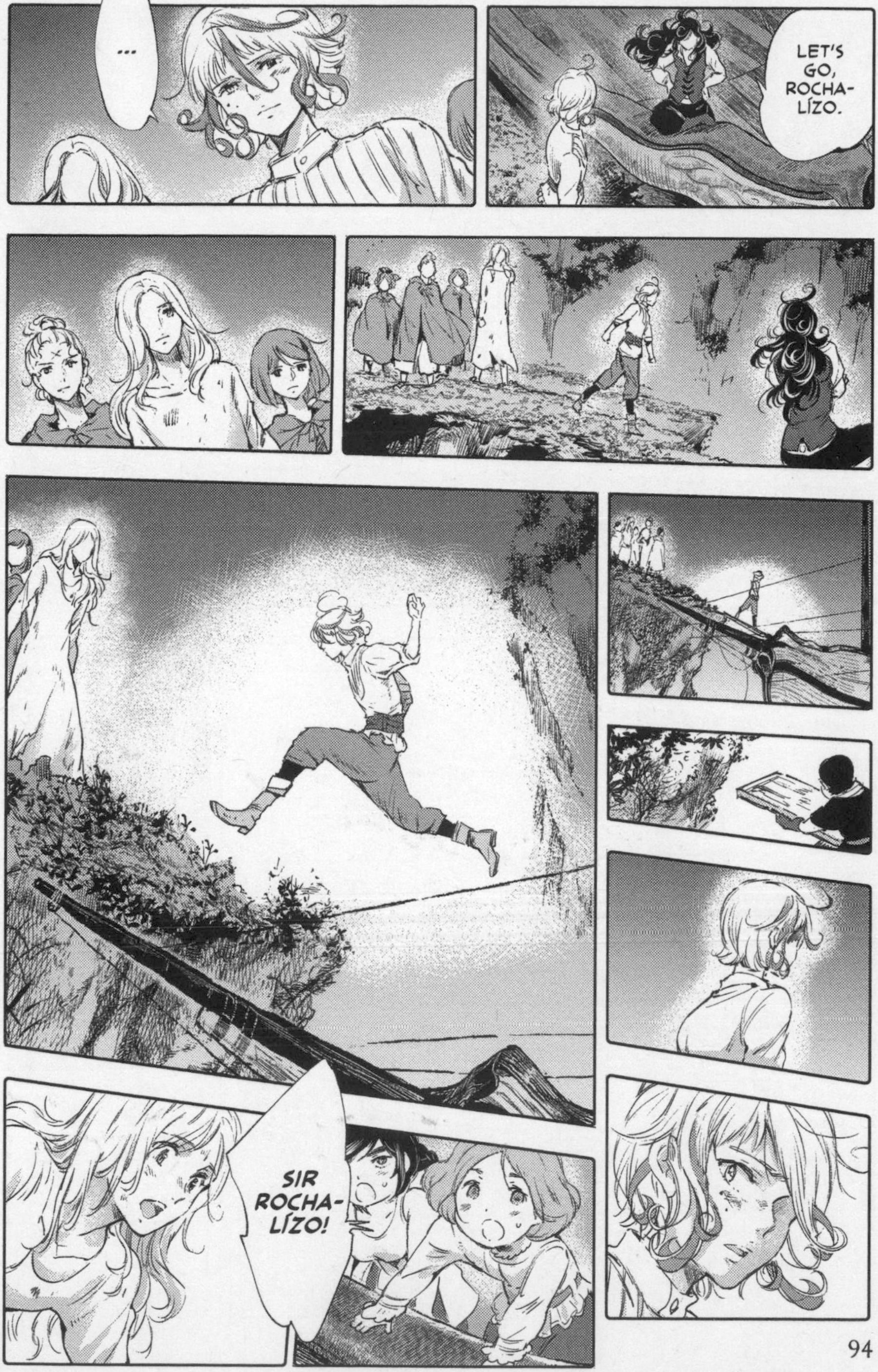
LET'S GO, ROCHA-LÍZO.
...
SIR ROCHA-LÍZO!

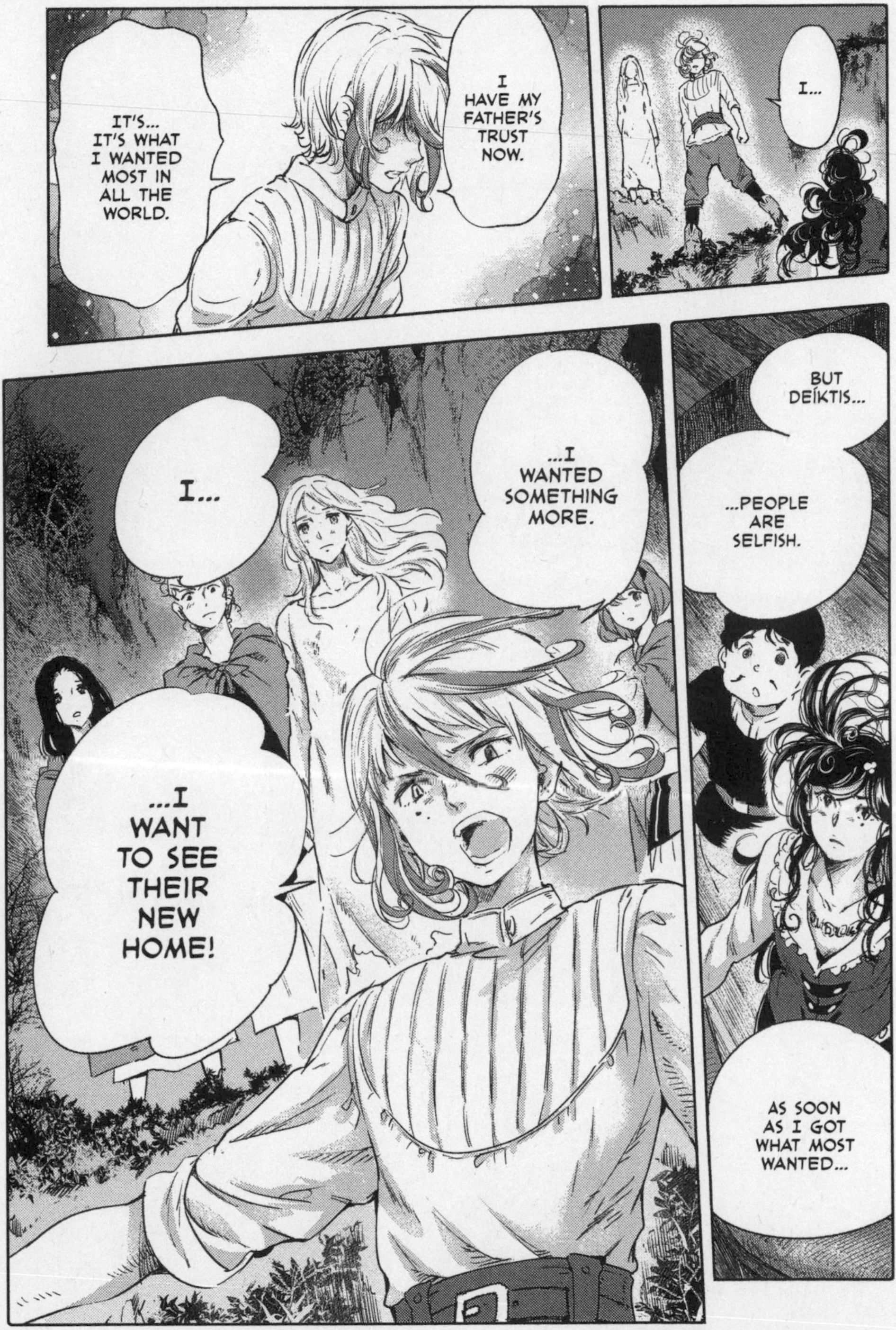
I...
I HAVE MY FATHER'S TRUST NOW.
IT'S... IT'S WHAT I WANTED MOST IN ALL THE WORLD.
BUT DEÍKTIS...
...PEOPLE ARE SELFISH.
AS SOON AS I GOT WHAT MOST WANTED...
...I WANTED SOMETHING MORE.
I...
...I WANT TO SEE THEIR NEW HOME!

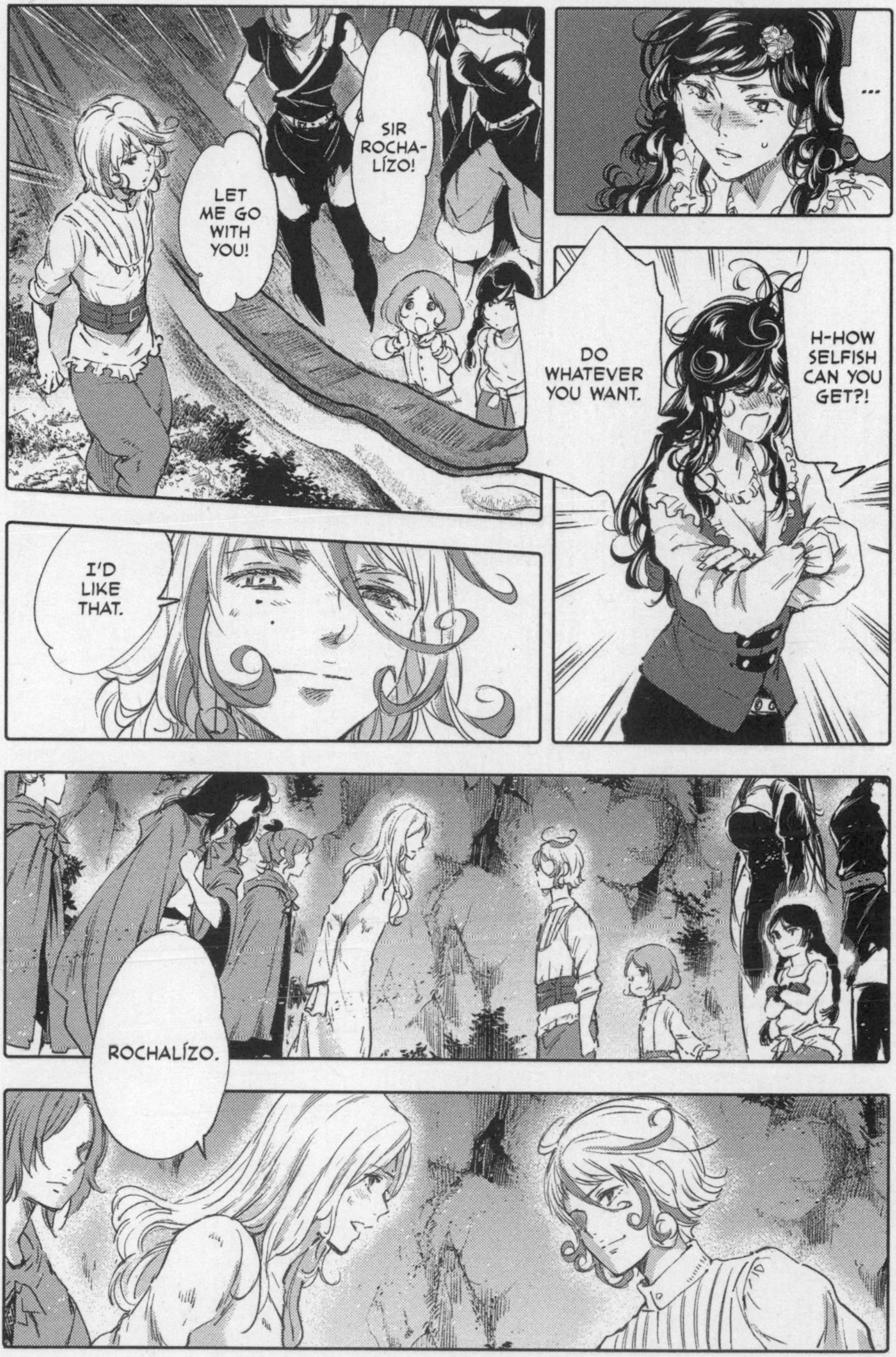
...
SIR ROCHALÍZO!
LET ME GO WITH YOU!
H-HOW SELFISH CAN YOU GET?!
DO WHATEVER YOU WANT.
I'D LIKE THAT.
ROCHALÍZO.

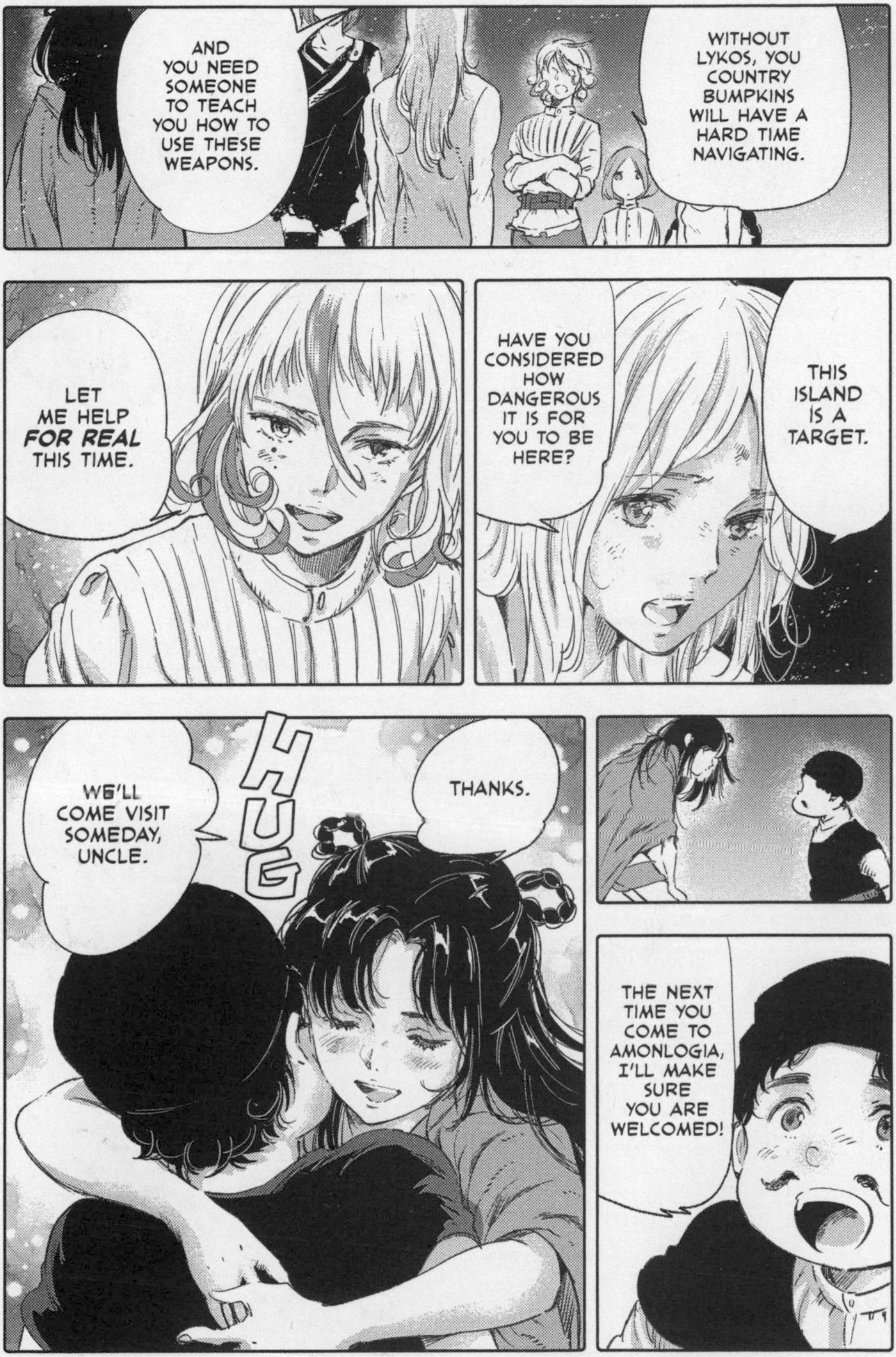
WITHOUT LYKOS, YOU COUNTRY BUMPKINS WILL HAVE A HARD TIME NAVIGATING.
AND YOU NEED SOMEONE TO TEACH YOU HOW TO USE THESE WEAPONS.
THIS ISLAND IS A TARGET.
HAVE YOU CONSIDERED HOW DANGEROUS IT IS FOR YOU TO BE HERE?
LET ME HELP *FOR REAL* THIS TIME.
THE NEXT TIME YOU COME TO AMONLOGIA, I'LL MAKE SURE YOU ARE WELCOMED!
THANKS.
HUG
WE'LL COME VISIT SOMEDAY, UNCLE.

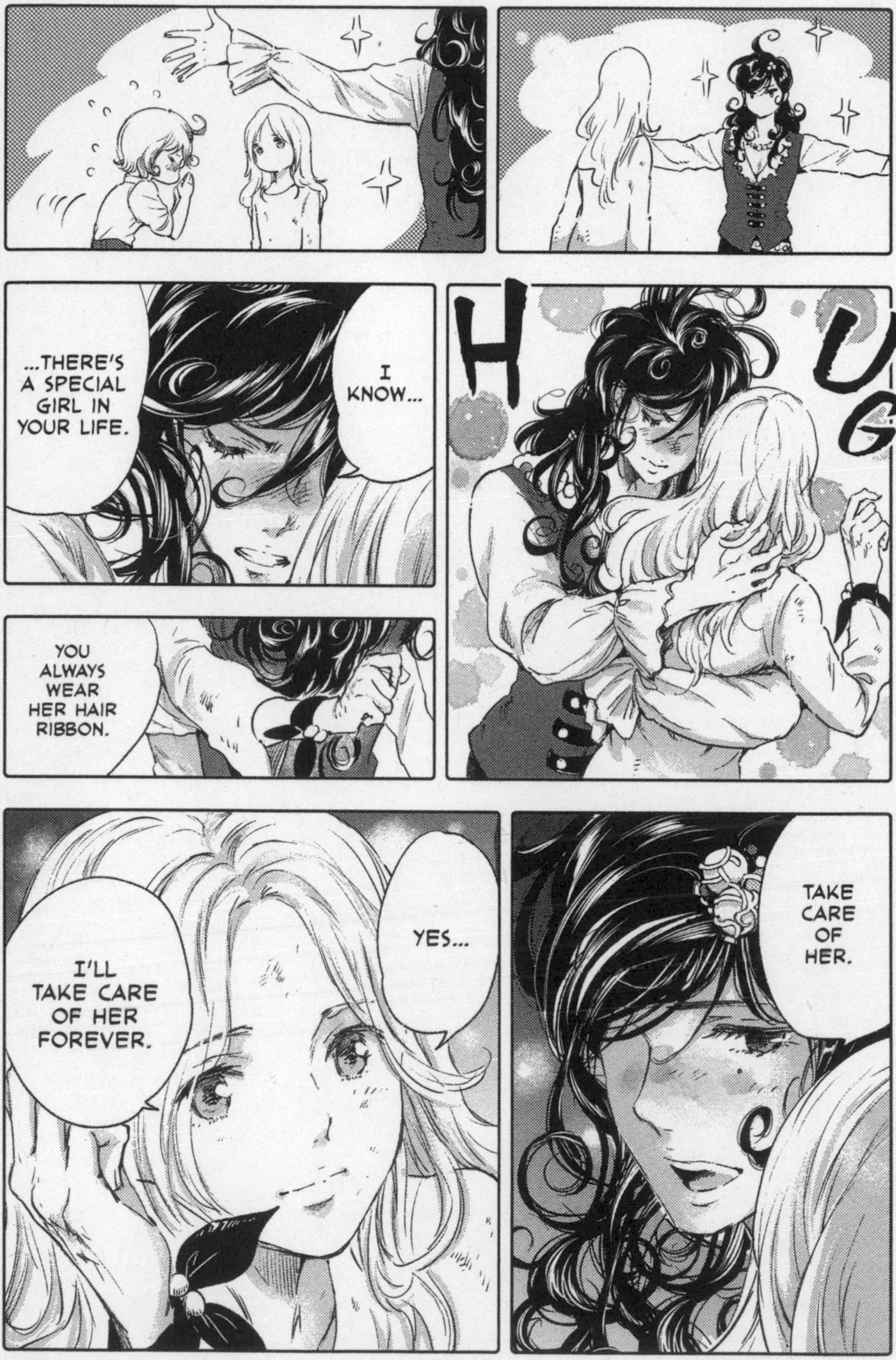
HUG
I KNOW...
...THERE'S A SPECIAL GIRL IN YOUR LIFE.
YOU ALWAYS WEAR HER HAIR RIBBON.
TAKE CARE OF HER.
YES...
I'LL TAKE CARE OF HER FOREVER.

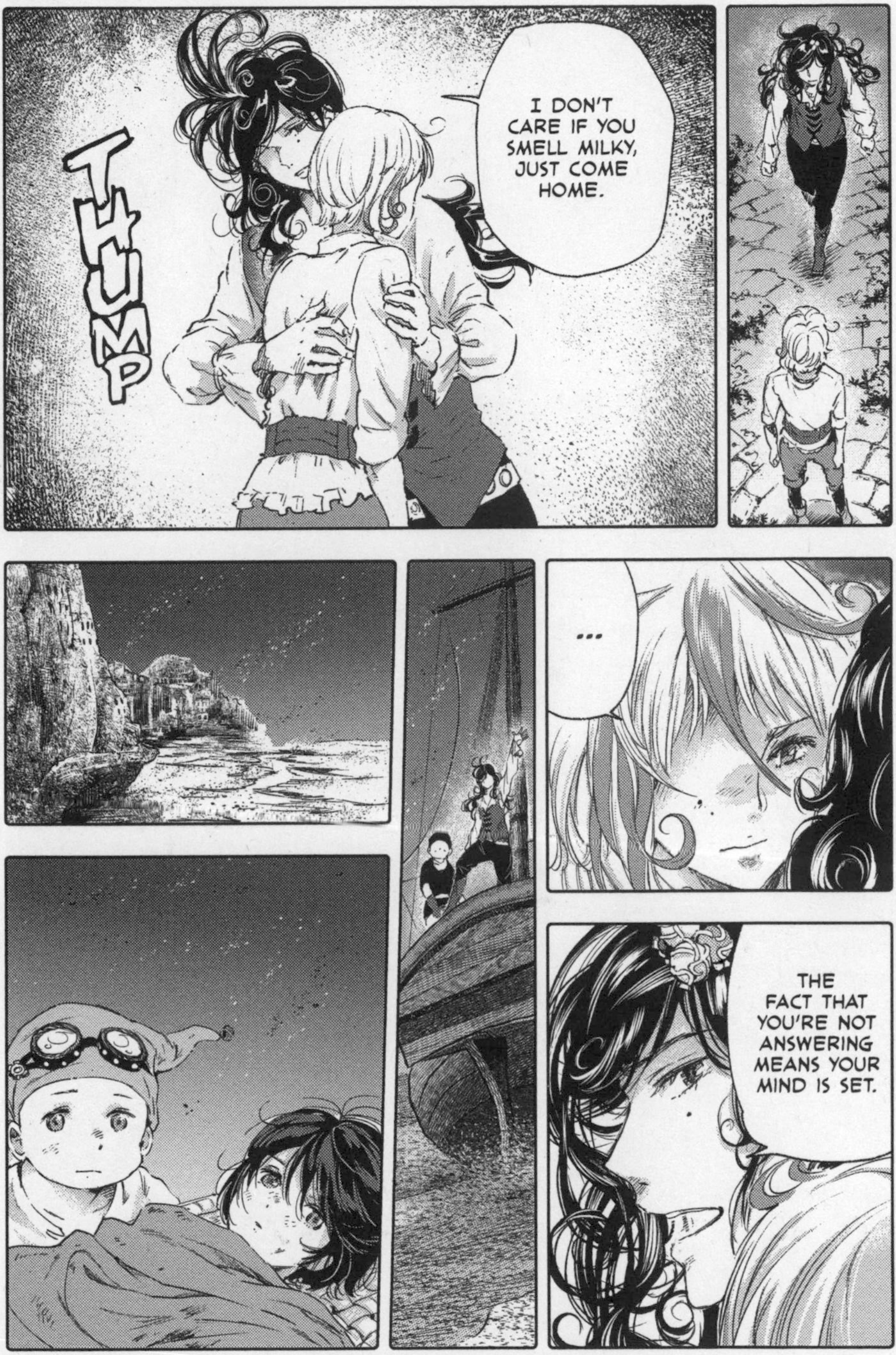
I DON'T CARE IF YOU SMELL MILKY, JUST COME HOME.
THUMP
...
THE FACT THAT YOU'RE NOT ANSWERING MEANS YOUR MIND IS SET.

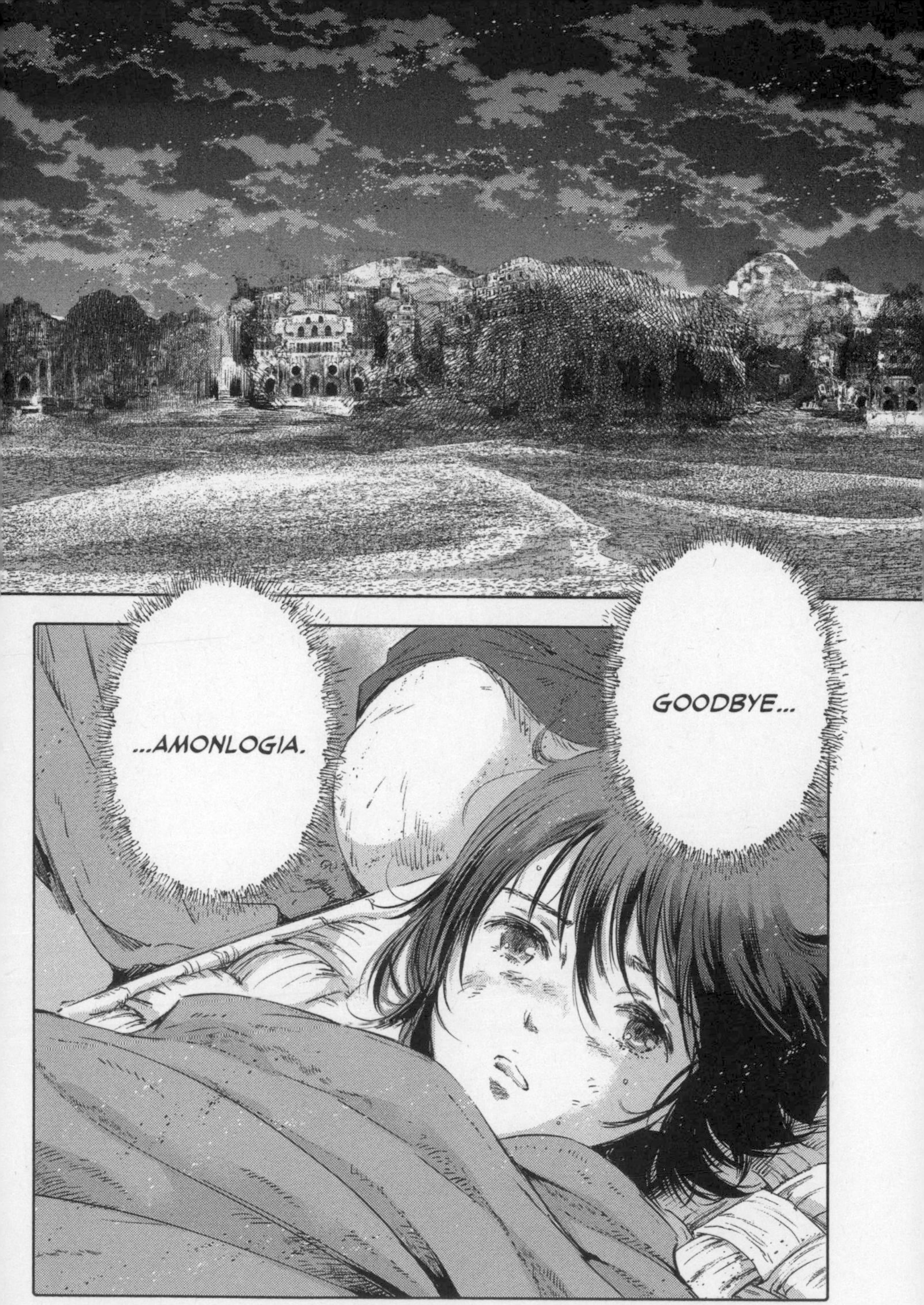
GOODBYE...
...AMONLOGIA.

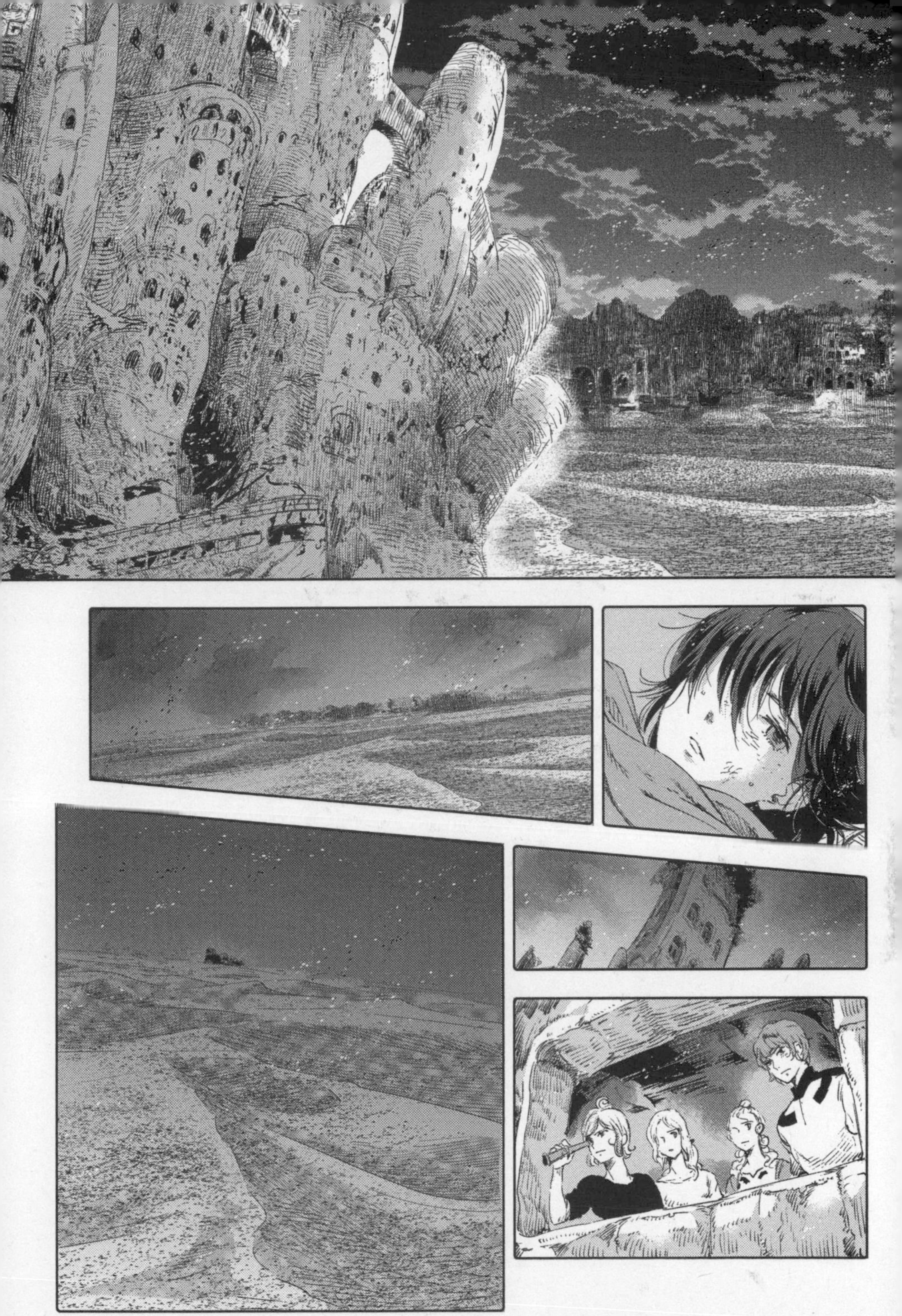

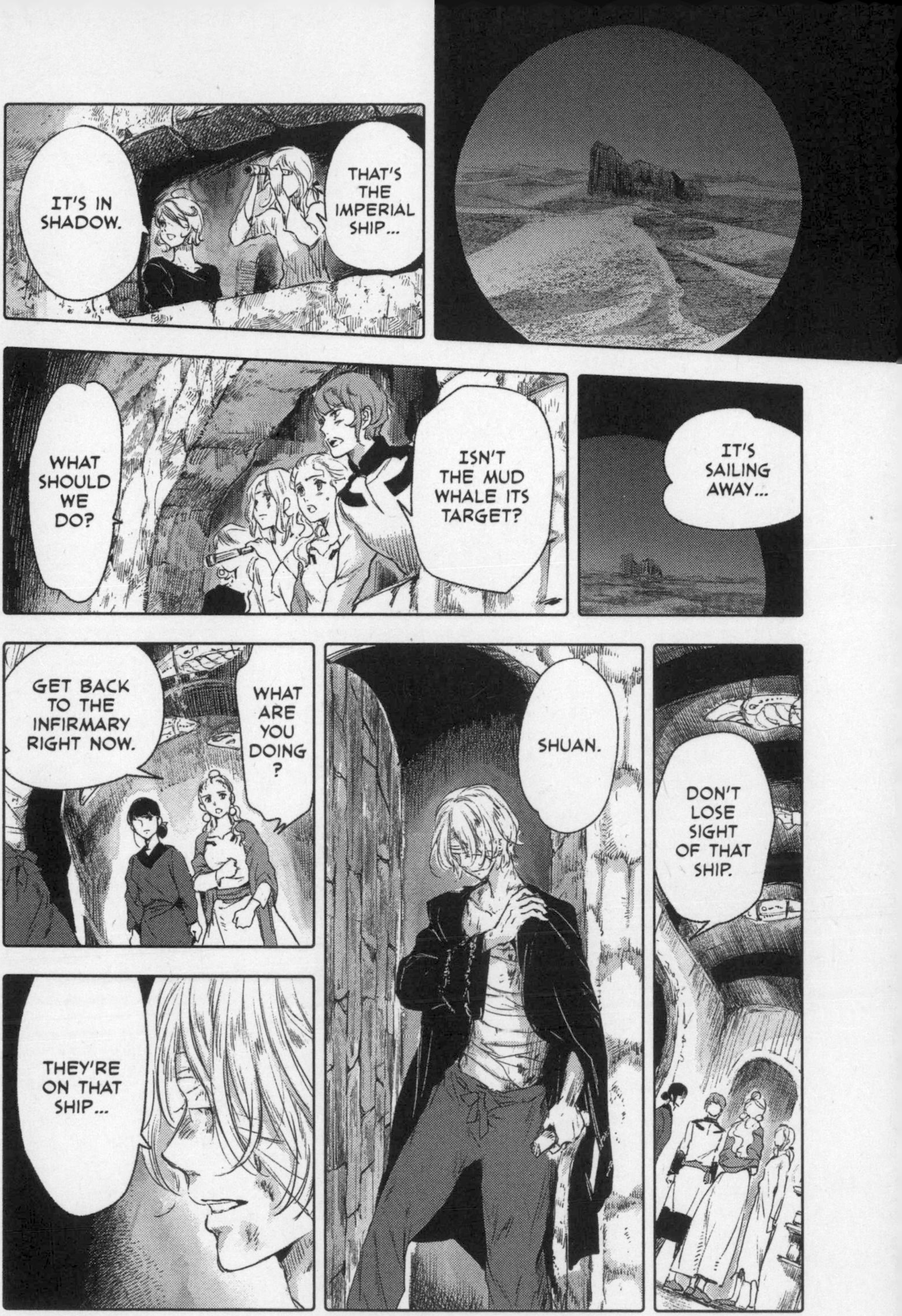

THAT'S THE IMPERIAL SHIP...
IT'S IN SHADOW.
IT'S SAILING AWAY...
ISN'T THE MUD WHALE ITS TARGET?
WHAT SHOULD WE DO?
DON'T LOSE SIGHT OF THAT SHIP.
SHUAN.
WHAT ARE YOU DOING?
GET BACK TO THE INFIRMARY RIGHT NOW.
THEY'RE ON THAT SHIP...

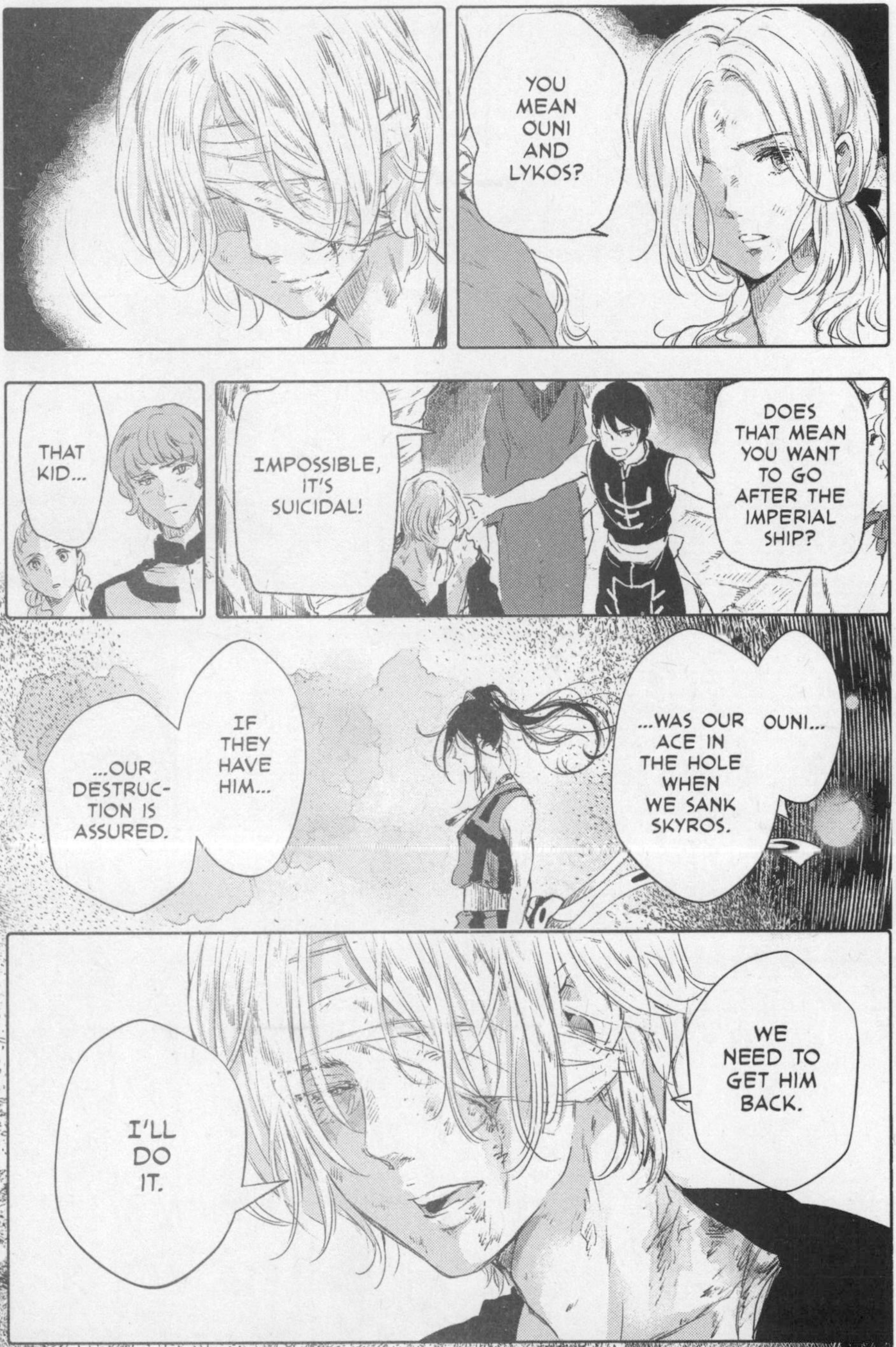
YOU MEAN OUNI AND LYKOS?
DOES THAT MEAN YOU WANT TO GO AFTER THE IMPERIAL SHIP?
IMPOSSIBLE, IT'S SUICIDAL!
THAT KID...
OUNI...
...WAS OUR ACE IN THE HOLE WHEN WE SANK SKYROS.
IF THEY HAVE HIM...
...OUR DESTRUCTION IS ASSURED.
WE NEED TO GET HIM BACK.
I'LL DO IT.

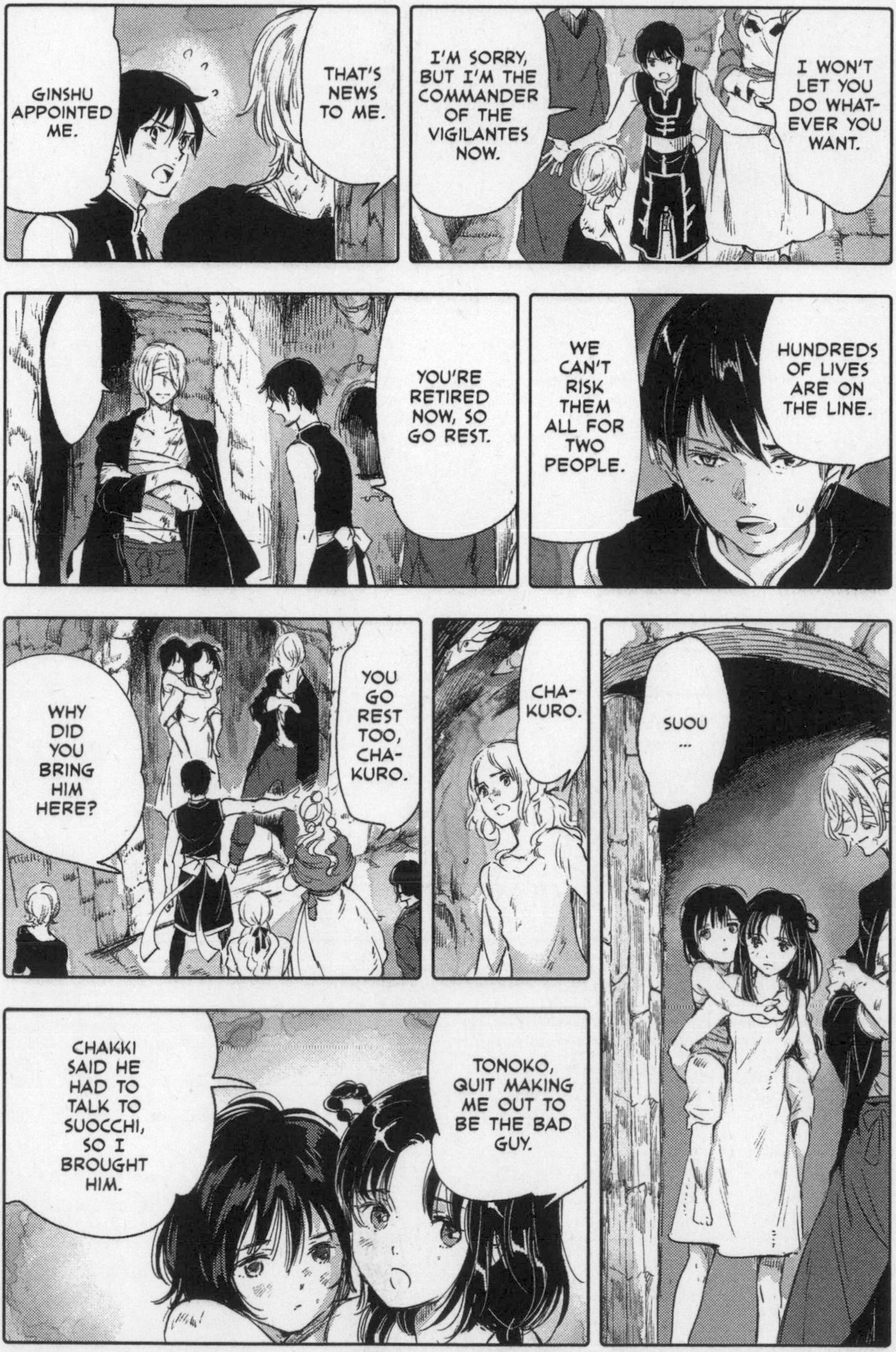
I WON'T LET YOU DO WHAT-EVER YOU WANT.
I'M SORRY, BUT I'M THE COMMANDER OF THE VIGILANTES NOW.
THAT'S NEWS TO ME.
GINSHU APPOINTED ME.
HUNDREDS OF LIVES ARE ON THE LINE.
WE CAN'T RISK THEM ALL FOR TWO PEOPLE.
YOU'RE RETIRED NOW, SO GO REST.
SUOU ...
CHA-KURO.
YOU GO REST TOO, CHA-KURO.
WHY DID YOU BRING HIM HERE?
TONOKO, QUIT MAKING ME OUT TO BE THE BAD GUY.
CHAKKI SAID HE HAD TO TALK TO SUOCCHI, SO I BROUGHT HIM.

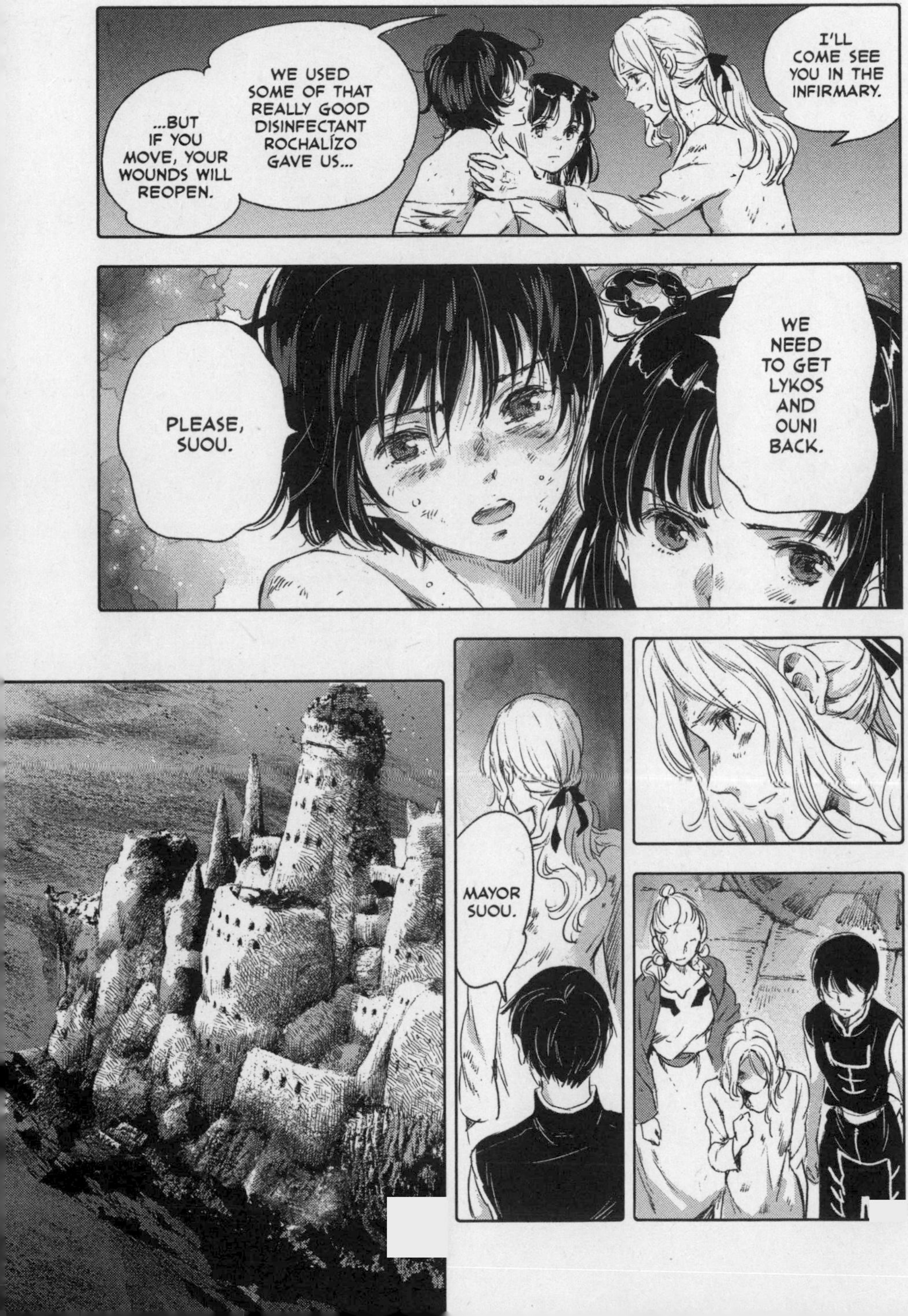
I'LL COME SEE YOU IN THE INFIRMARY.
WE USED SOME OF THAT REALLY GOOD DISINFECTANT ROCHALÍZO GAVE US...
...BUT IF YOU MOVE, YOUR WOUNDS WILL REOPEN.
WE NEED TO GET LYKOS AND OUNI BACK.
PLEASE, SUOU.
MAYOR SUOU.

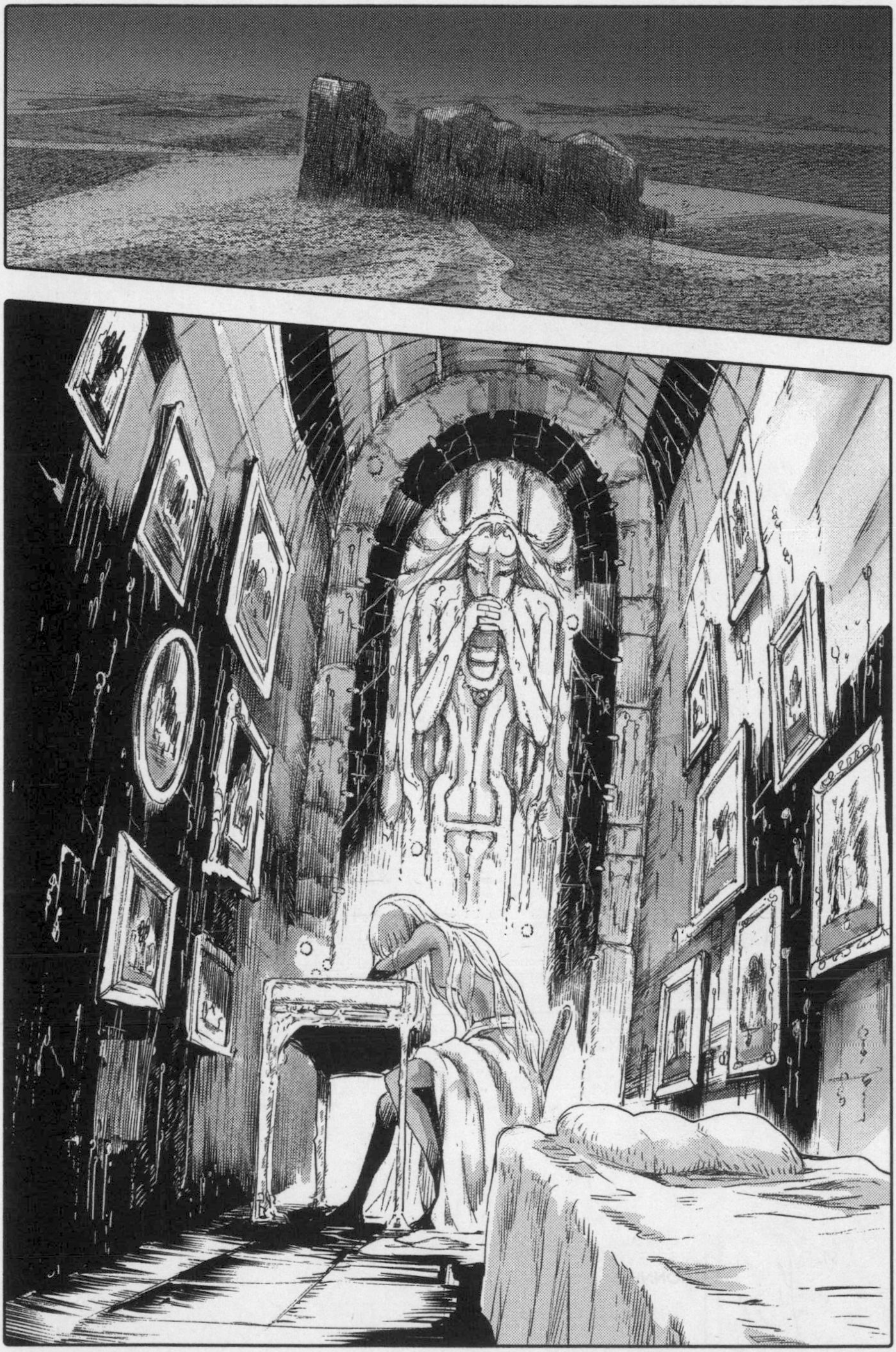

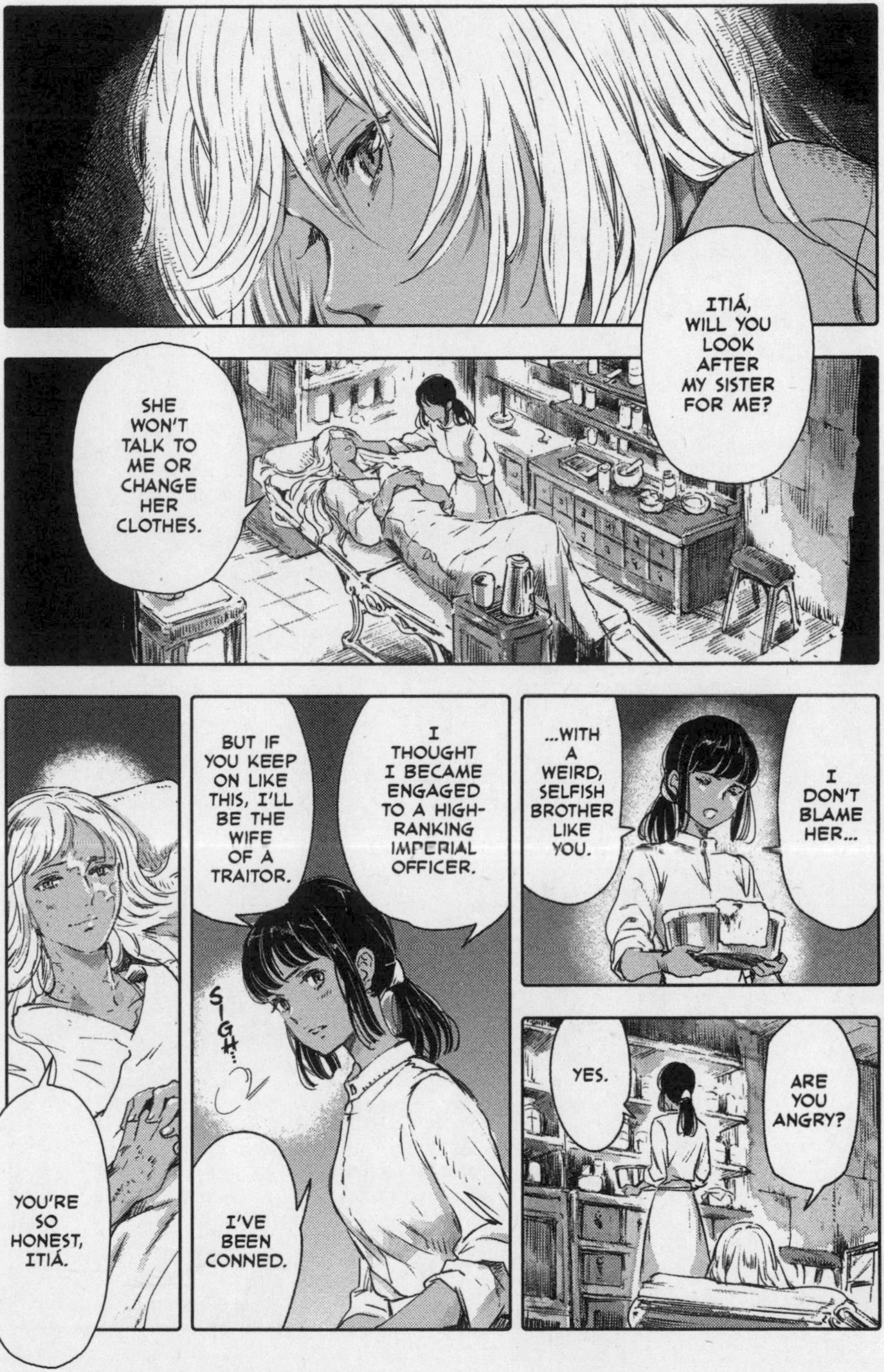
ITIÁ, WILL YOU LOOK AFTER MY SISTER FOR ME?
SHE WON'T TALK TO ME OR CHANGE HER CLOTHES.
I DON'T BLAME HER...
...WITH A WEIRD, SELFISH BROTHER LIKE YOU.
ARE YOU ANGRY?
YES.
I THOUGHT I BECAME ENGAGED TO A HIGH-RANKING IMPERIAL OFFICER.
BUT IF YOU KEEP ON LIKE THIS, I'LL BE THE WIFE OF A TRAITOR.
SIGH...
I'VE BEEN CONNED.
YOU'RE SO HONEST, ITIÁ.

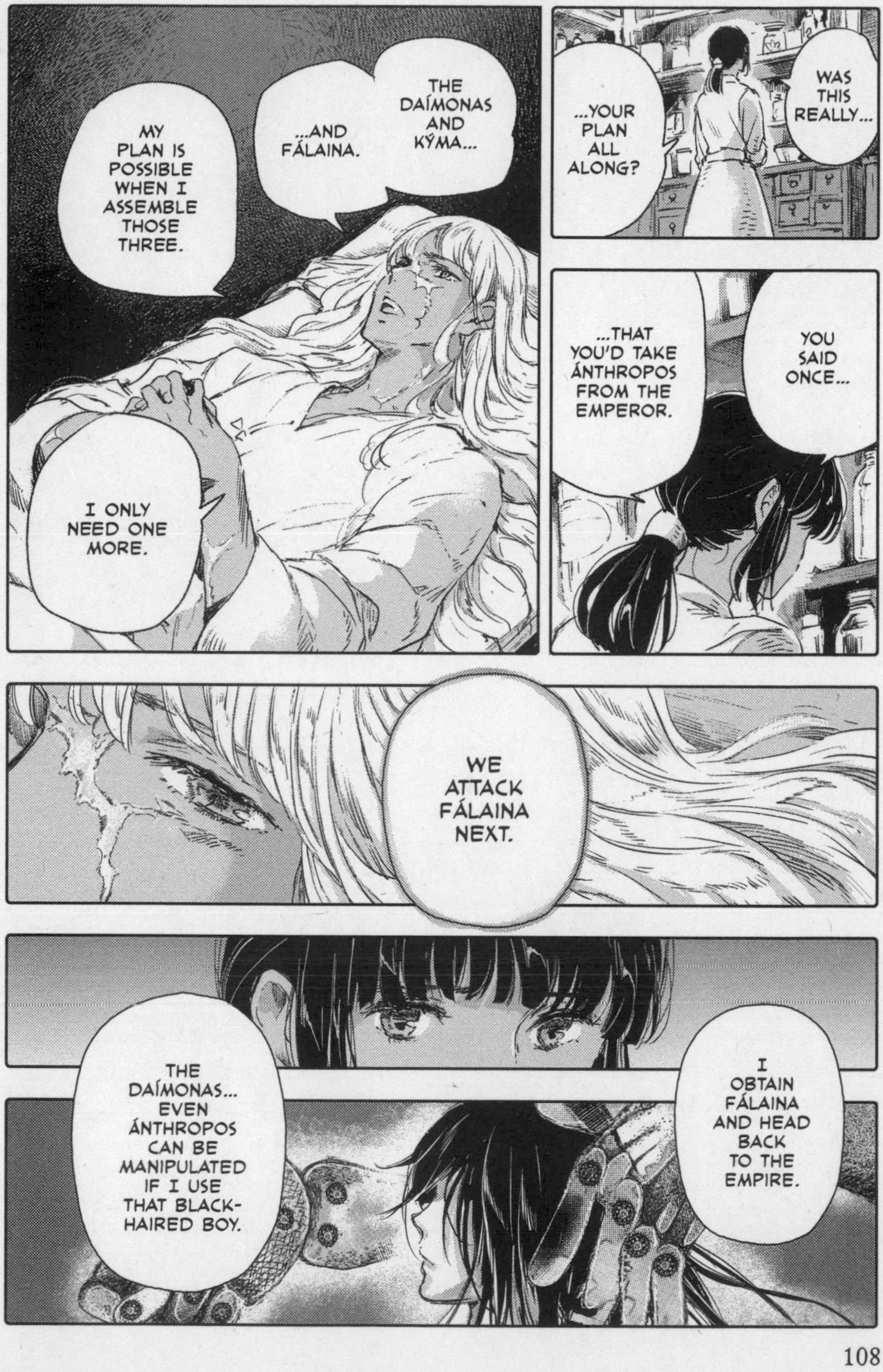
WAS THIS REALLY...
...YOUR PLAN ALL ALONG?
YOU SAID ONCE...
...THAT YOU'D TAKE ÁNTHROPOS FROM THE EMPEROR.
THE DAÍMONAS AND KÝMA...
...AND FÁLAINA.
MY PLAN IS POSSIBLE WHEN I ASSEMBLE THOSE THREE.
I ONLY NEED ONE MORE.
WE ATTACK FÁLAINA NEXT.
I OBTAIN FÁLAINA AND HEAD BACK TO THE EMPIRE.
THE DAÍMONAS... EVEN ÁNTHROPOS CAN BE MANIPULATED IF I USE THAT BLACK-HAIRED BOY.

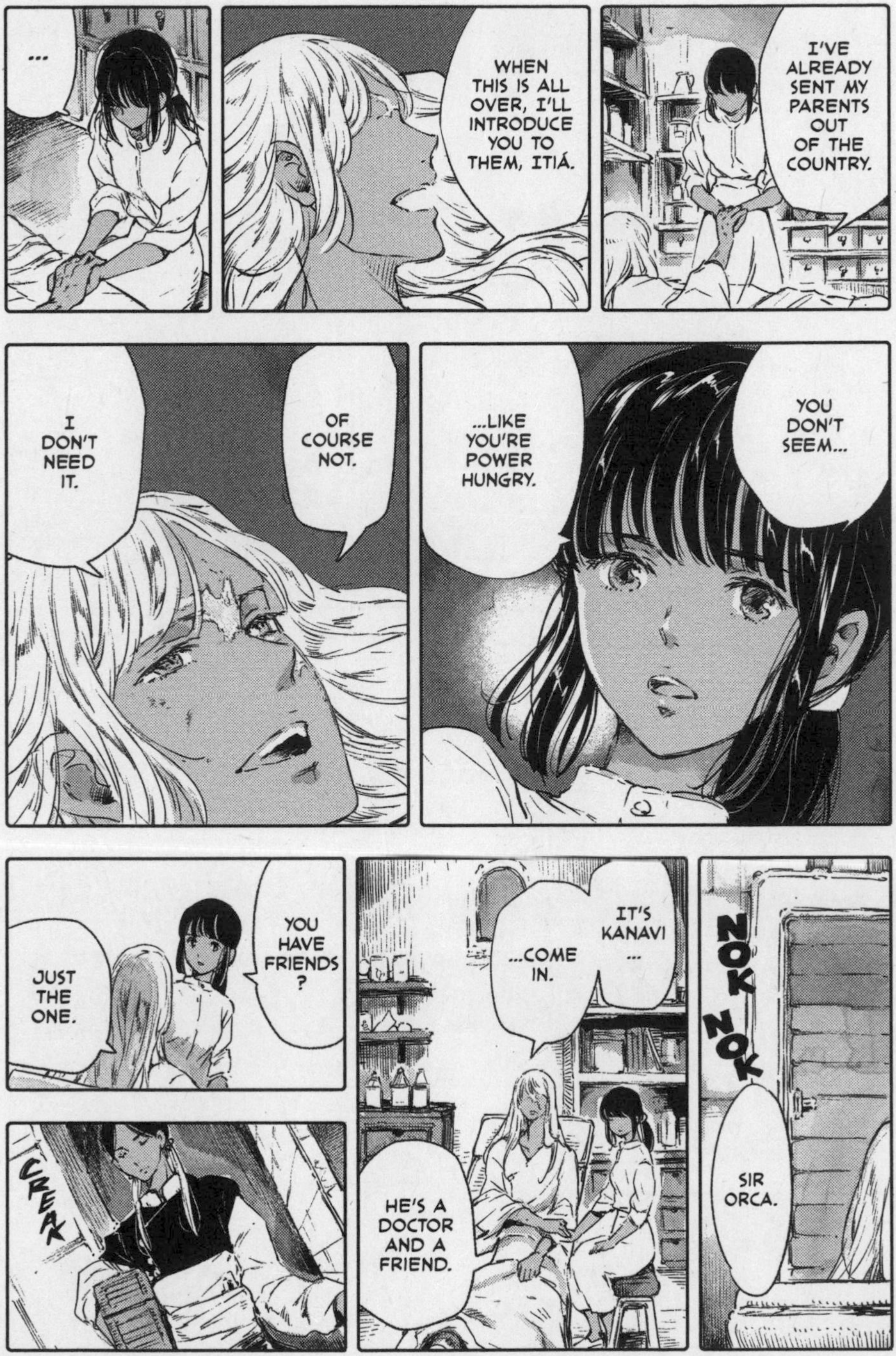

I'VE ALREADY SENT MY PARENTS OUT OF THE COUNTRY.
WHEN THIS IS ALL OVER, I'LL INTRODUCE YOU TO THEM, ITIÁ.
...
YOU DON'T SEEM...
...LIKE YOU'RE POWER HUNGRY.
OF COURSE NOT.
I DON'T NEED IT.
NOK NOK
SIR ORCA.
IT'S KANAVI ...
...COME IN.
HE'S A DOCTOR AND A FRIEND.
YOU HAVE FRIENDS?
JUST THE ONE.
CREAK

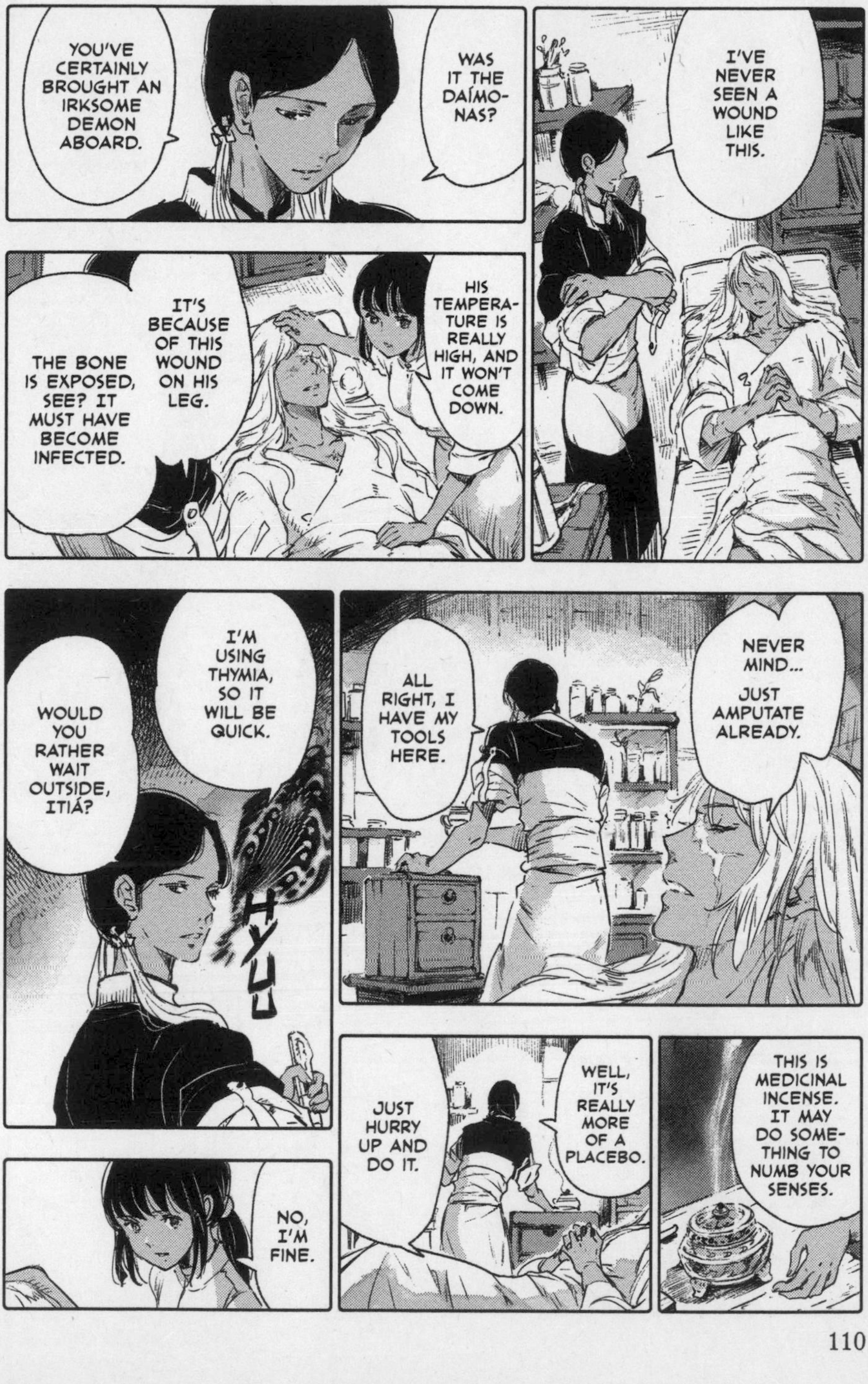
I'VE NEVER SEEN A WOUND LIKE THIS.
WAS IT THE DAÍMONAS?
YOU'VE CERTAINLY BROUGHT AN IRKSOME DEMON ABOARD.
HIS TEMPERATURE IS REALLY HIGH, AND IT WON'T COME DOWN.
IT'S BECAUSE OF THIS WOUND ON HIS LEG.
THE BONE IS EXPOSED, SEE? IT MUST HAVE BECOME INFECTED.
NEVER MIND... JUST AMPUTATE ALREADY.
ALL RIGHT, I HAVE MY TOOLS HERE.
THIS IS MEDICINAL INCENSE. IT MAY DO SOMETHING TO NUMB YOUR SENSES.
WELL, IT'S REALLY MORE OF A PLACEBO.
JUST HURRY UP AND DO IT.
I'M USING THYMIA, SO IT WILL BE QUICK.
WOULD YOU RATHER WAIT OUTSIDE, ITIÁ?
HYUU
NO, I'M FINE.

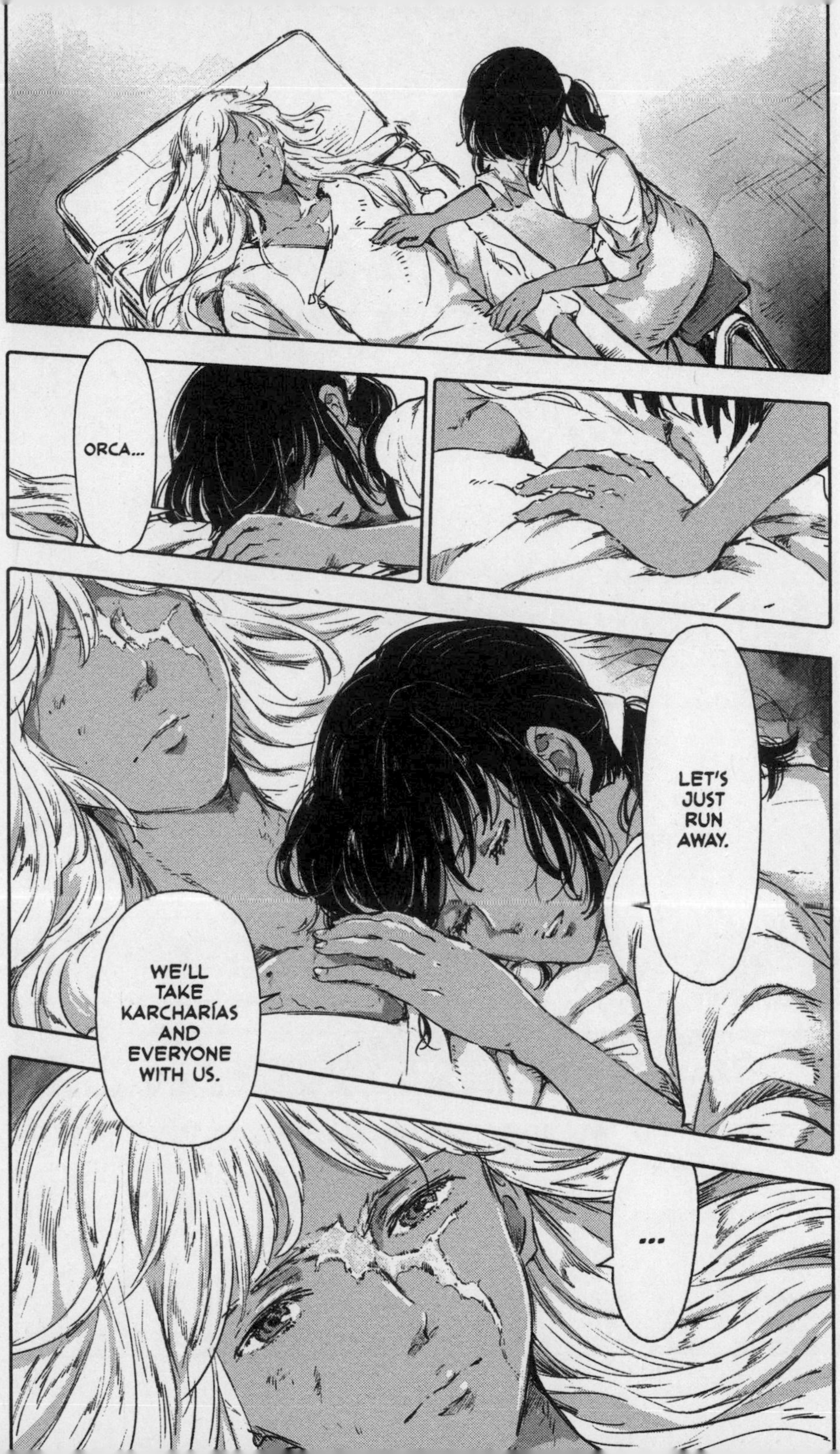
ORCA...
LET'S JUST RUN AWAY.
WE'LL TAKE KARCHARÍAS AND EVERYONE WITH US.
...

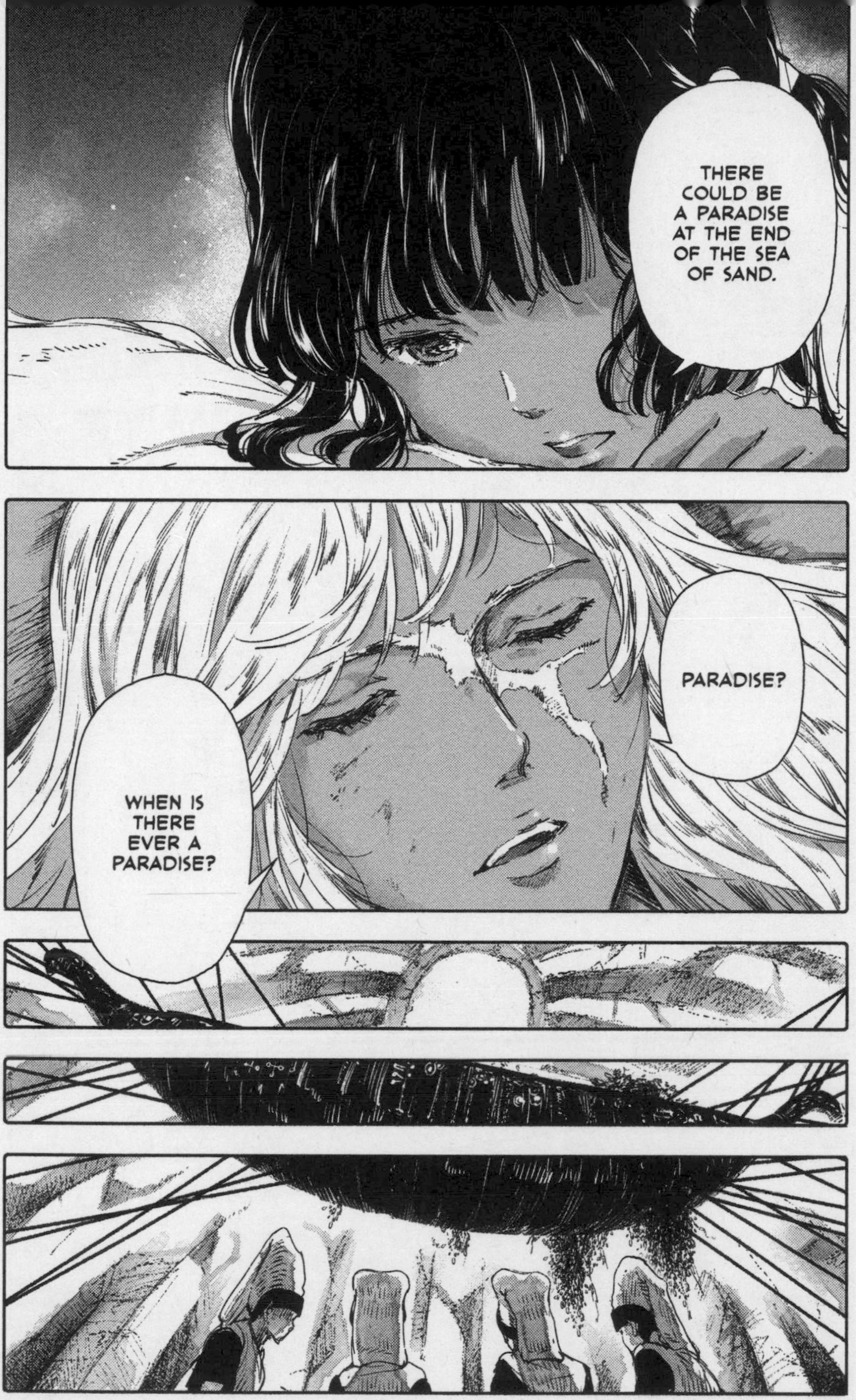
THERE COULD BE A PARADISE AT THE END OF THE SEA OF SAND.
PARADISE?
WHEN IS THERE EVER A PARADISE?

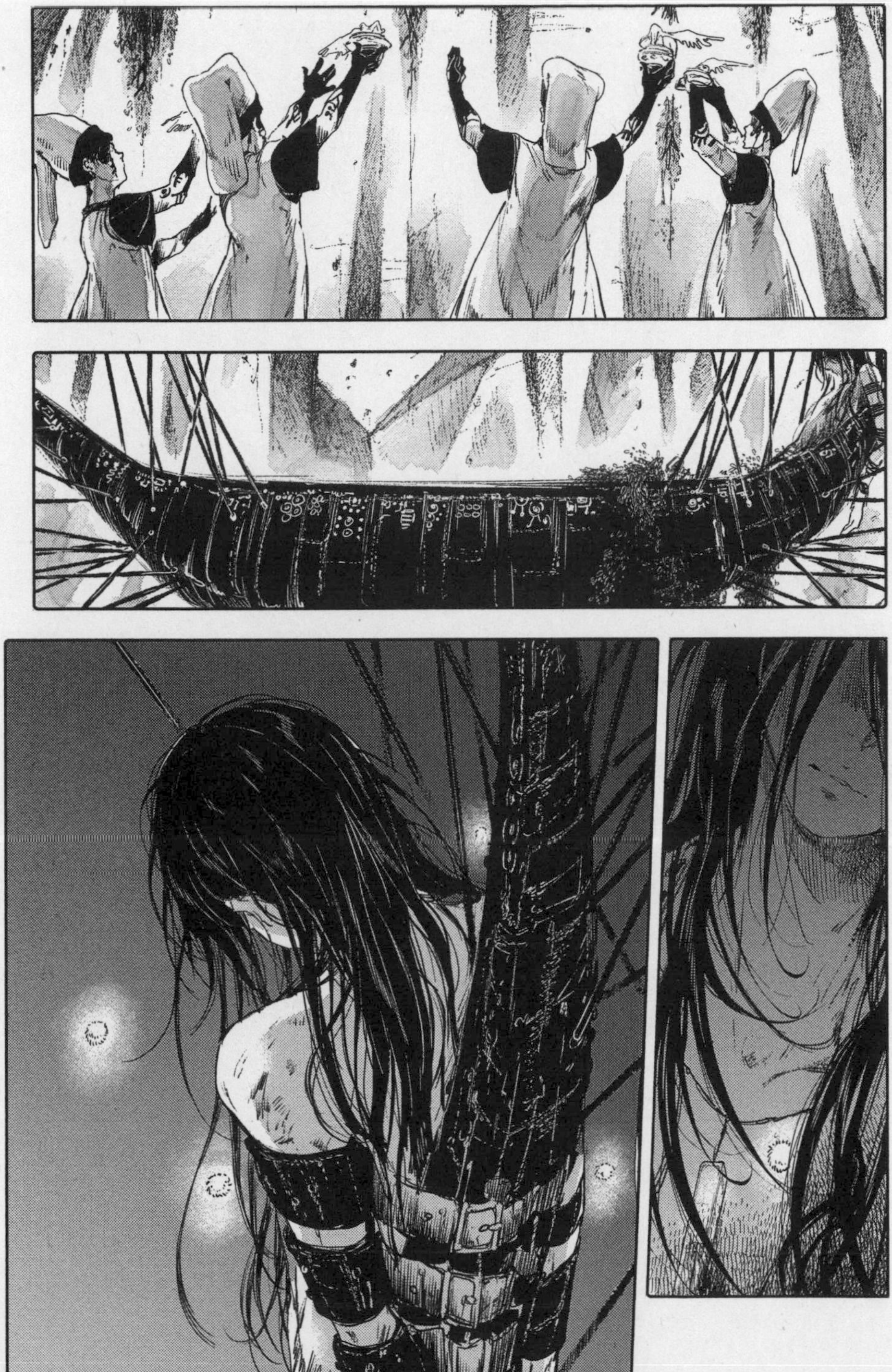

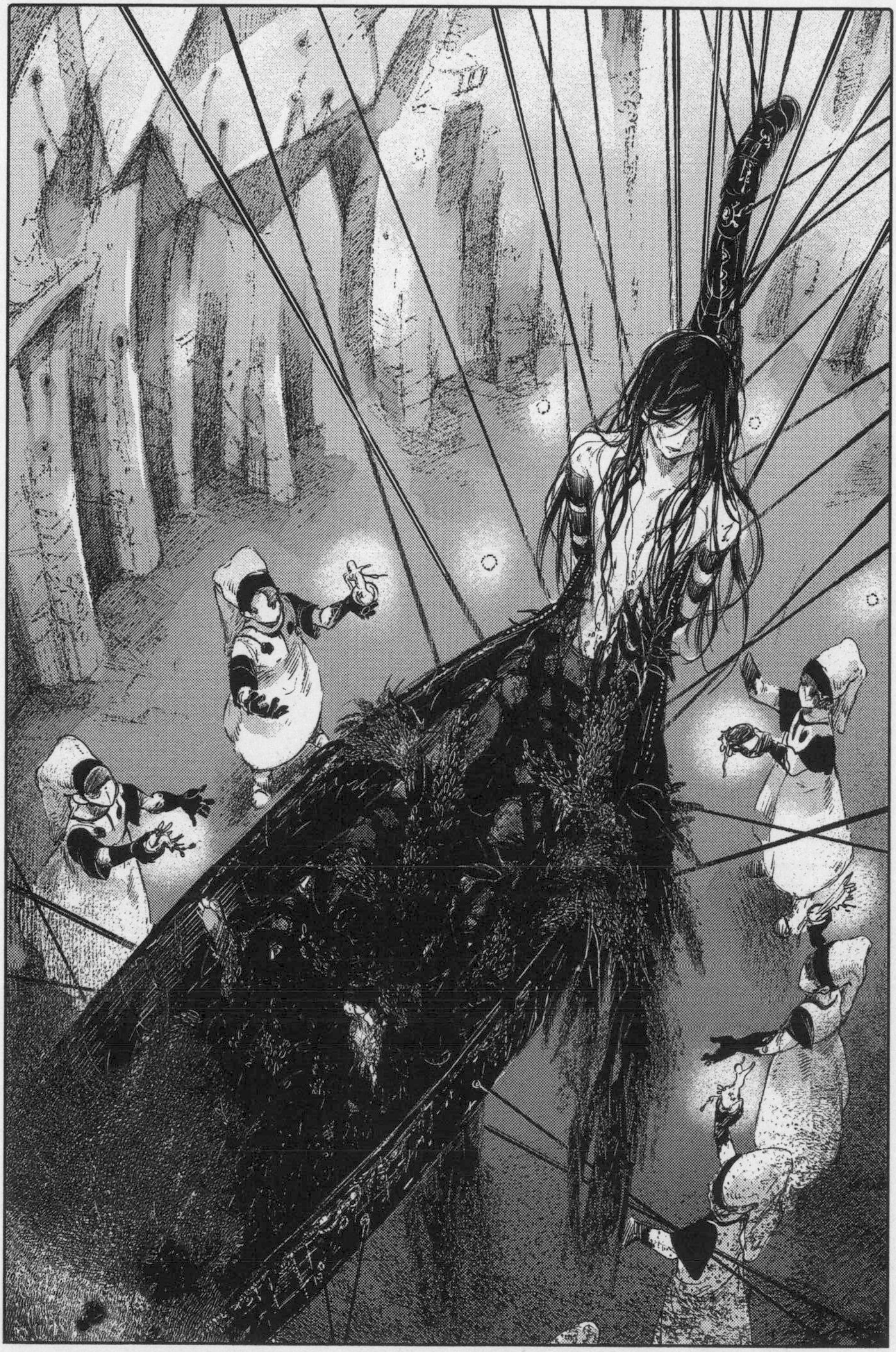

Goodbye, Amonlogia -The End-

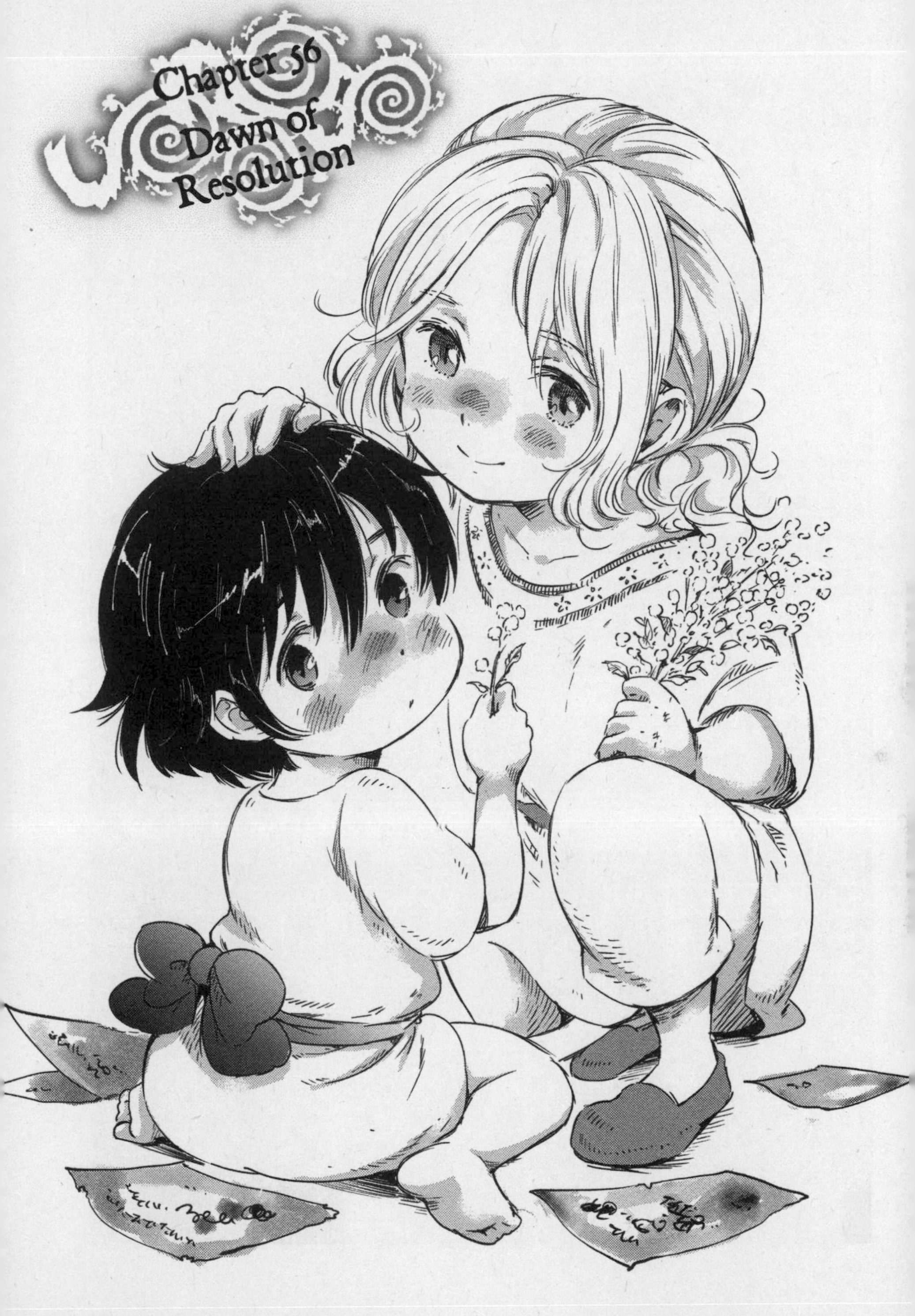
Chapter 56
Dawn of
Resolution

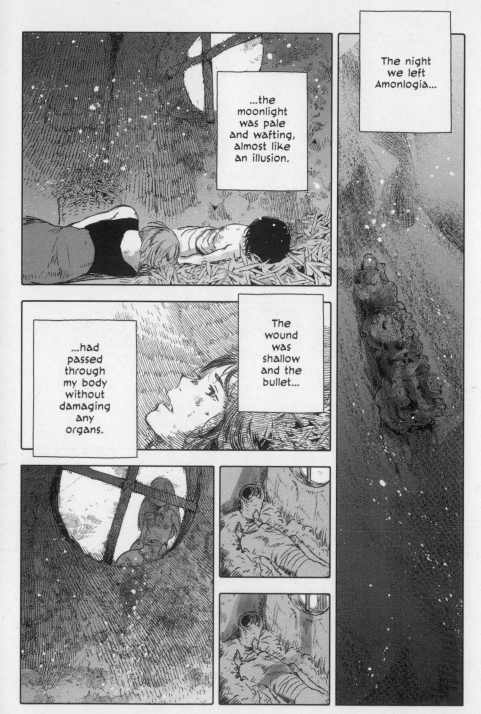

The night we left Amonlogia...

...the moonlight was pale and wafting, almost like an illusion.

The wound was shallow and the bullet...

...had passed through my body without damaging any organs.

116

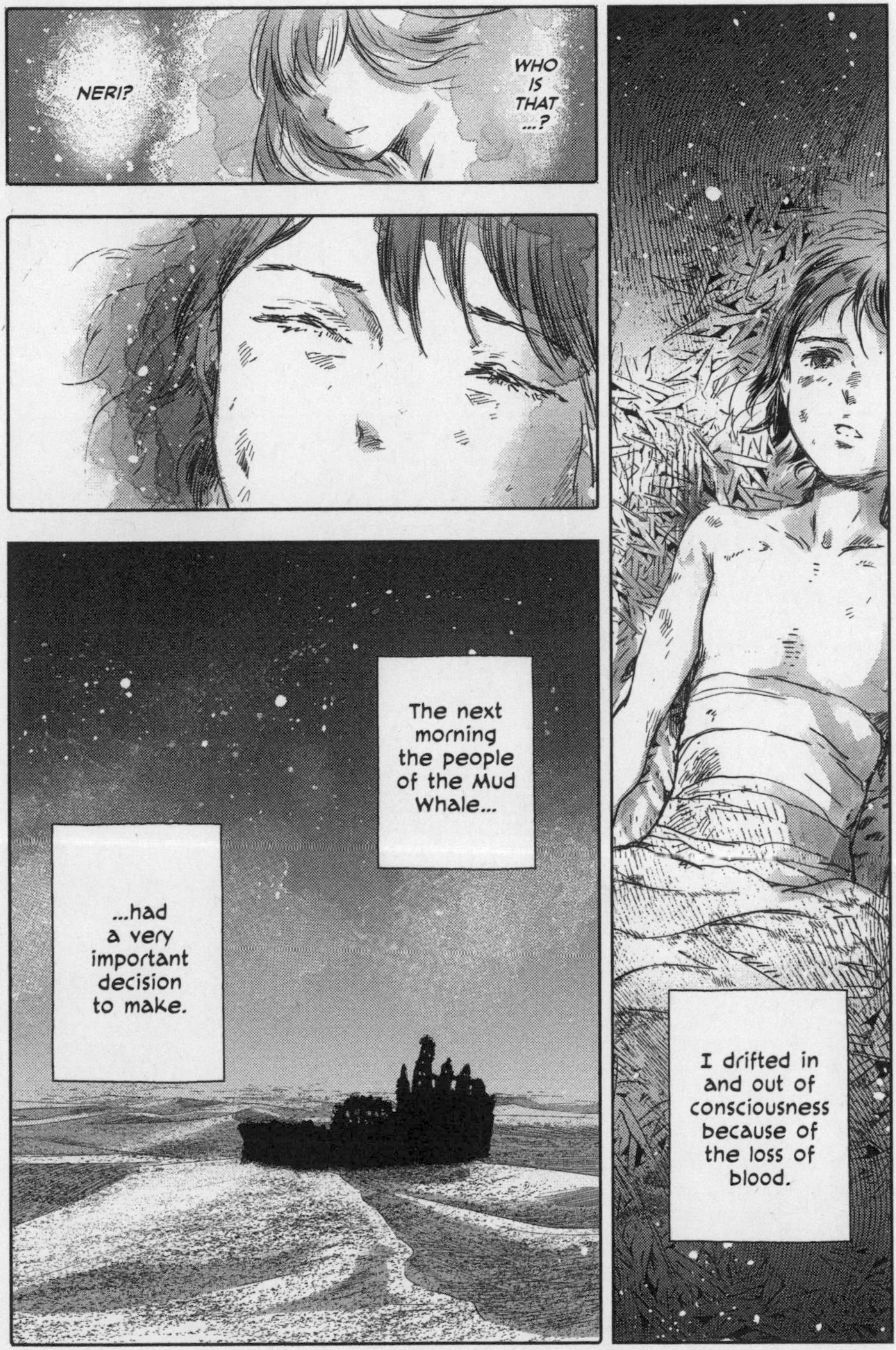
I drifted in and out of consciousness because of the loss of blood.
WHO IS THAT ...?
NERI?
The next morning the people of the Mud Whale...
...had a very important decision to make.

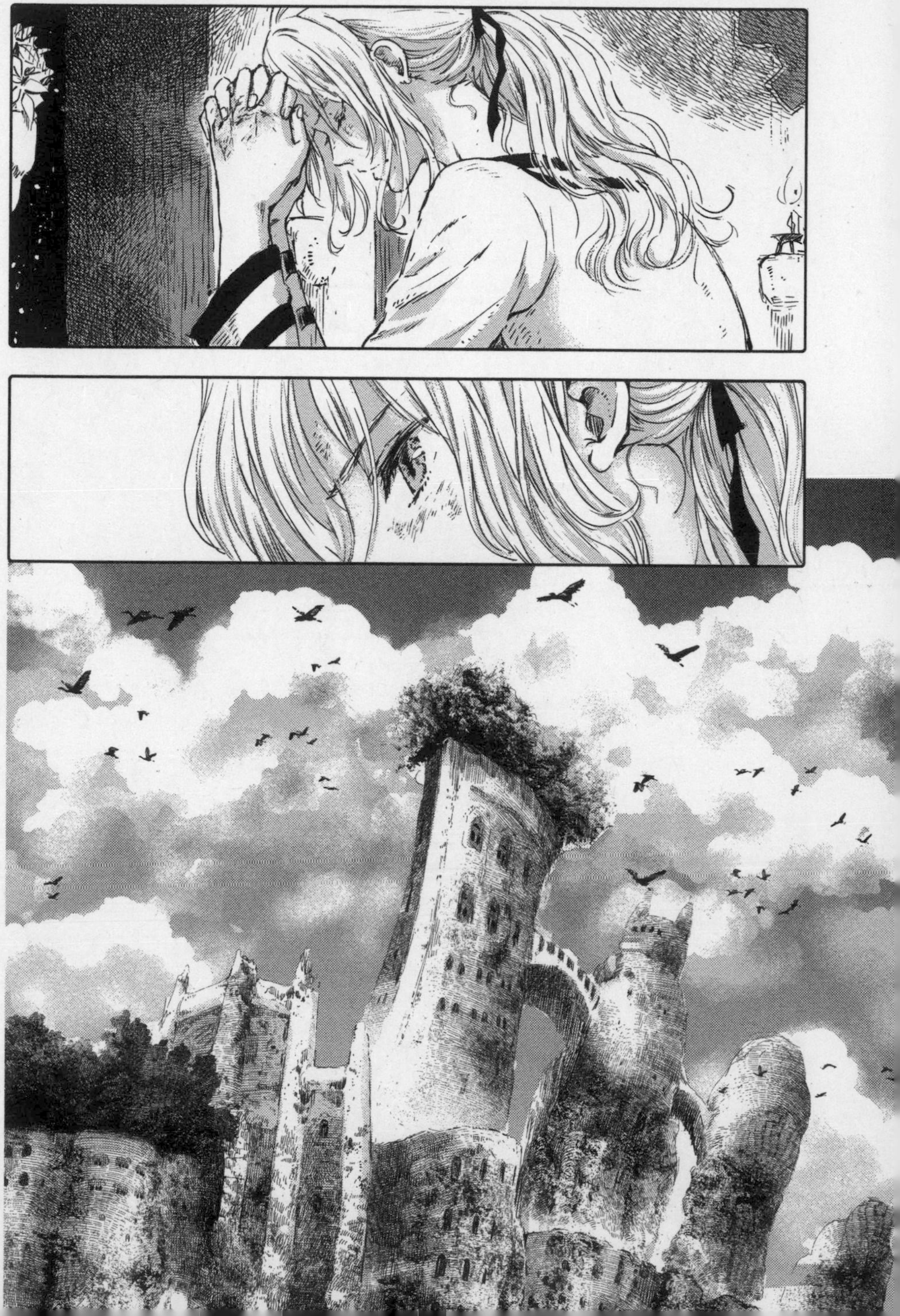

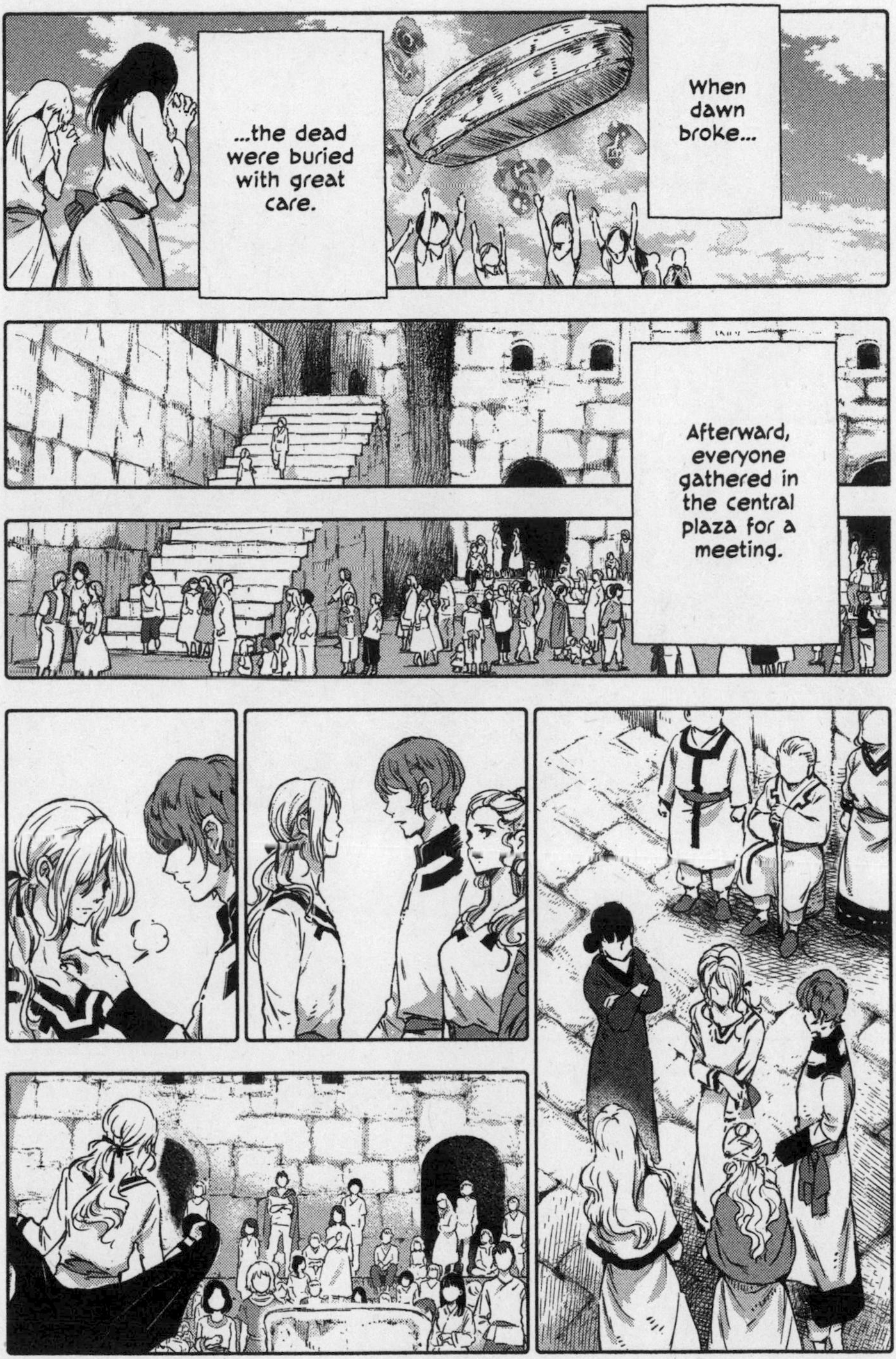
When dawn broke...
...the dead were buried with great care.
Afterward, everyone gathered in the central plaza for a meeting.

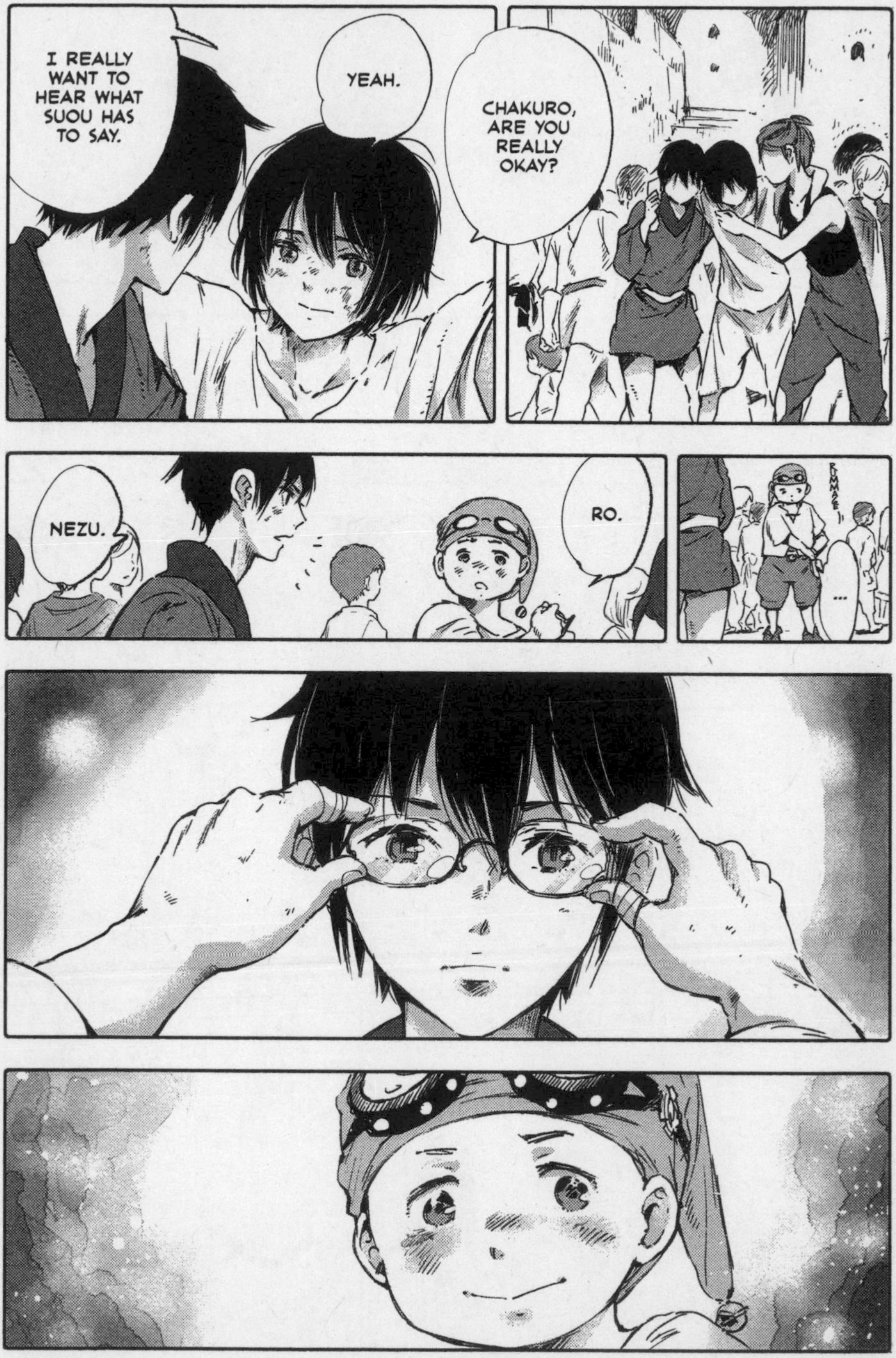
CHAKURO, ARE YOU REALLY OKAY?
YEAH.
I REALLY WANT TO HEAR WHAT SUOU HAS TO SAY.
RUMMAGE
...
RO.
NEZU.

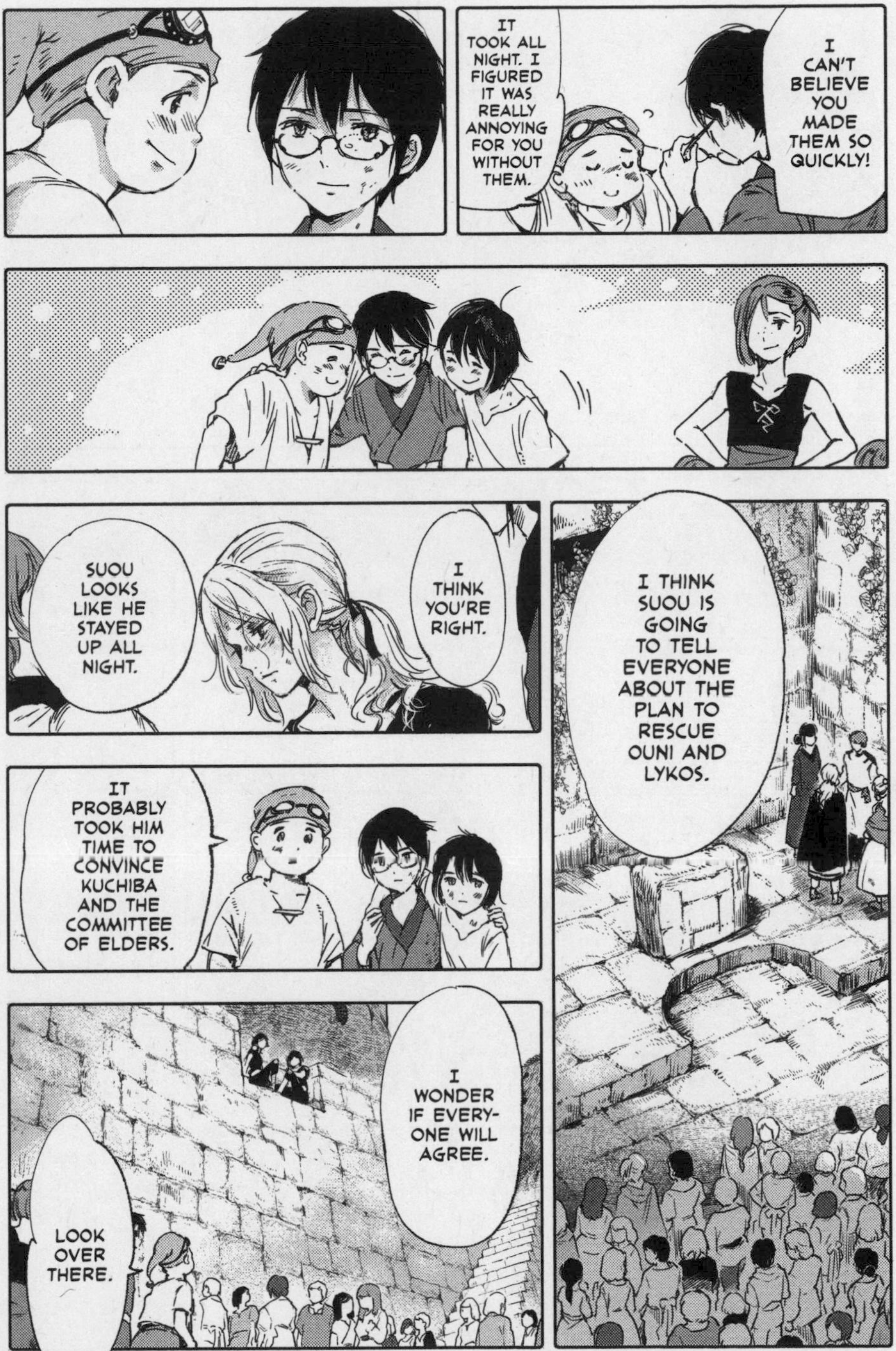
I CAN'T BELIEVE YOU MADE THEM SO QUICKLY!
IT TOOK ALL NIGHT. I FIGURED IT WAS REALLY ANNOYING FOR YOU WITHOUT THEM.
I THINK SUOU IS GOING TO TELL EVERYONE ABOUT THE PLAN TO RESCUE OUNI AND LYKOS.
I THINK YOU'RE RIGHT.
SUOU LOOKS LIKE HE STAYED UP ALL NIGHT.
IT PROBABLY TOOK HIM TIME TO CONVINCE KUCHIBA AND THE COMMITTEE OF ELDERS.
I WONDER IF EVERY-ONE WILL AGREE.
LOOK OVER THERE.

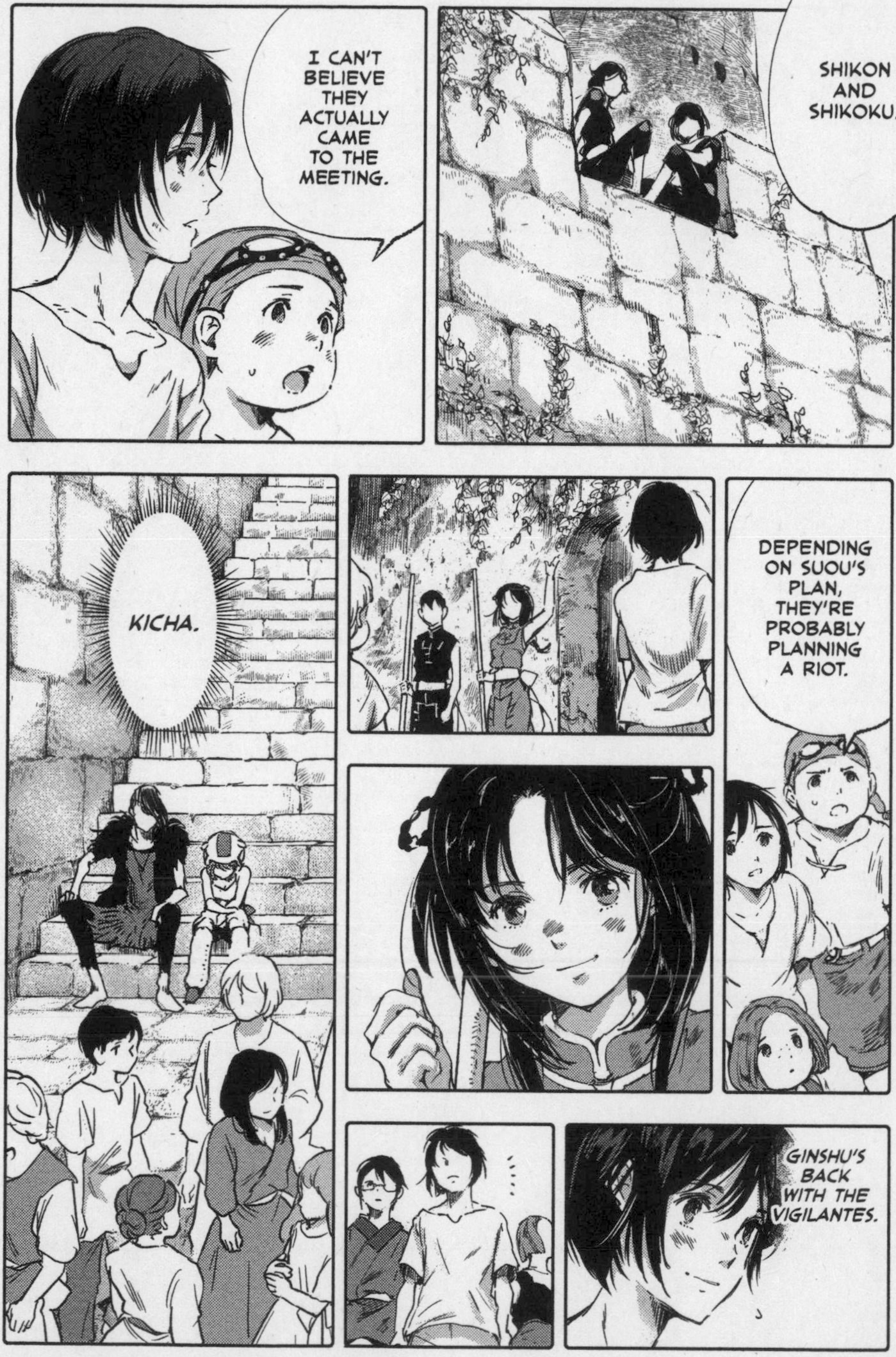

SHIKON AND SHIKOKU.
I CAN'T BELIEVE THEY ACTUALLY CAME TO THE MEETING.
DEPENDING ON SUOU'S PLAN, THEY'RE PROBABLY PLANNING A RIOT.
GINSHU'S BACK WITH THE VIGILANTES.
...
KICHA.

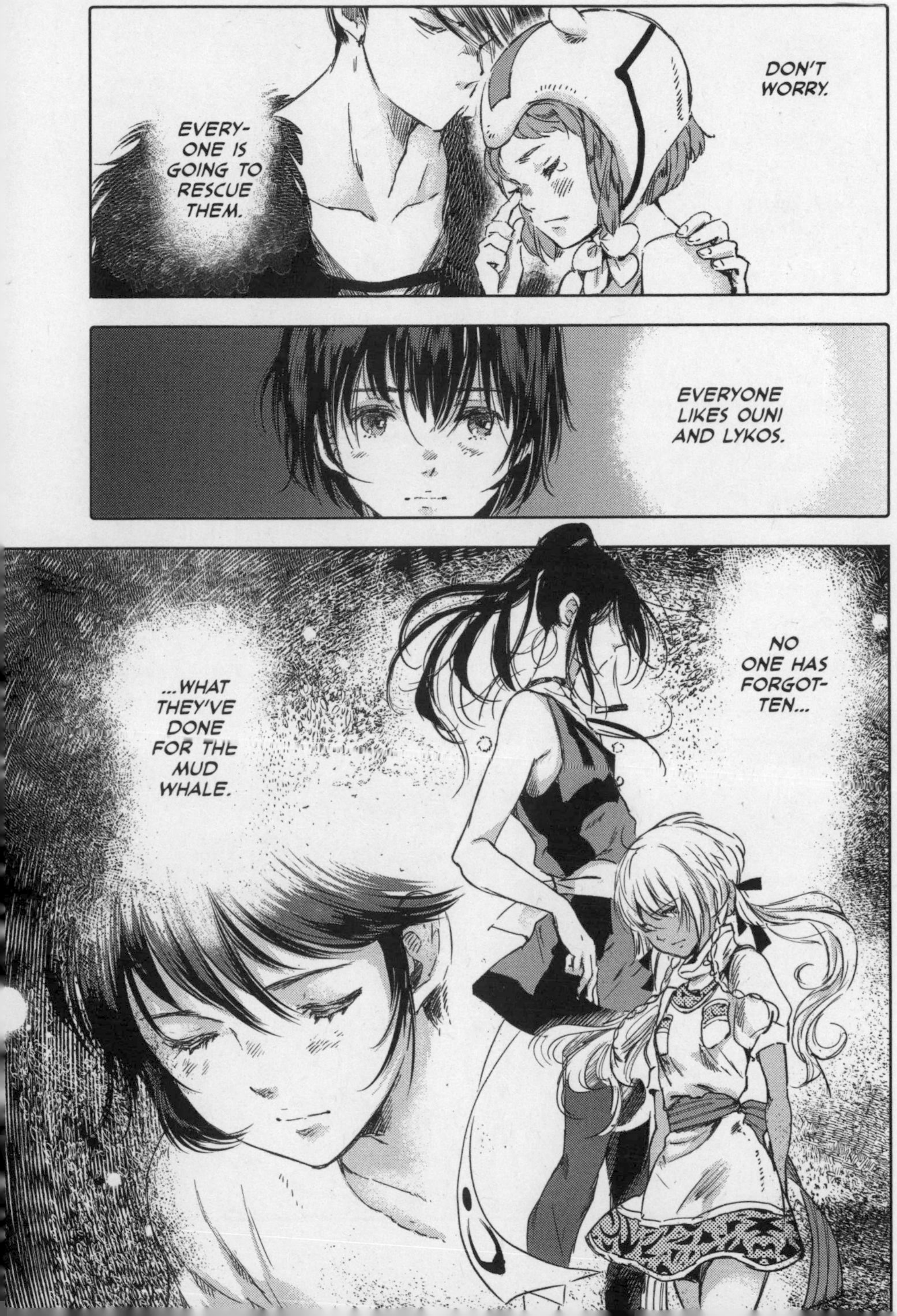
DON'T WORRY.
EVERY-ONE IS GOING TO RESCUE THEM.
EVERYONE LIKES OUNI AND LYKOS.
NO ONE HAS FORGOT-TEN...
...WHAT THEY'VE DONE FOR THE MUD WHALE.

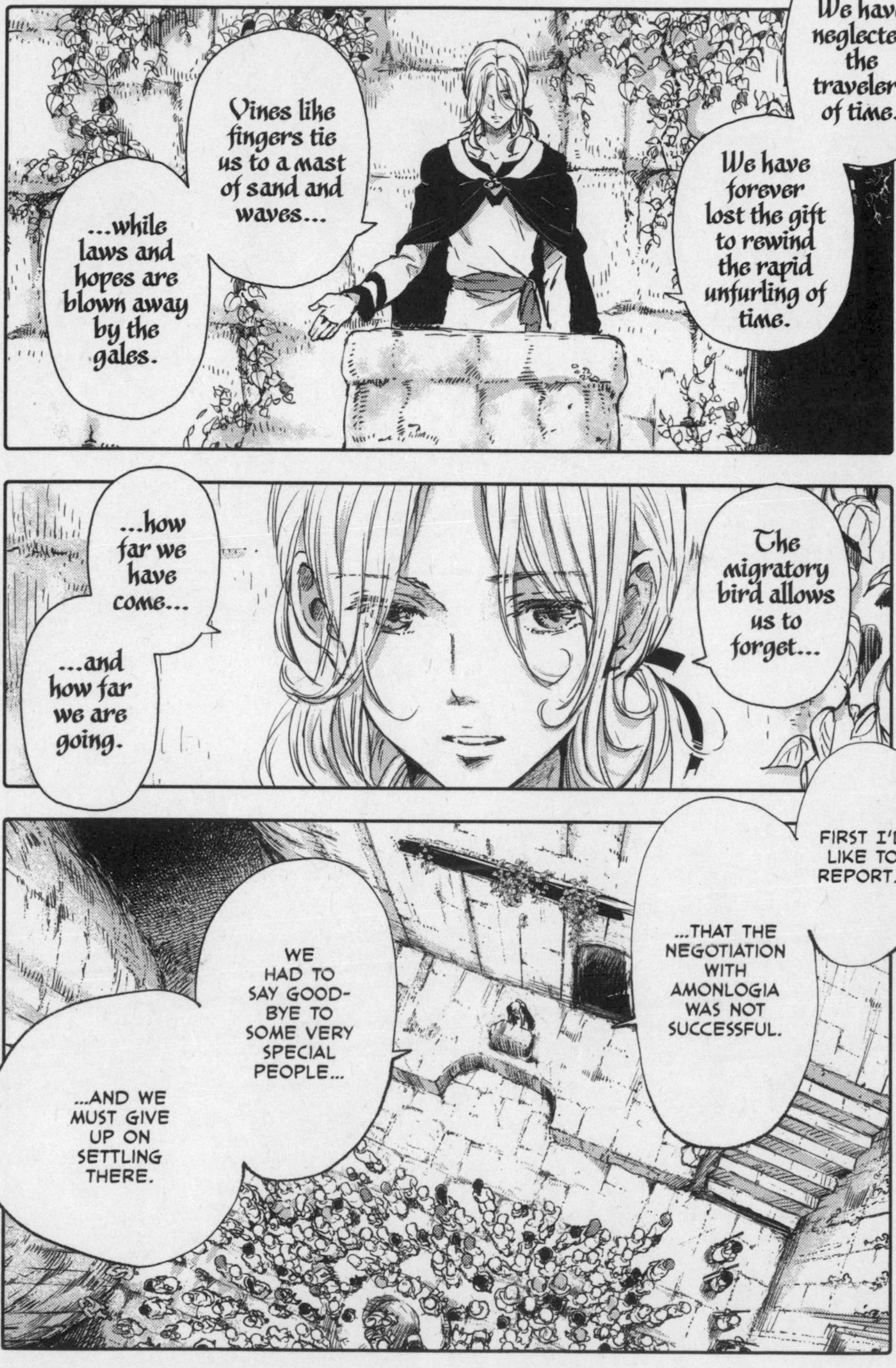
We have neglected the travelers of time.
We have forever lost the gift to rewind the rapid unfurling of time.
Vines like fingers tie us to a mast of sand and waves...
...while laws and hopes are blown away by the gales.
The migratory bird allows us to forget...
...how far we have come...
...and how far we are going.
FIRST I'D LIKE TO REPORT...
...THAT THE NEGOTIATION WITH AMONLOGIA WAS NOT SUCCESSFUL.
WE HAD TO SAY GOOD-BYE TO SOME VERY SPECIAL PEOPLE...
...AND WE MUST GIVE UP ON SETTLING THERE.

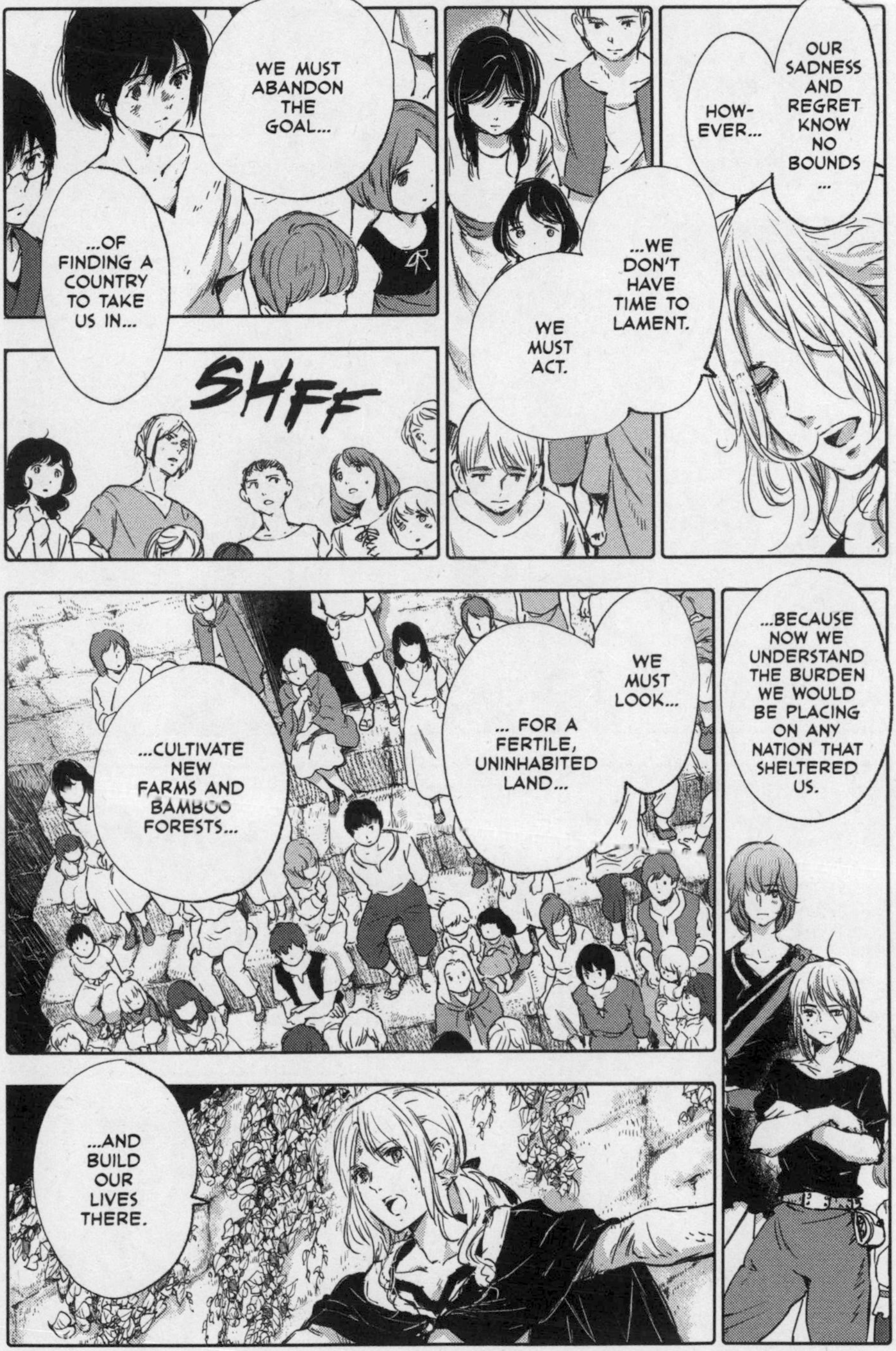
OUR SADNESS AND REGRET KNOW NO BOUNDS ...
HOW-EVER...
...WE DON'T HAVE TIME TO LAMENT.
WE MUST ACT.
WE MUST ABANDON THE GOAL...
...OF FINDING A COUNTRY TO TAKE US IN...
SHFF
...BECAUSE NOW WE UNDERSTAND THE BURDEN WE WOULD BE PLACING ON ANY NATION THAT SHELTERED US.
WE MUST LOOK...
... FOR A FERTILE, UNINHABITED LAND...
...CULTIVATE NEW FARMS AND BAMBOO FORESTS...
...AND BUILD OUR LIVES THERE.

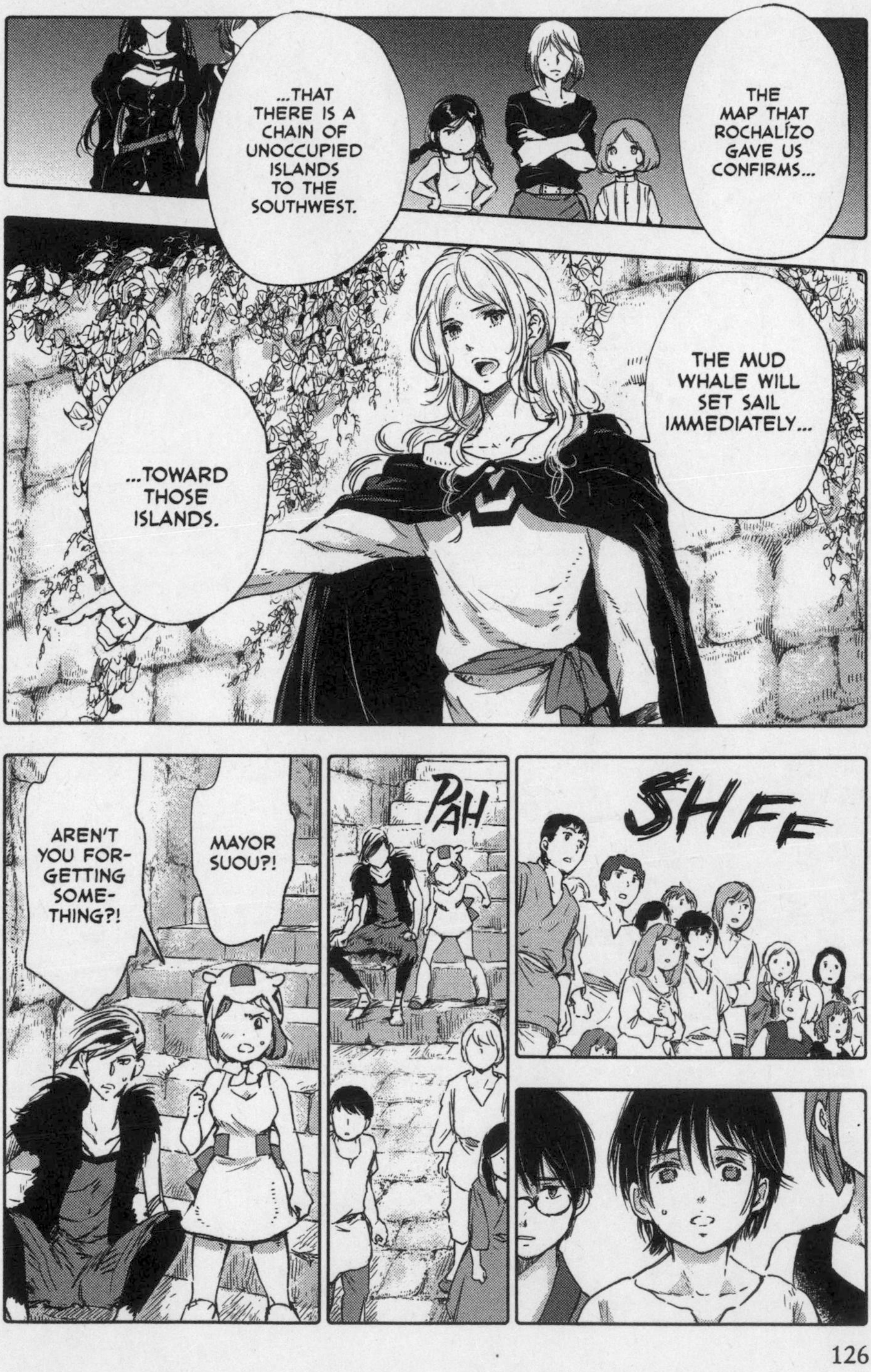
THE MAP THAT ROCHALÍZO GAVE US CONFIRMS...
...THAT THERE IS A CHAIN OF UNOCCUPIED ISLANDS TO THE SOUTHWEST.
THE MUD WHALE WILL SET SAIL IMMEDIATELY...
...TOWARD THOSE ISLANDS.
SHFF
PAH
MAYOR SUOU?!
AREN'T YOU FOR-GETTING SOME-THING?!

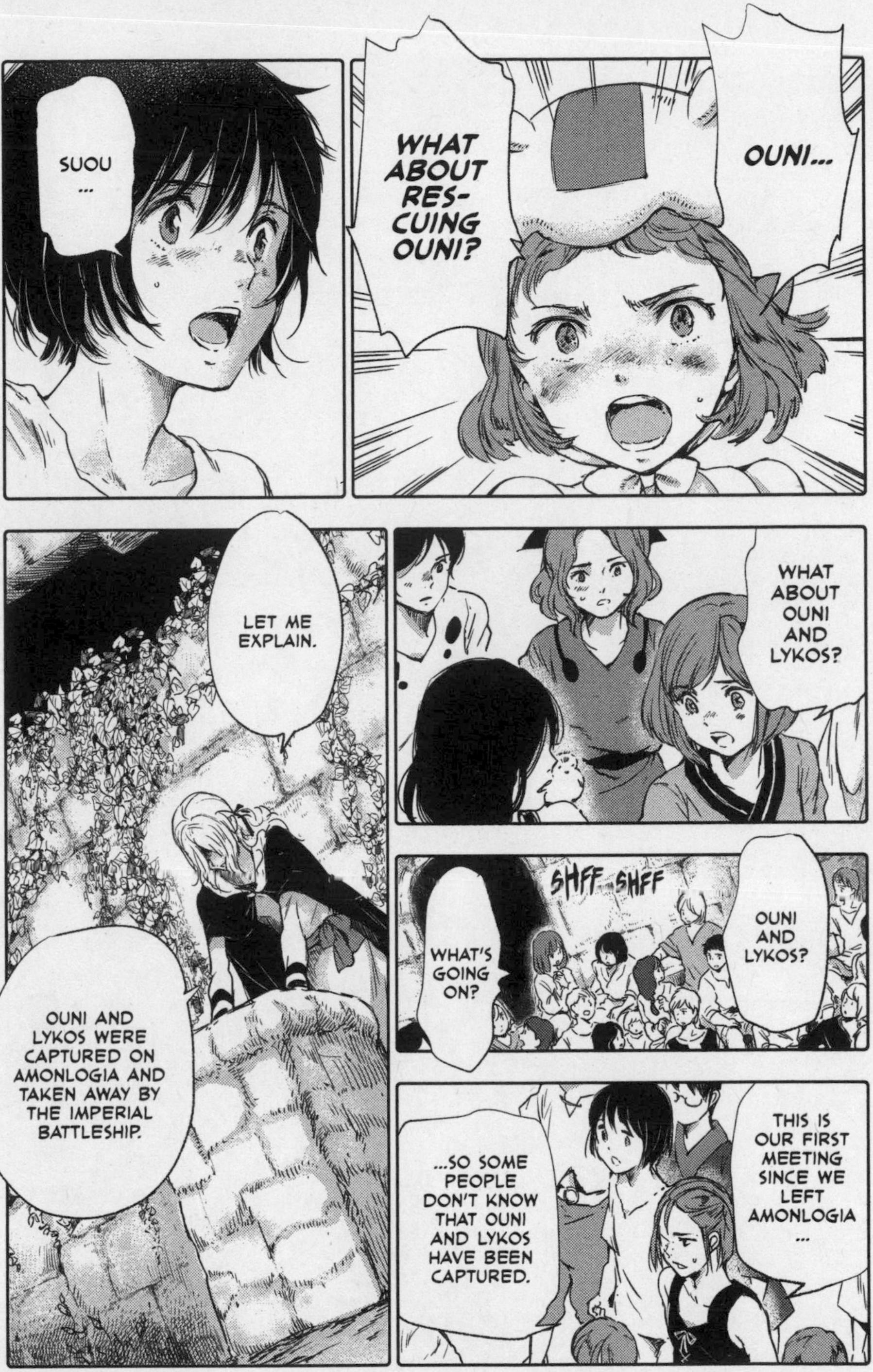
OUNI...
WHAT ABOUT RES-CUING OUNI?
SUOU ...
WHAT ABOUT OUNI AND LYKOS?
OUNI AND LYKOS?
SHFF SHFF
WHAT'S GOING ON?
THIS IS OUR FIRST MEETING SINCE WE LEFT AMONLOGIA ...
...SO SOME PEOPLE DON'T KNOW THAT OUNI AND LYKOS HAVE BEEN CAPTURED.
LET ME EXPLAIN.
OUNI AND LYKOS WERE CAPTURED ON AMONLOGIA AND TAKEN AWAY BY THE IMPERIAL BATTLESHIP.

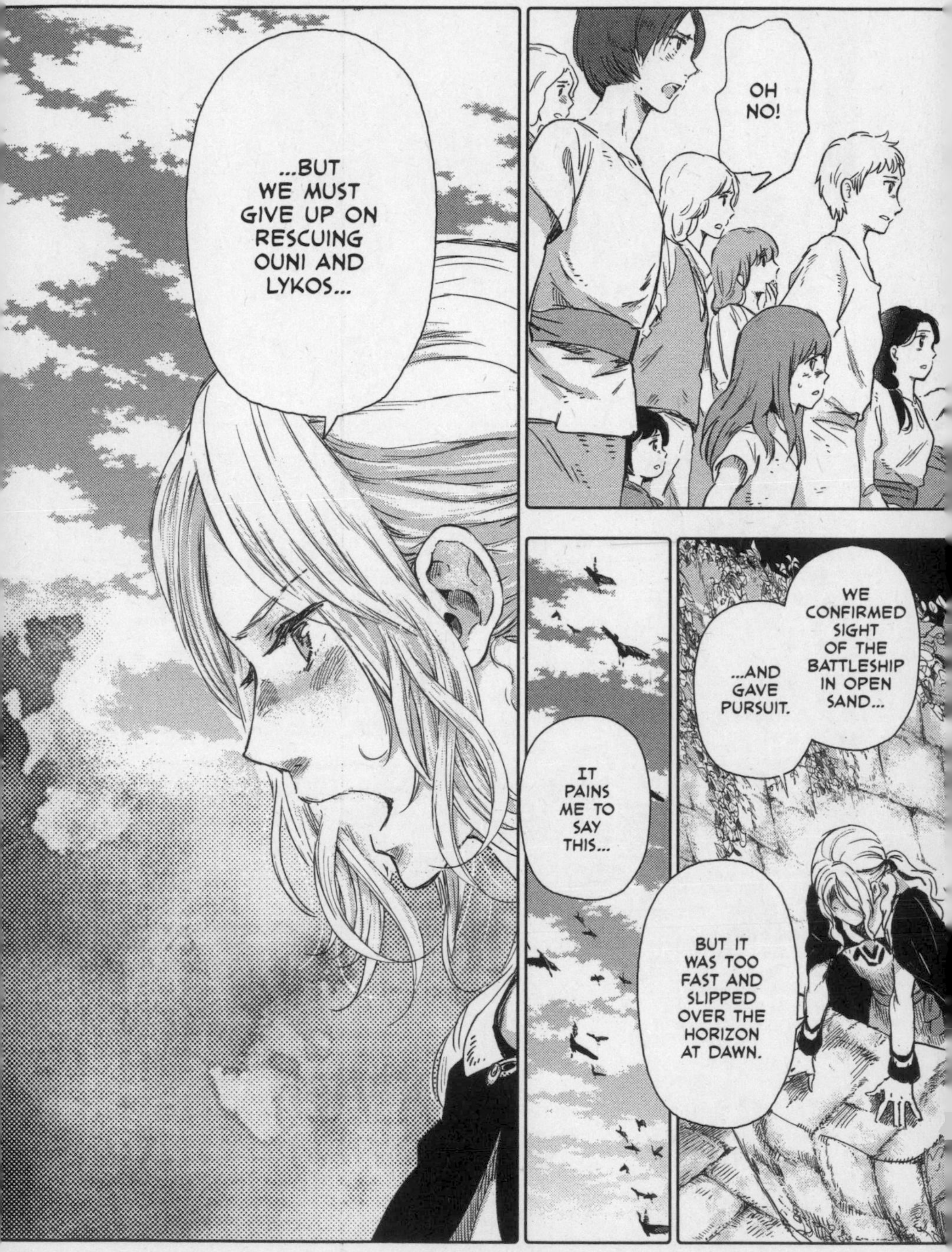
OH NO!
WE CONFIRMED SIGHT OF THE BATTLESHIP IN OPEN SAND...
...AND GAVE PURSUIT.
BUT IT WAS TOO FAST AND SLIPPED OVER THE HORIZON AT DAWN.
IT PAINS ME TO SAY THIS...
...BUT WE MUST GIVE UP ON RESCUING OUNI AND LYKOS...

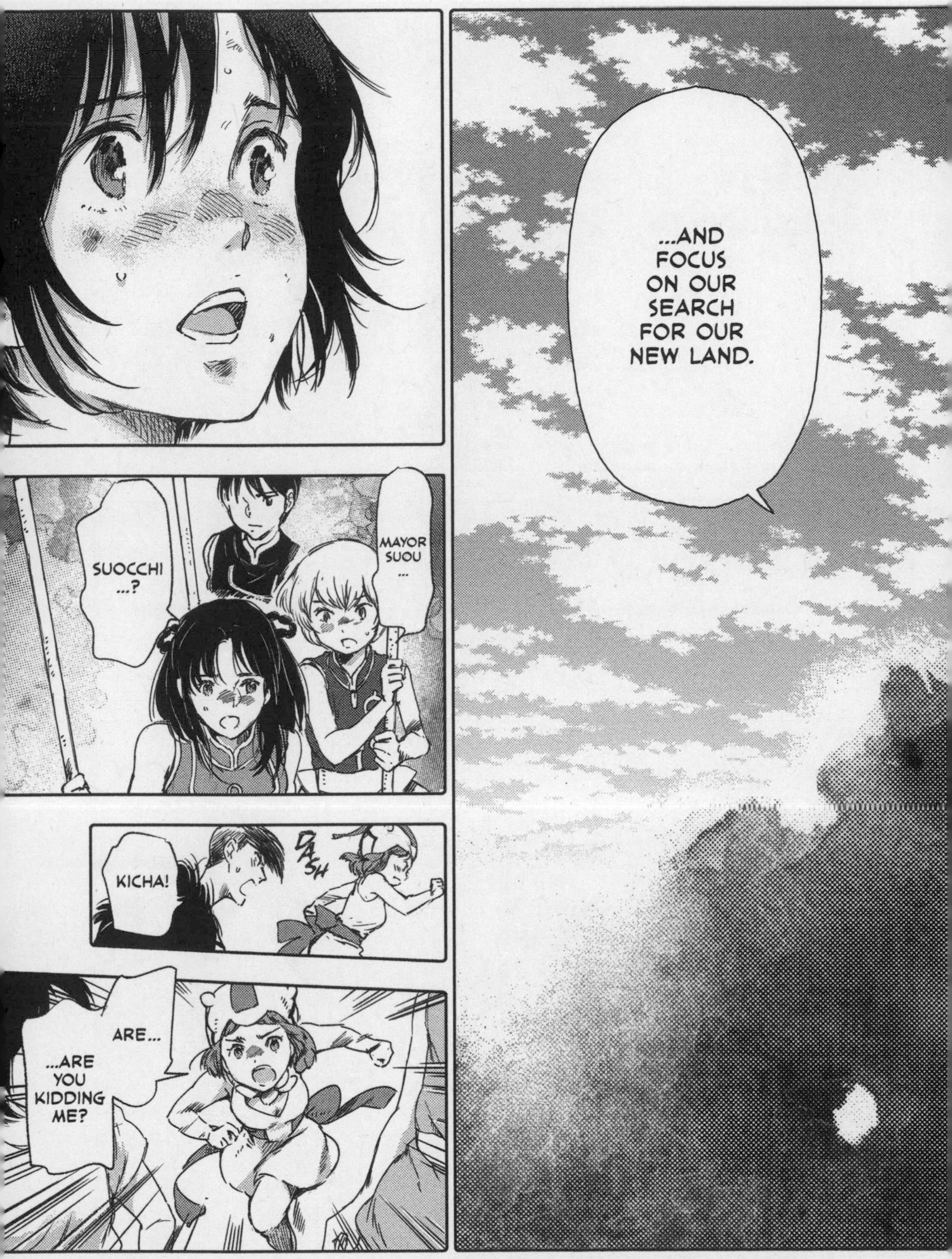
...AND FOCUS ON OUR SEARCH FOR OUR NEW LAND.
MAYOR SUOU ...
SUOCCHI ...?
DASH
KICHA!
ARE...
...ARE YOU KIDDING ME?

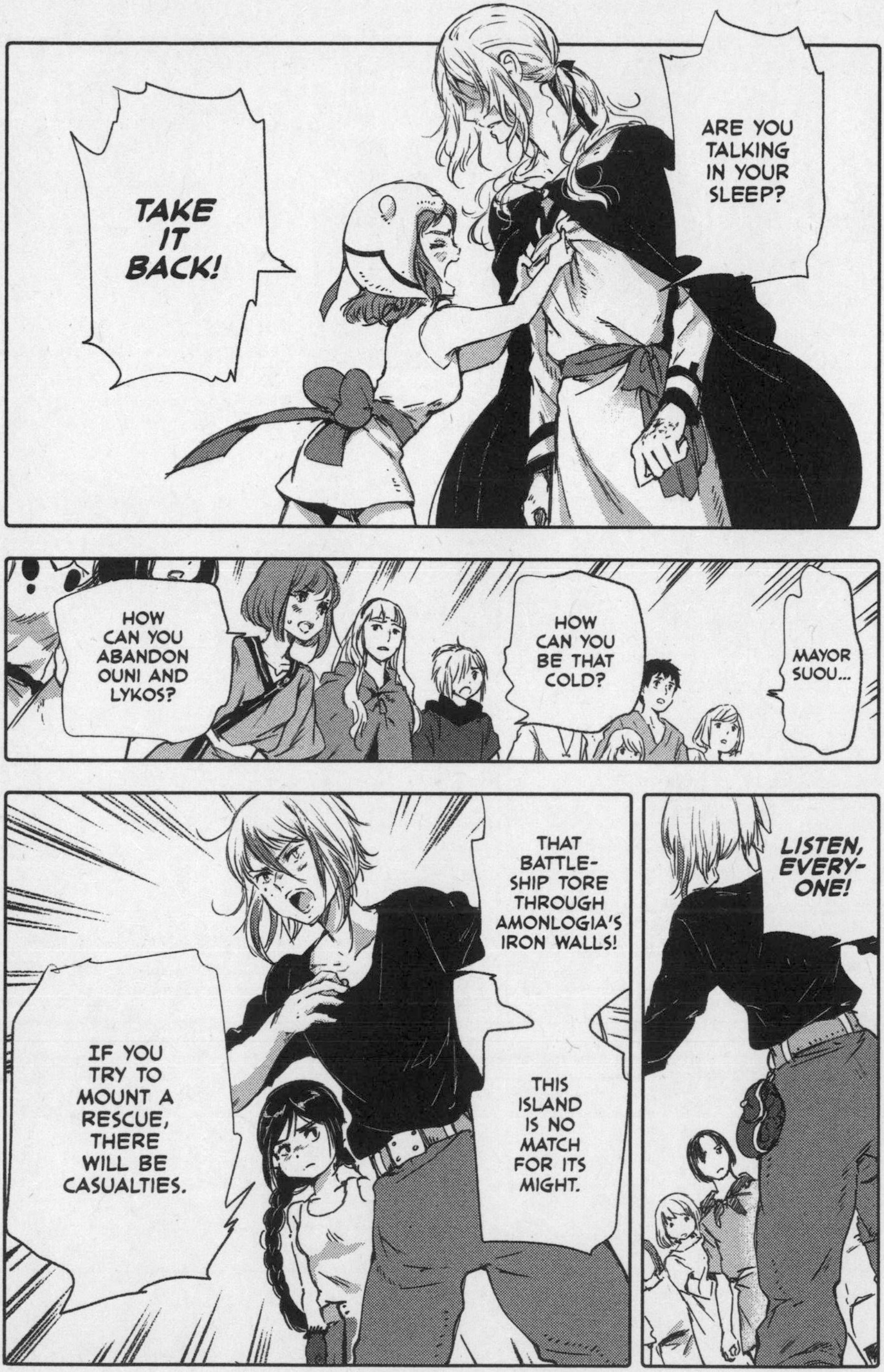
ARE YOU TALKING IN YOUR SLEEP?
TAKE IT BACK!
MAYOR SUOU...
HOW CAN YOU BE THAT COLD?
HOW CAN YOU ABANDON OUNI AND LYKOS?
LISTEN, EVERYONE!
THAT BATTLESHIP TORE THROUGH AMONLOGIA'S IRON WALLS!
THIS ISLAND IS NO MATCH FOR ITS MIGHT.
IF YOU TRY TO MOUNT A RESCUE, THERE WILL BE CASUALTIES.

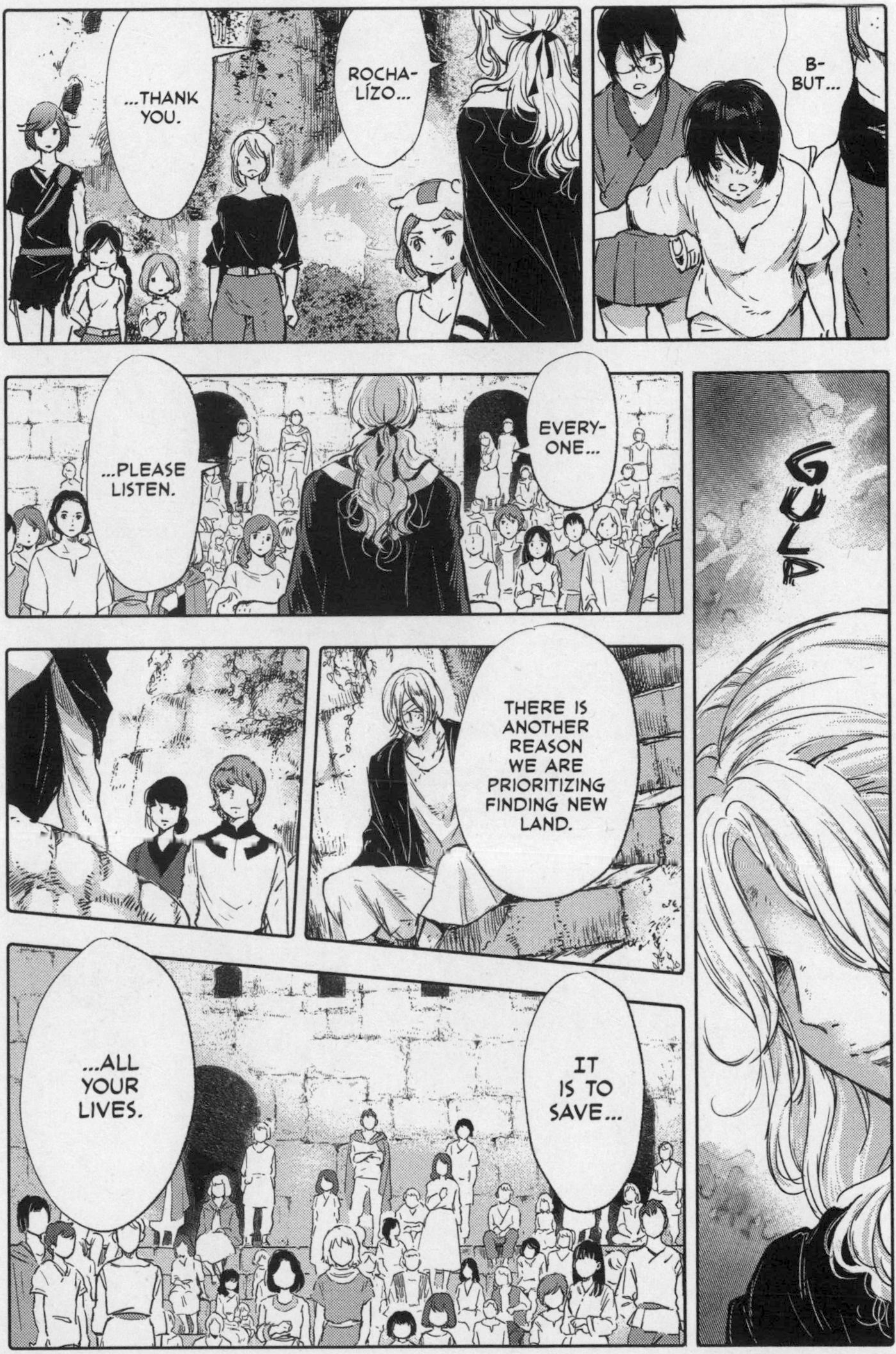
B-BUT...
ROCHA-LÍZO...
...THANK YOU.
GULP
EVERY-ONE...
...PLEASE LISTEN.
THERE IS ANOTHER REASON WE ARE PRIORITIZING FINDING NEW LAND.
IT IS TO SAVE...
...ALL YOUR LIVES.

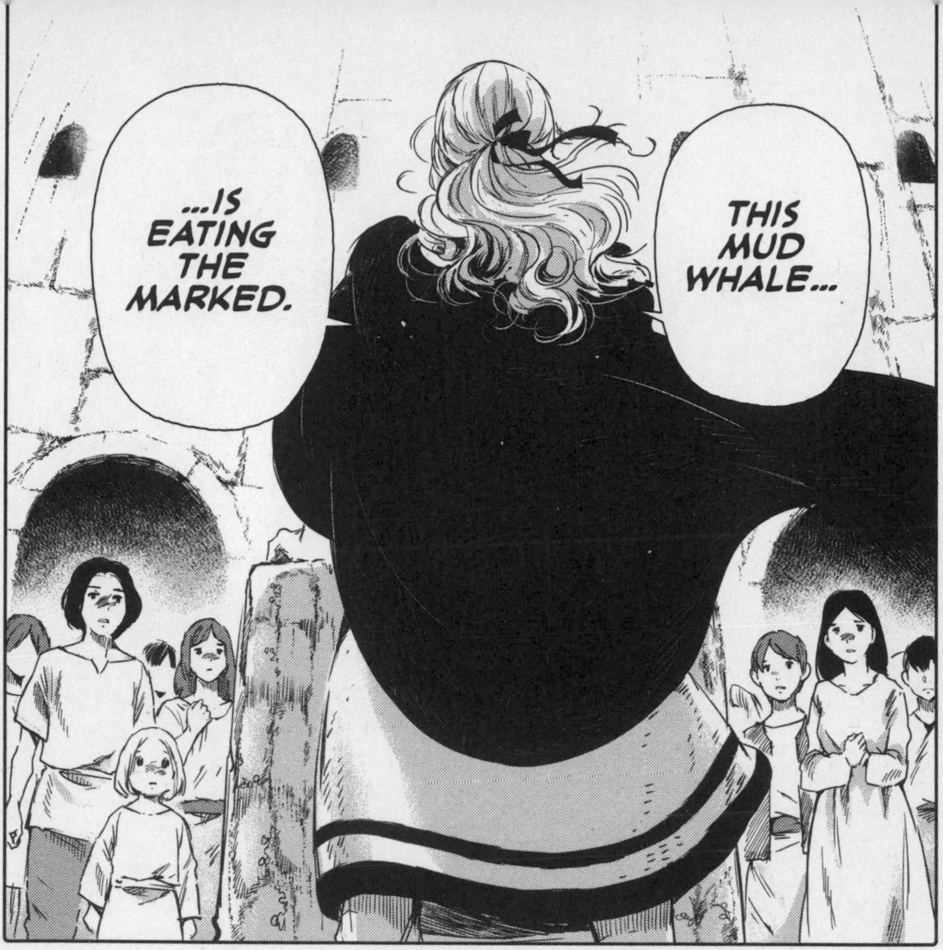
THIS MUD WHALE...
...IS EATING THE MARKED.
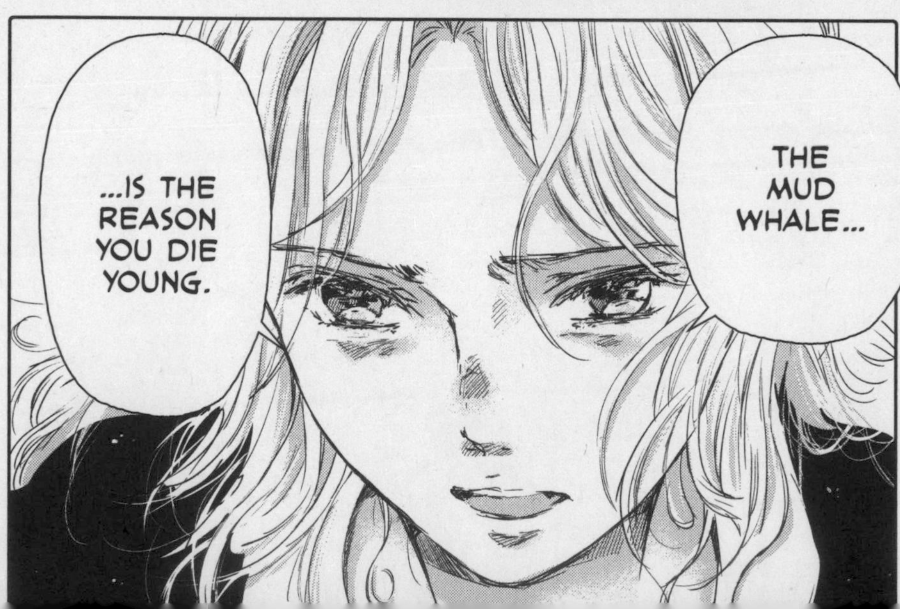
THE MUD WHALE...
...IS THE REASON YOU DIE YOUNG.

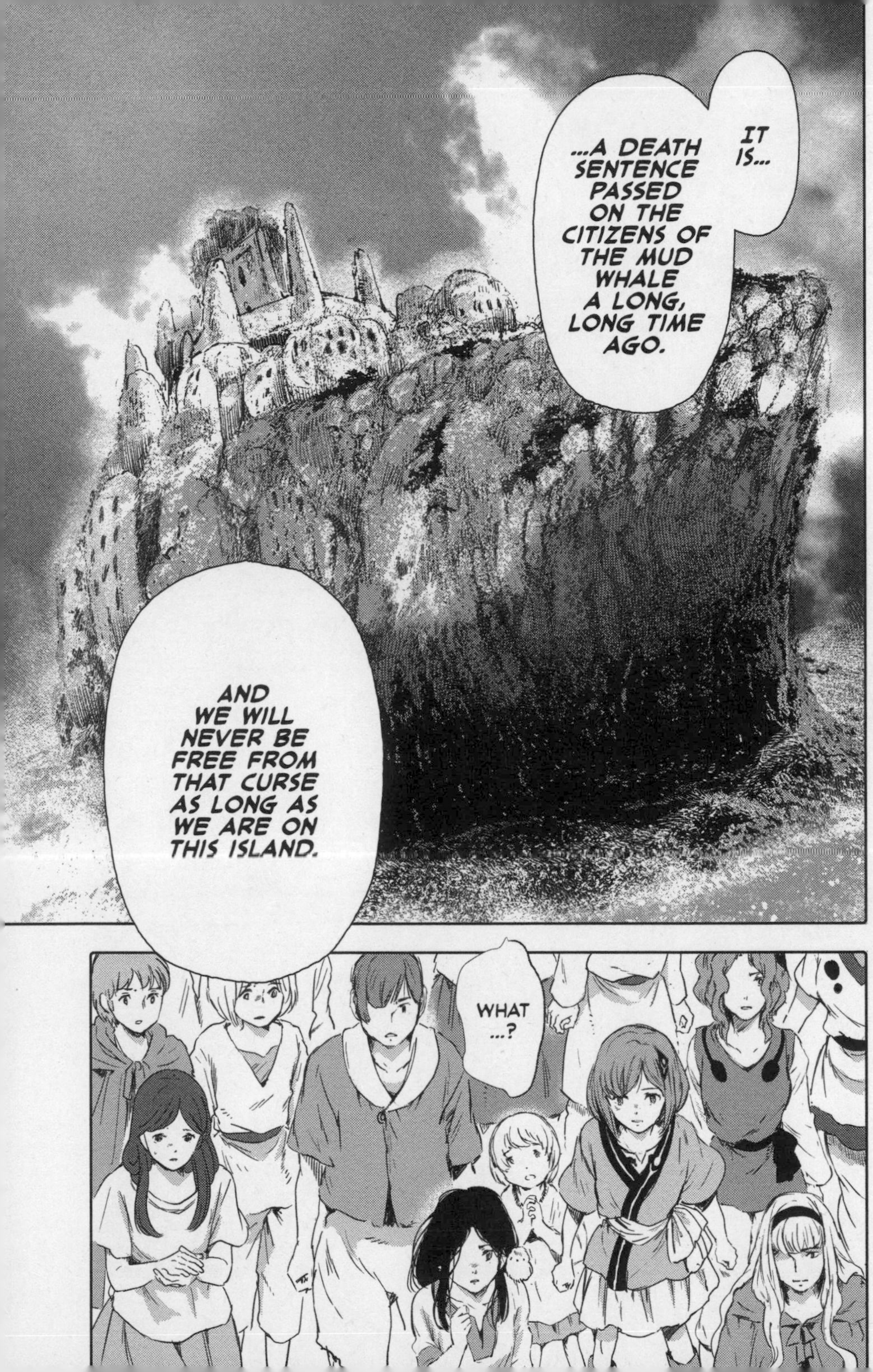
IT IS...
...A DEATH SENTENCE PASSED ON THE CITIZENS OF THE MUD WHALE A LONG, LONG TIME AGO.
AND WE WILL NEVER BE FREE FROM THAT CURSE AS LONG AS WE ARE ON THIS ISLAND.
WHAT ...?

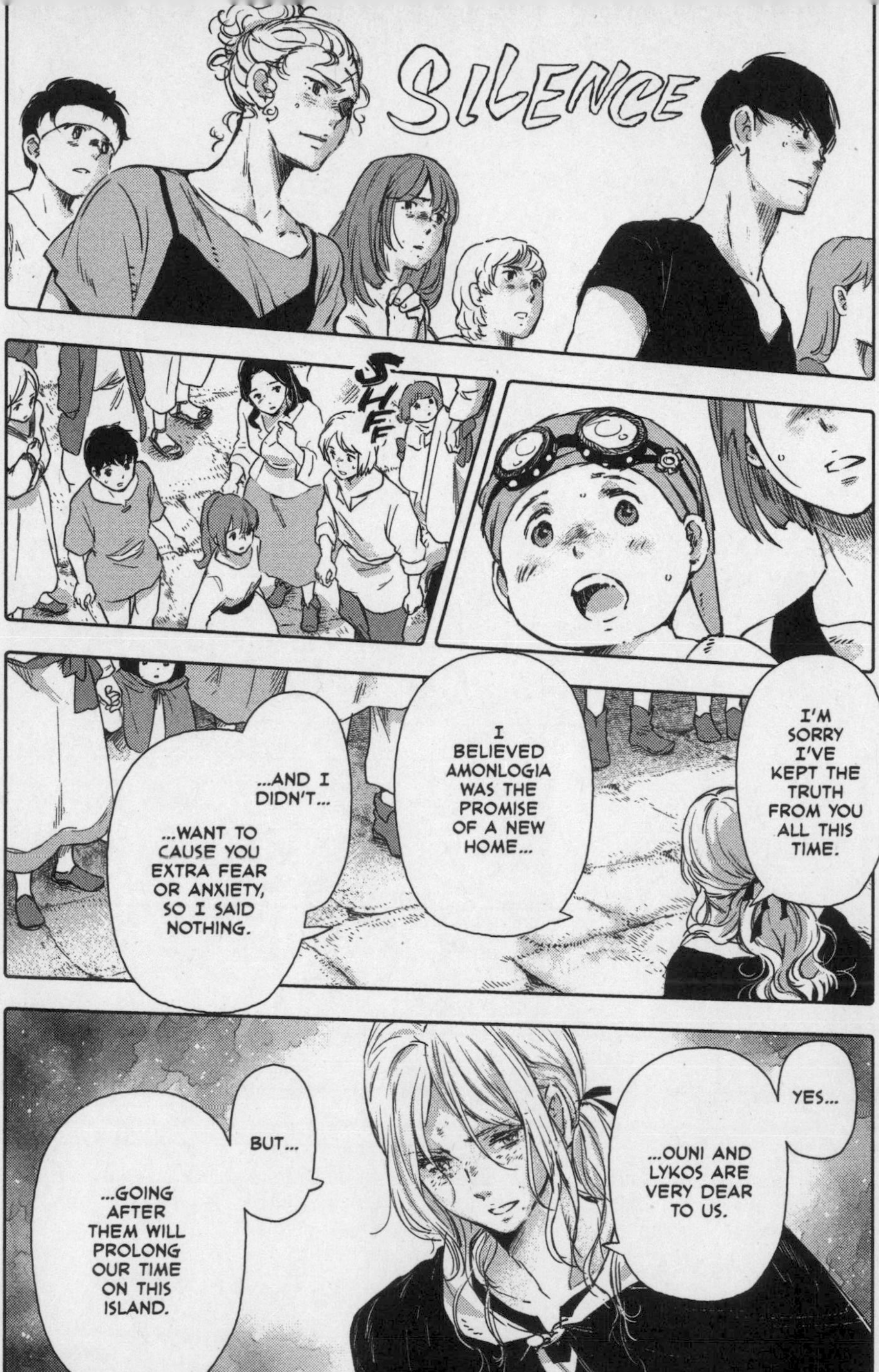
SILENCE
SHF
I'M SORRY I'VE KEPT THE TRUTH FROM YOU ALL THIS TIME.
I BELIEVED AMONLOGIA WAS THE PROMISE OF A NEW HOME...
...AND I DIDN'T...
...WANT TO CAUSE YOU EXTRA FEAR OR ANXIETY, SO I SAID NOTHING.
YES...
...OUNI AND LYKOS ARE VERY DEAR TO US.
BUT...
...GOING AFTER THEM WILL PROLONG OUR TIME ON THIS ISLAND.

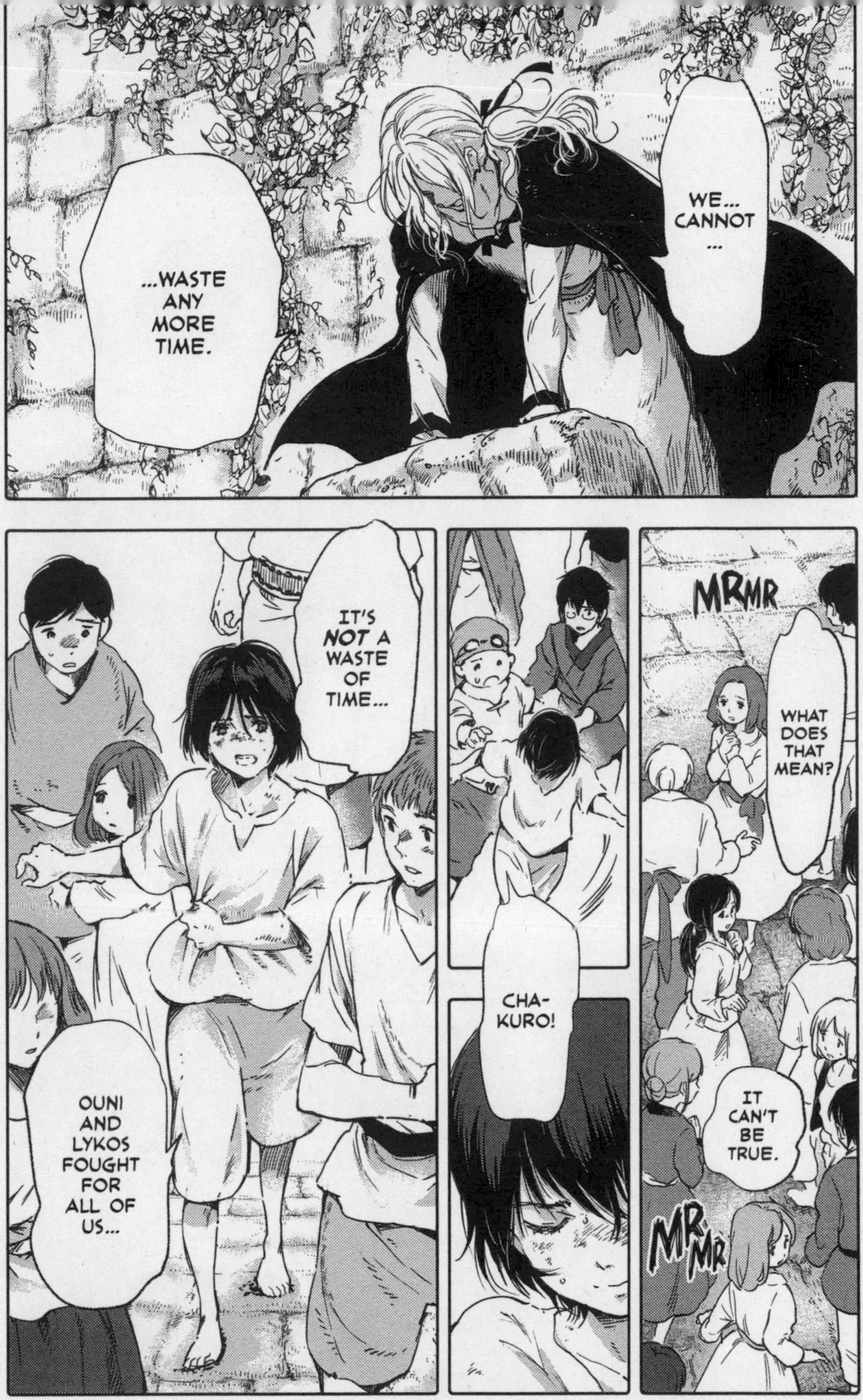
WE... CANNOT ...
...WASTE ANY MORE TIME.
MRMR
WHAT DOES THAT MEAN?
IT CAN'T BE TRUE.
MR MR
CHA-KURO!
IT'S *NOT* A WASTE OF TIME...
OUNI AND LYKOS FOUGHT FOR ALL OF US...

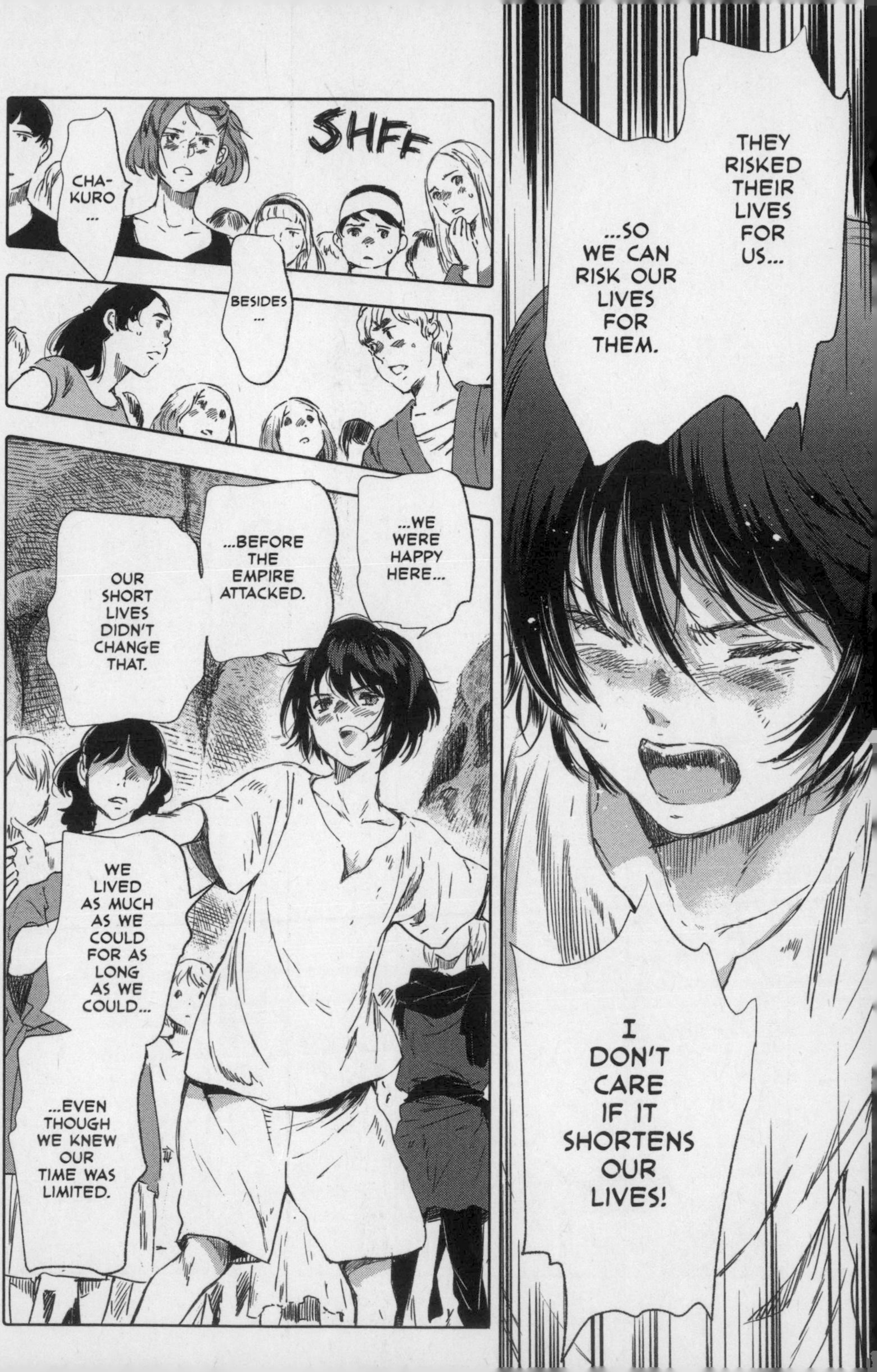
THEY RISKED THEIR LIVES FOR US...
...SO WE CAN RISK OUR LIVES FOR THEM.
I DON'T CARE IF IT SHORTENS OUR LIVES!
SHFF
CHA-KURO...
BESIDES...
...WE WERE HAPPY HERE...
...BEFORE THE EMPIRE ATTACKED.
OUR SHORT LIVES DIDN'T CHANGE THAT.
WE LIVED AS MUCH AS WE COULD FOR AS LONG AS WE COULD...
...EVEN THOUGH WE KNEW OUR TIME WAS LIMITED.

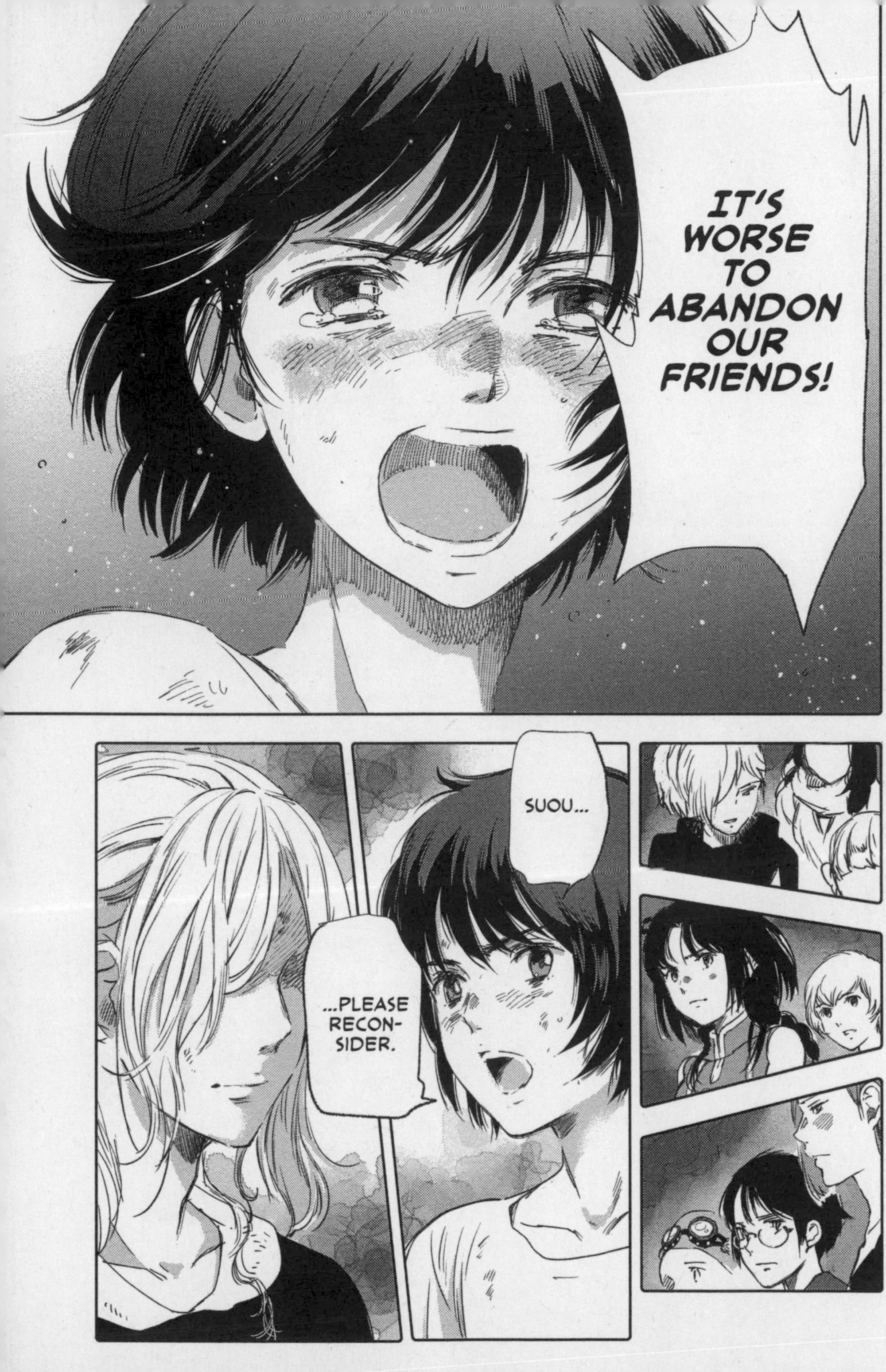
IT'S WORSE TO ABANDON OUR FRIENDS!
SUOU...
...PLEASE RECON-SIDER.

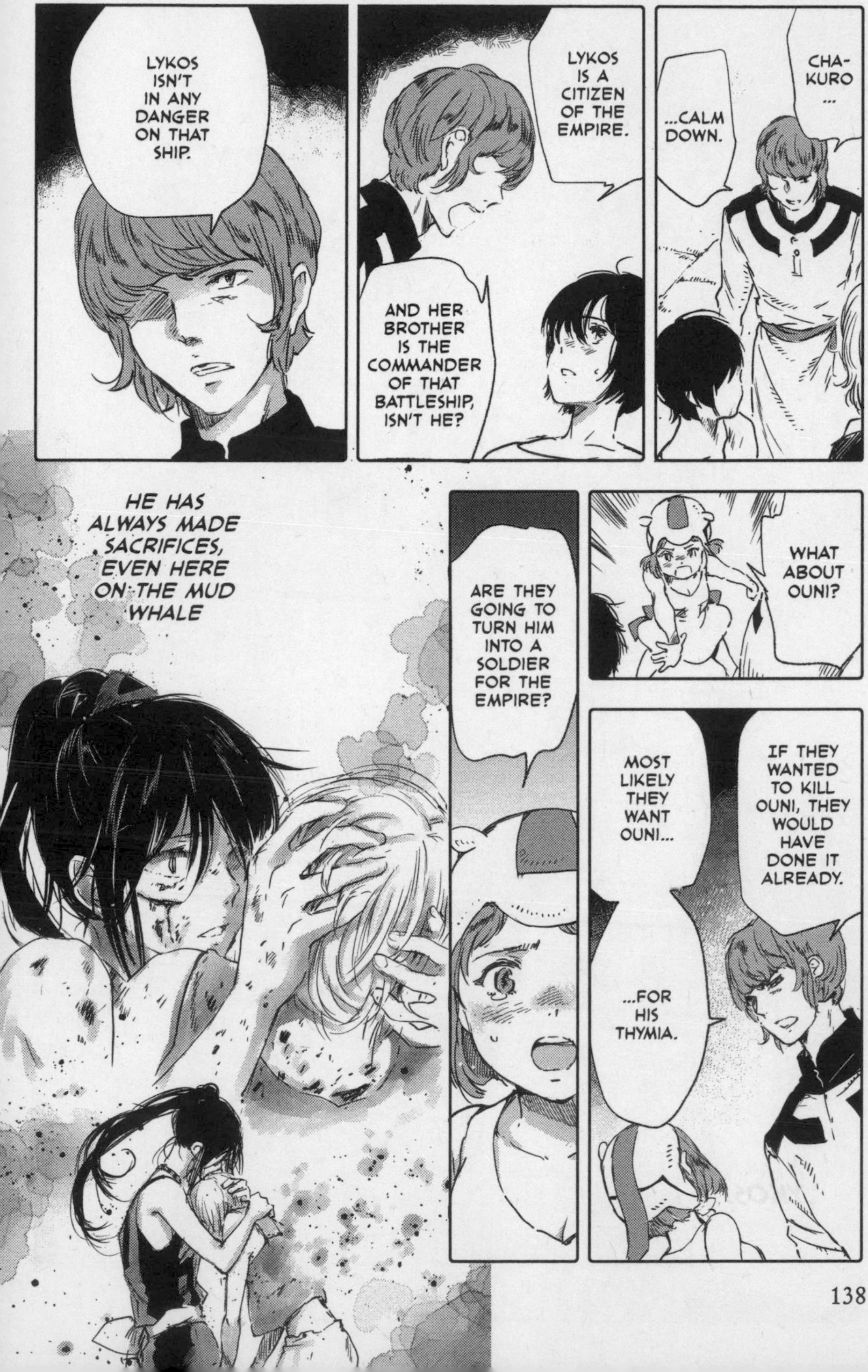

CHA-KURO ...
...CALM DOWN.
LYKOS IS A CITIZEN OF THE EMPIRE.
AND HER BROTHER IS THE COMMANDER OF THAT BATTLESHIP, ISN'T HE?
LYKOS ISN'T IN ANY DANGER ON THAT SHIP.
WHAT ABOUT OUNI?
IF THEY WANTED TO KILL OUNI, THEY WOULD HAVE DONE IT ALREADY.
MOST LIKELY THEY WANT OUNI...
...FOR HIS THYMIA.
ARE THEY GOING TO TURN HIM INTO A SOLDIER FOR THE EMPIRE?
HE HAS ALWAYS MADE SACRIFICES, EVEN HERE ON THE MUD WHALE

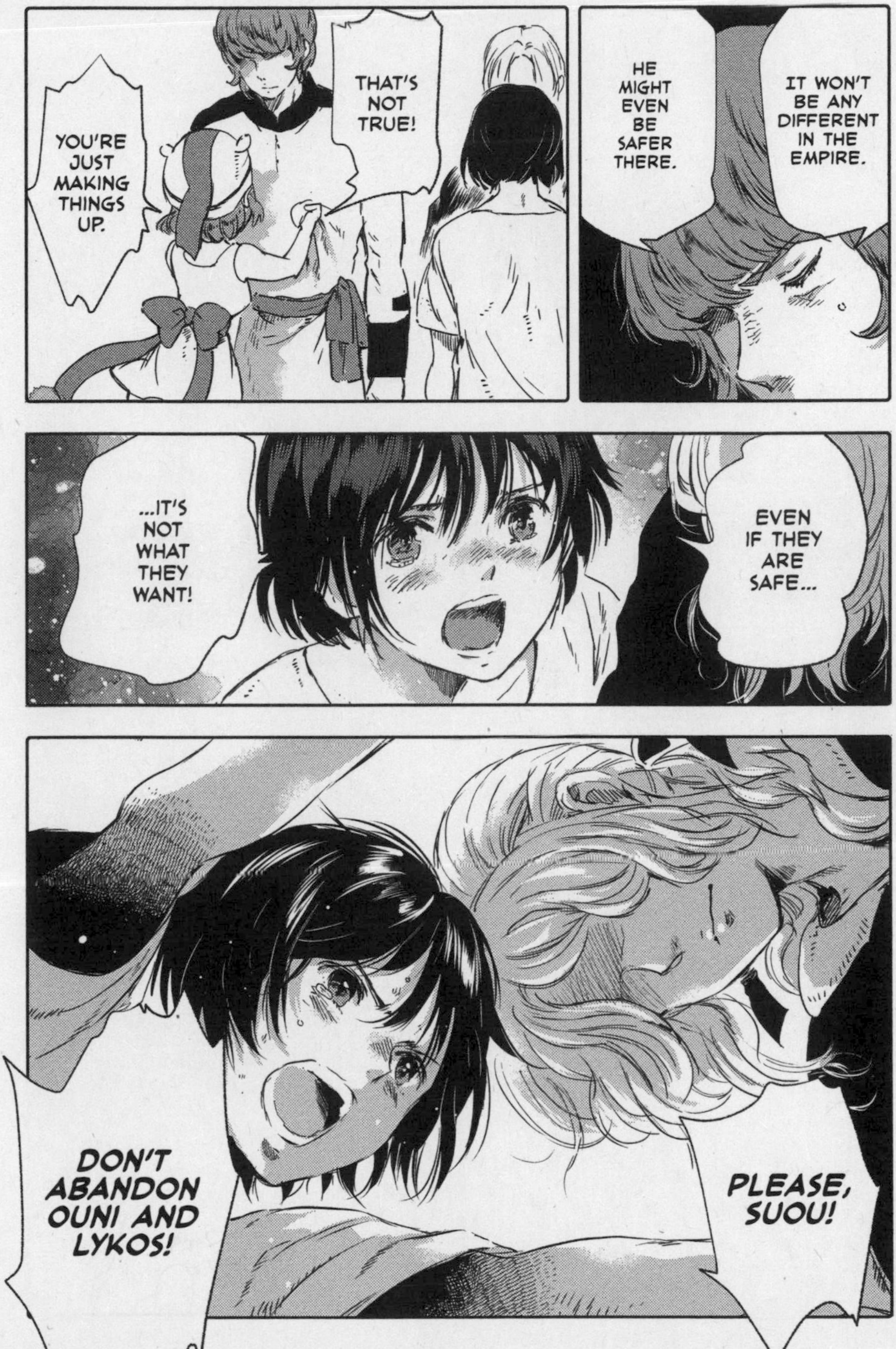
IT WON'T BE ANY DIFFERENT IN THE EMPIRE.
HE MIGHT EVEN BE SAFER THERE.
THAT'S NOT TRUE!
YOU'RE JUST MAKING THINGS UP.
EVEN IF THEY ARE SAFE...
...IT'S NOT WHAT THEY WANT!
PLEASE, SUOU!
DON'T ABANDON OUNI AND LYKOS!

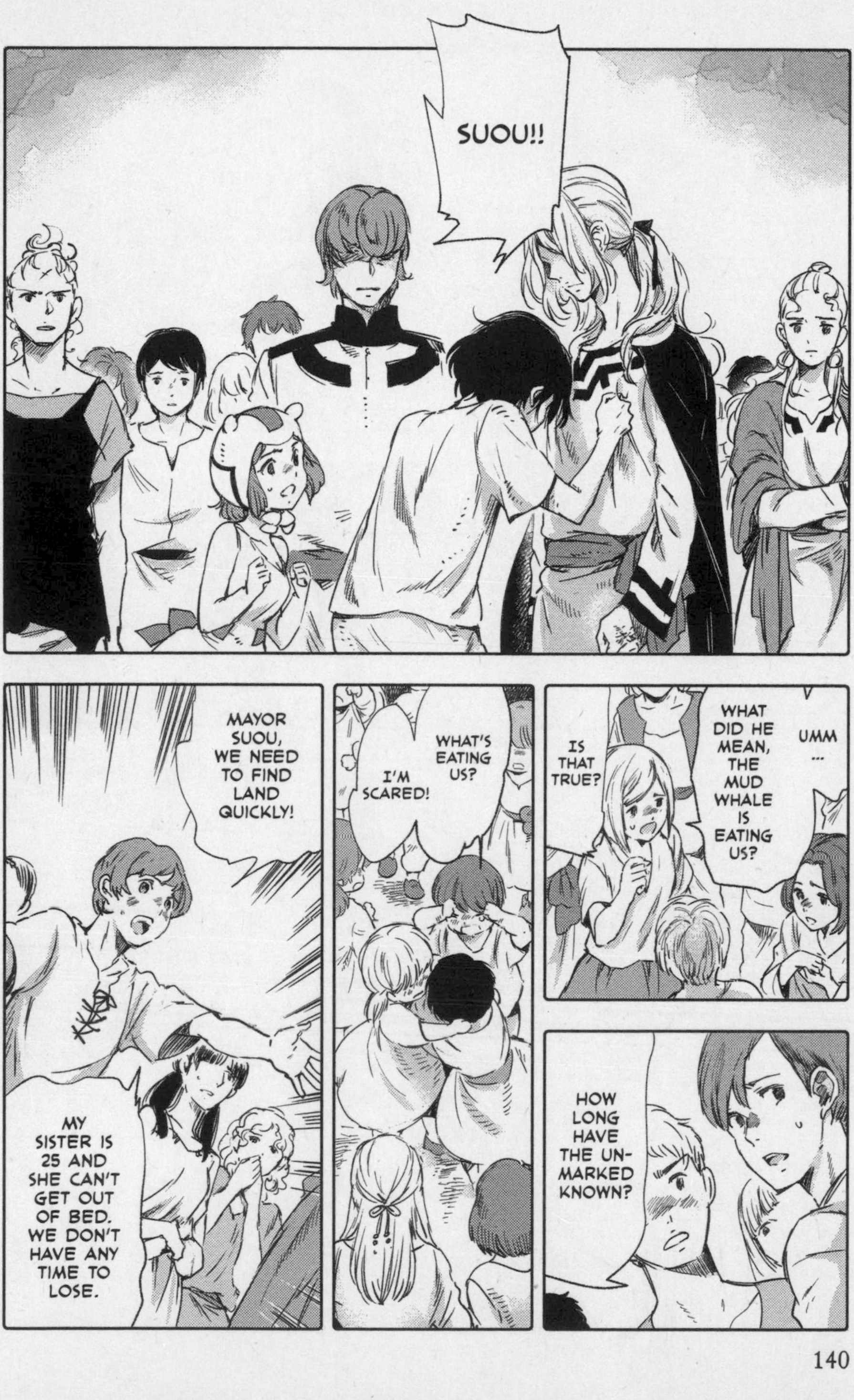
SUOU!!
UMM...
WHAT DID HE MEAN, THE MUD WHALE IS EATING US?
IS THAT TRUE?
HOW LONG HAVE THE UN-MARKED KNOWN?
WHAT'S EATING US?
I'M SCARED!
MAYOR SUOU, WE NEED TO FIND LAND QUICKLY!
MY SISTER IS 25 AND SHE CAN'T GET OUT OF BED. WE DON'T HAVE ANY TIME TO LOSE.

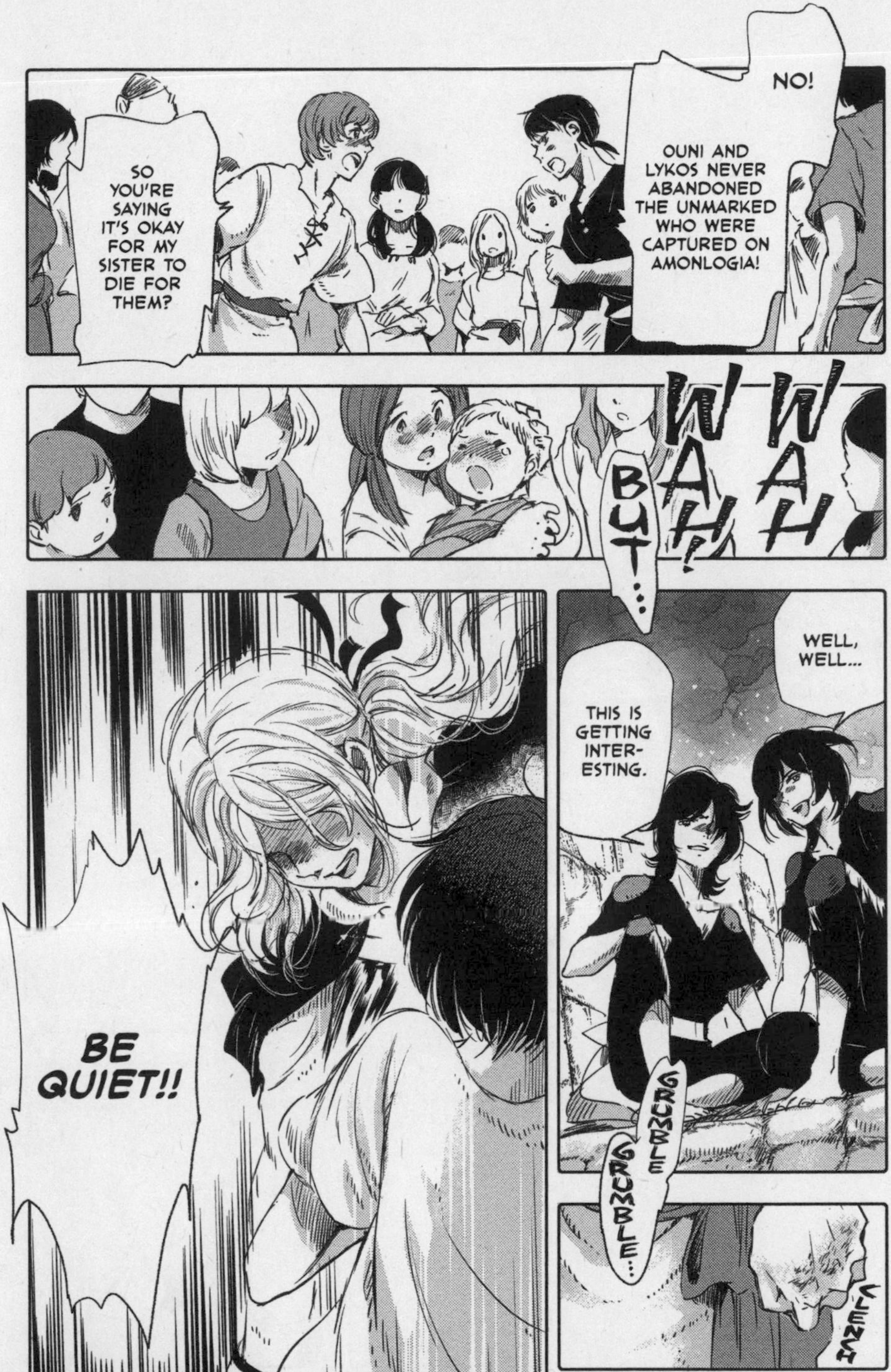
NO!
OUNI AND LYKOS NEVER ABANDONED THE UNMARKED WHO WERE CAPTURED ON AMONLOGIA!
SO YOU'RE SAYING IT'S OKAY FOR MY SISTER TO DIE FOR THEM?
WAH WAH
BUT...
WELL, WELL...
THIS IS GETTING INTER-ESTING.
GRUMBLE GRUMBLE...
CLENCH
BE QUIET!!

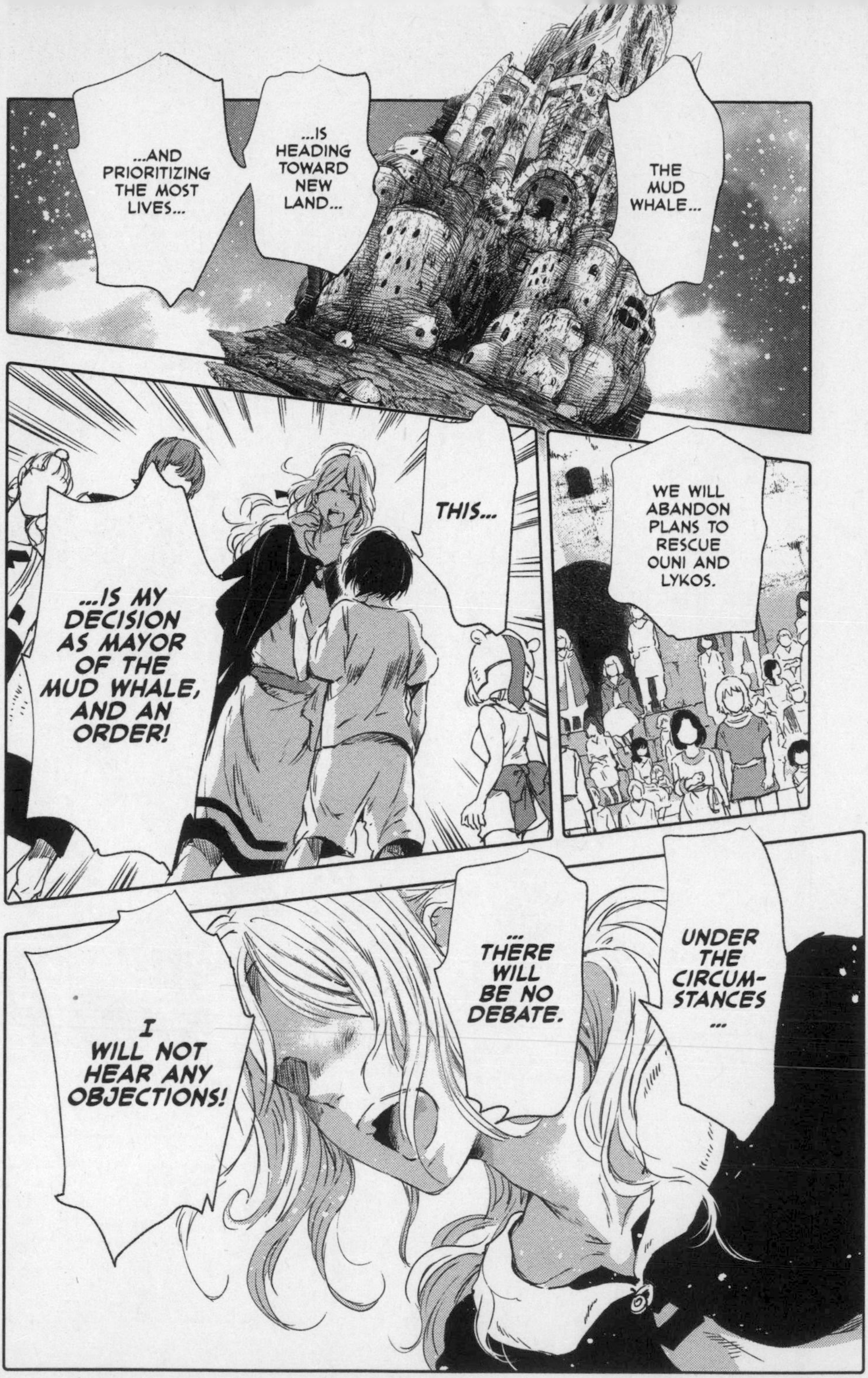
THE MUD WHALE...
...IS HEADING TOWARD NEW LAND...
...AND PRIORITIZING THE MOST LIVES...
WE WILL ABANDON PLANS TO RESCUE OUNI AND LYKOS.
THIS...
...IS MY DECISION AS MAYOR OF THE MUD WHALE, AND AN ORDER!
UNDER THE CIRCUM-STANCES...
...THERE WILL BE NO DEBATE.
I WILL NOT HEAR ANY OBJECTIONS!

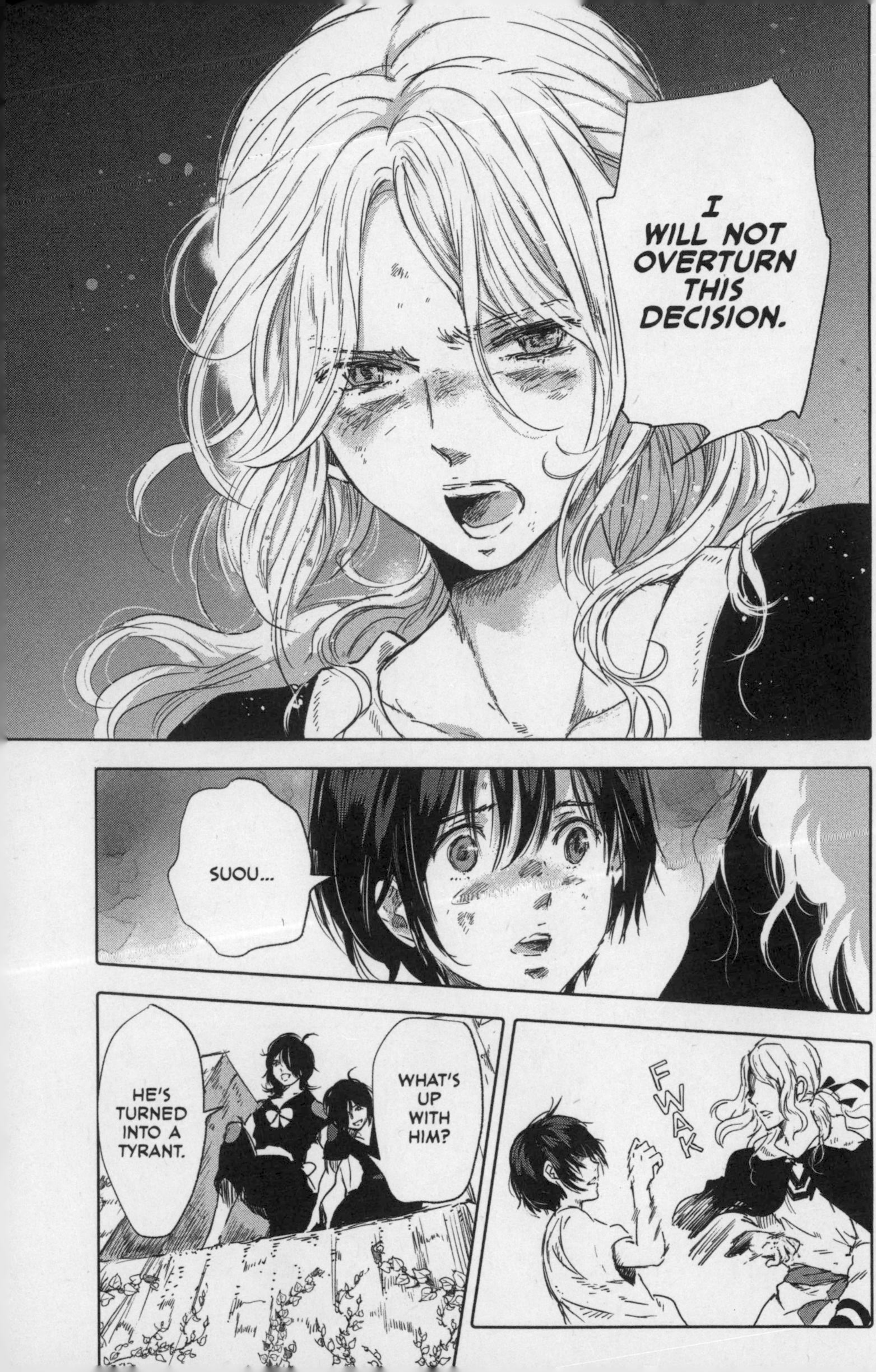
I WILL NOT OVERTURN THIS DECISION.
SUOU...
FWAK
WHAT'S UP WITH HIM?
HE'S TURNED INTO A TYRANT.

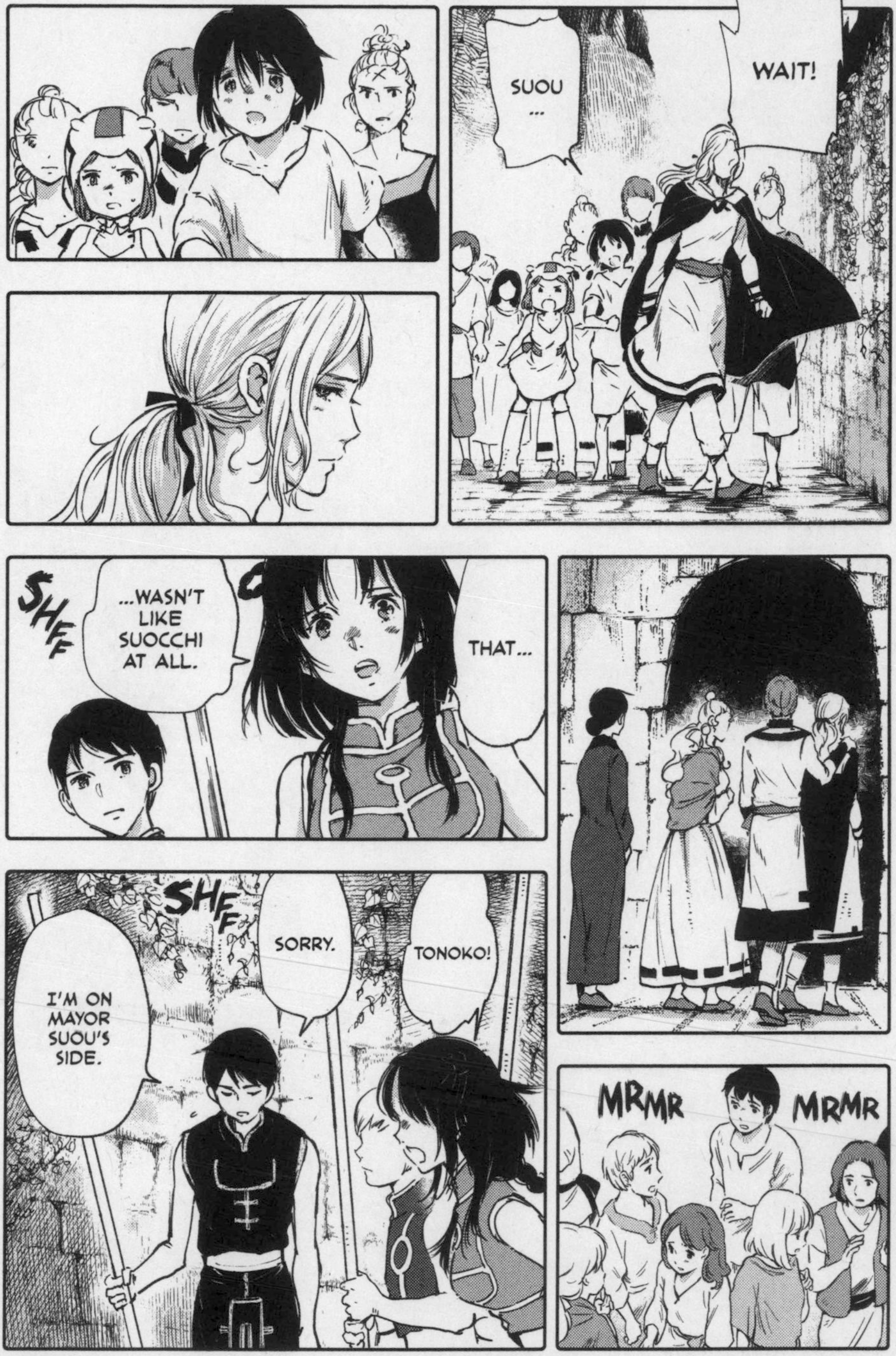
WAIT!
SUOU ...
THAT...
...WASN'T LIKE SUOCCHI AT ALL.
SHFF
TONOKO!
SORRY.
SHFF
I'M ON MAYOR SUOU'S SIDE.
MRMR
MRMR

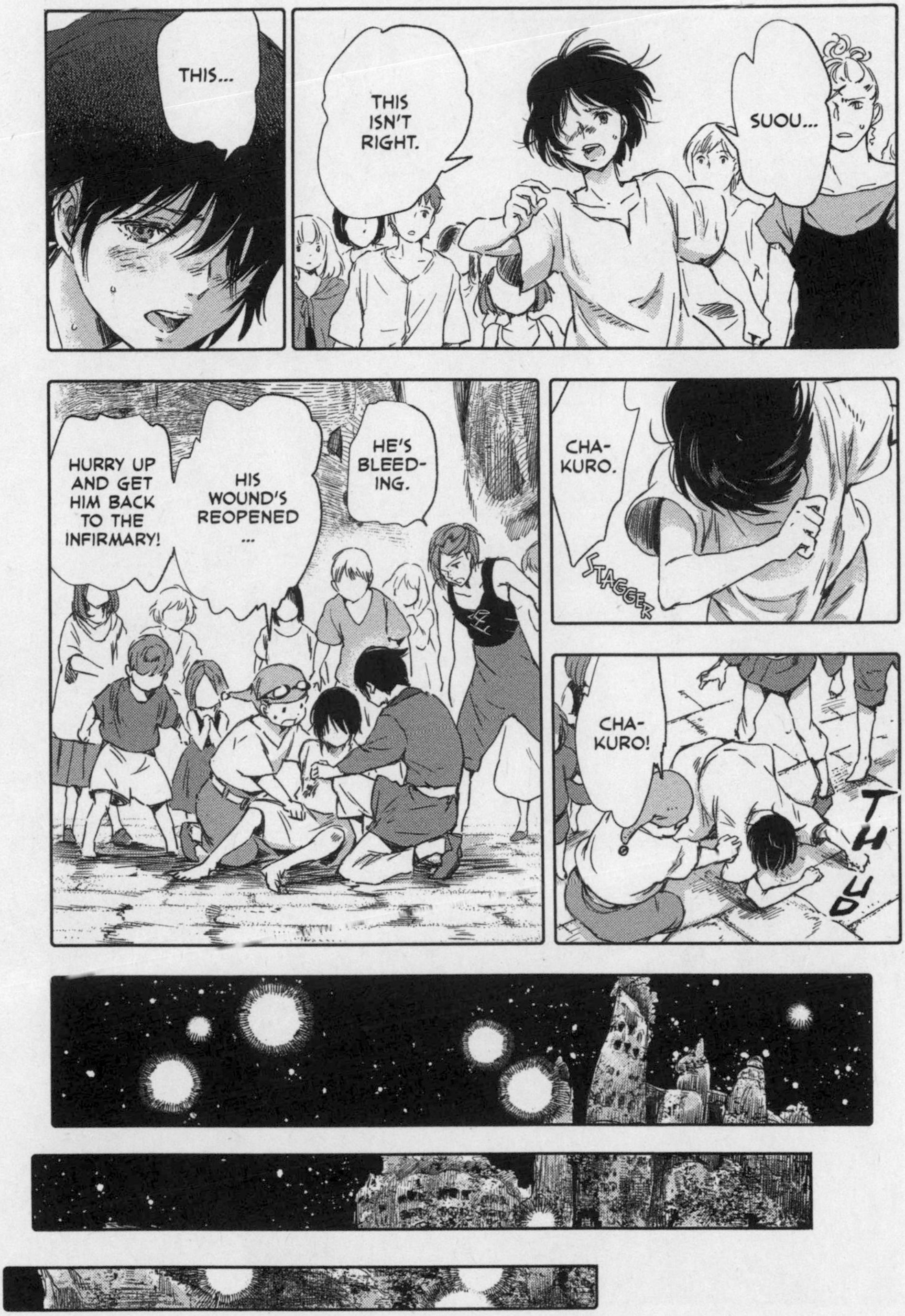
SUOU...
THIS ISN'T RIGHT.
THIS...
CHA-KURO.
STAGGER
CHA-KURO!
THUD
HE'S BLEED-ING.
HIS WOUND'S REOPENED ...
HURRY UP AND GET HIM BACK TO THE INFIRMARY!

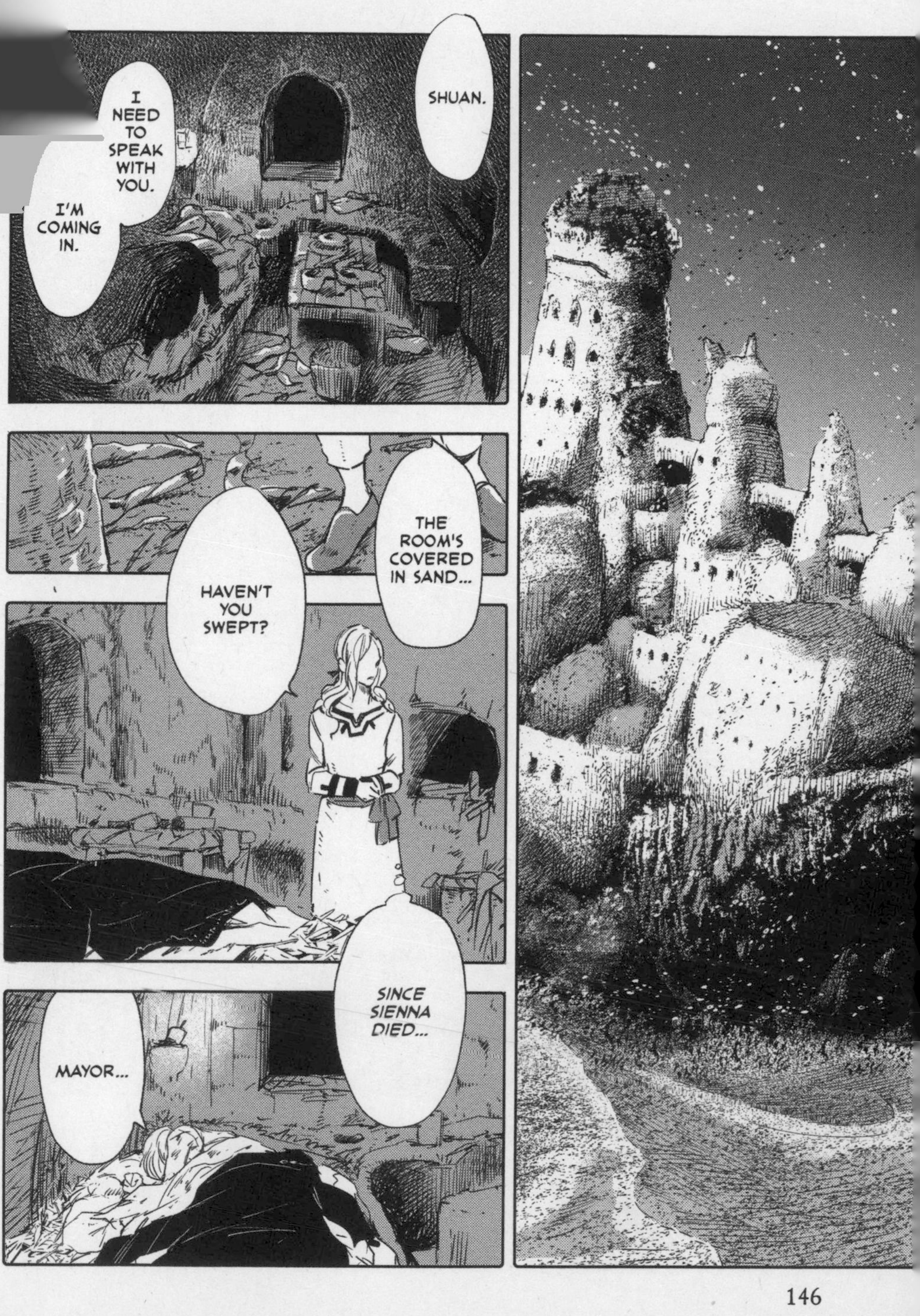
SHUAN.
I NEED TO SPEAK WITH YOU.
I'M COMING IN.
THE ROOM'S COVERED IN SAND...
HAVEN'T YOU SWEPT?
SINCE SIENNA DIED...
MAYOR...

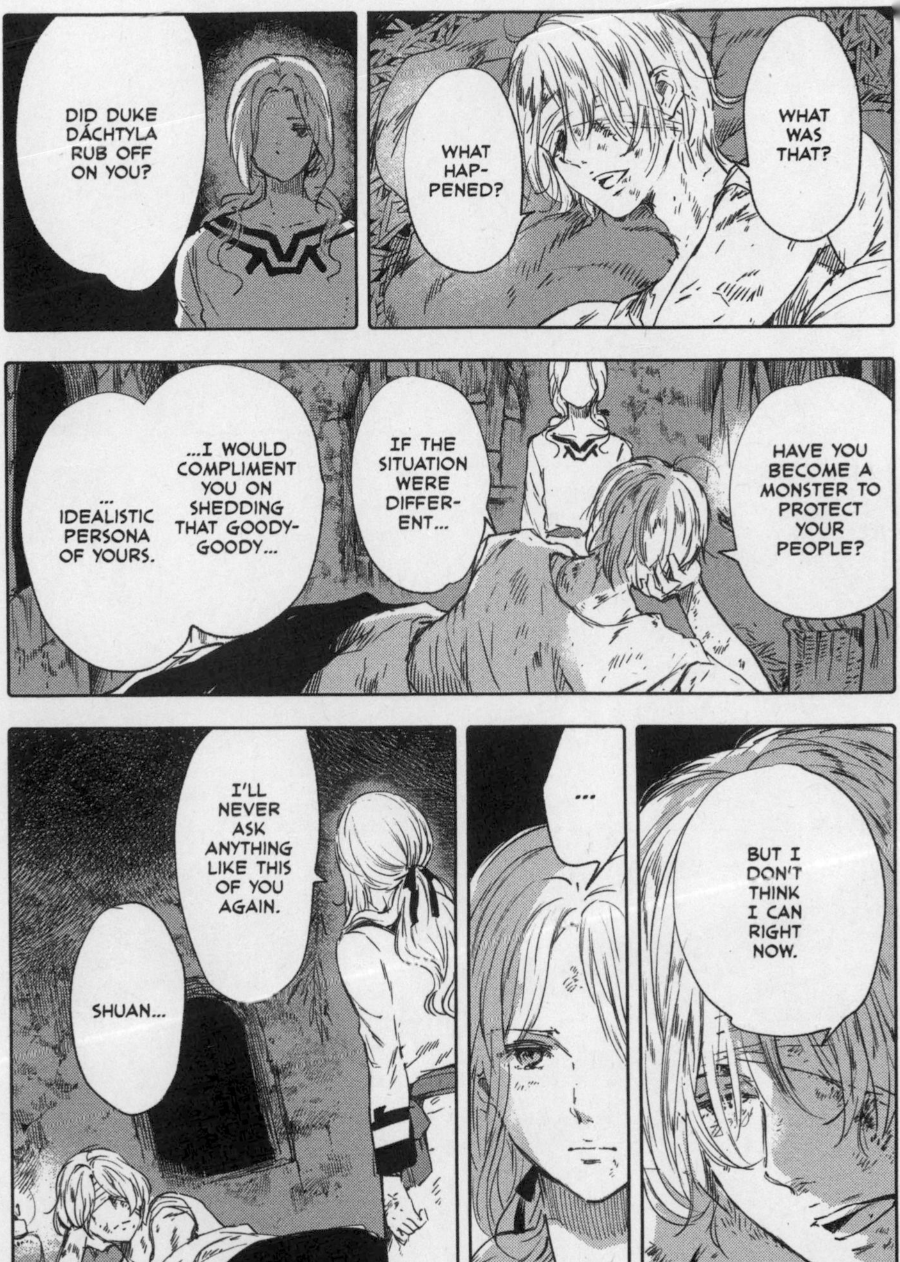
WHAT WAS THAT?
WHAT HAPPENED?
DID DUKE DÁCHTYLA RUB OFF ON YOU?
HAVE YOU BECOME A MONSTER TO PROTECT YOUR PEOPLE?
IF THE SITUATION WERE DIFFERENT...
...I WOULD COMPLIMENT YOU ON SHEDDING THAT GOODY-GOODY...
... IDEALISTIC PERSONA OF YOURS.
BUT I DON'T THINK I CAN RIGHT NOW.
...
I'LL NEVER ASK ANYTHING LIKE THIS OF YOU AGAIN.
SHUAN...

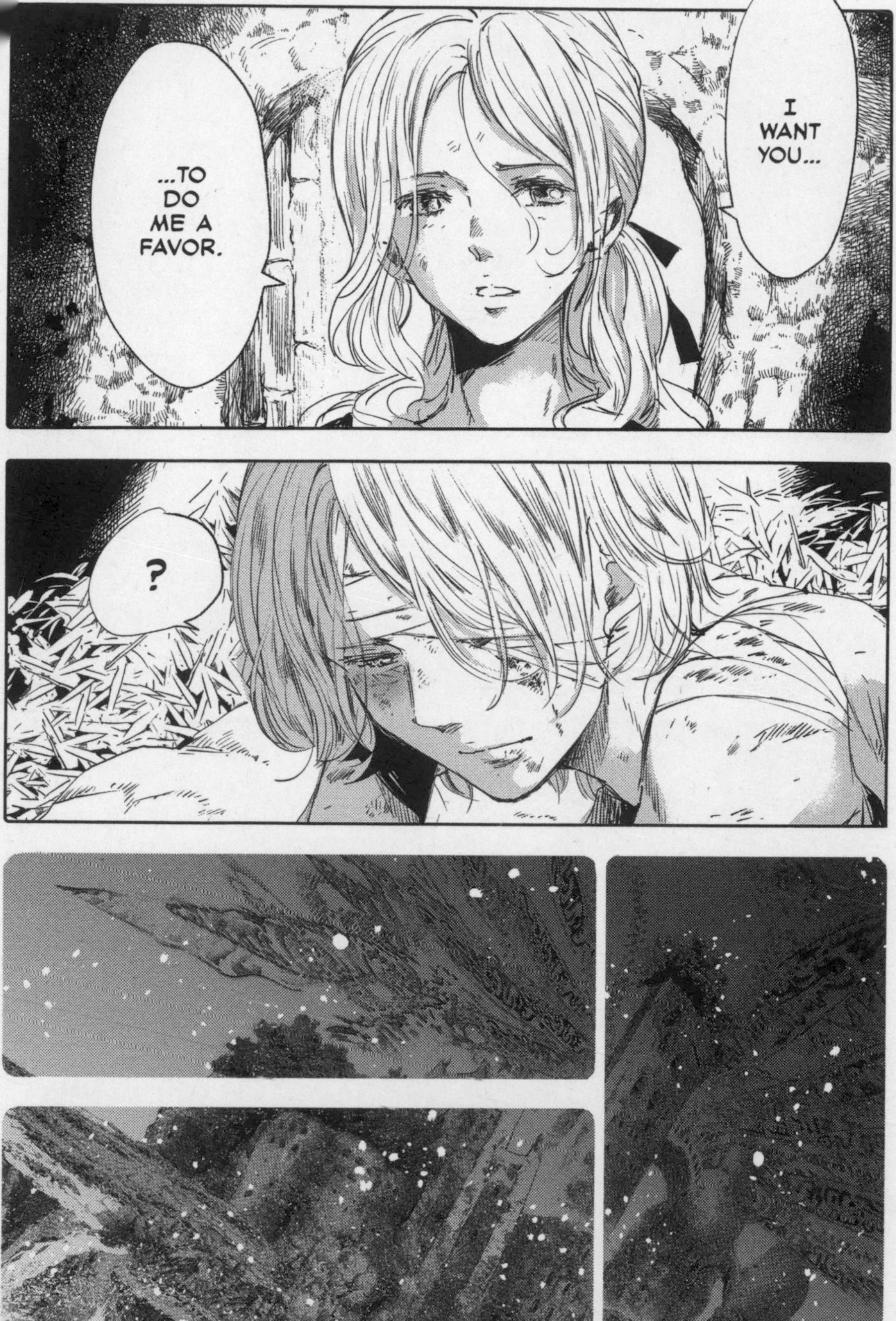
I WANT YOU...
...TO DO ME A FAVOR.
?

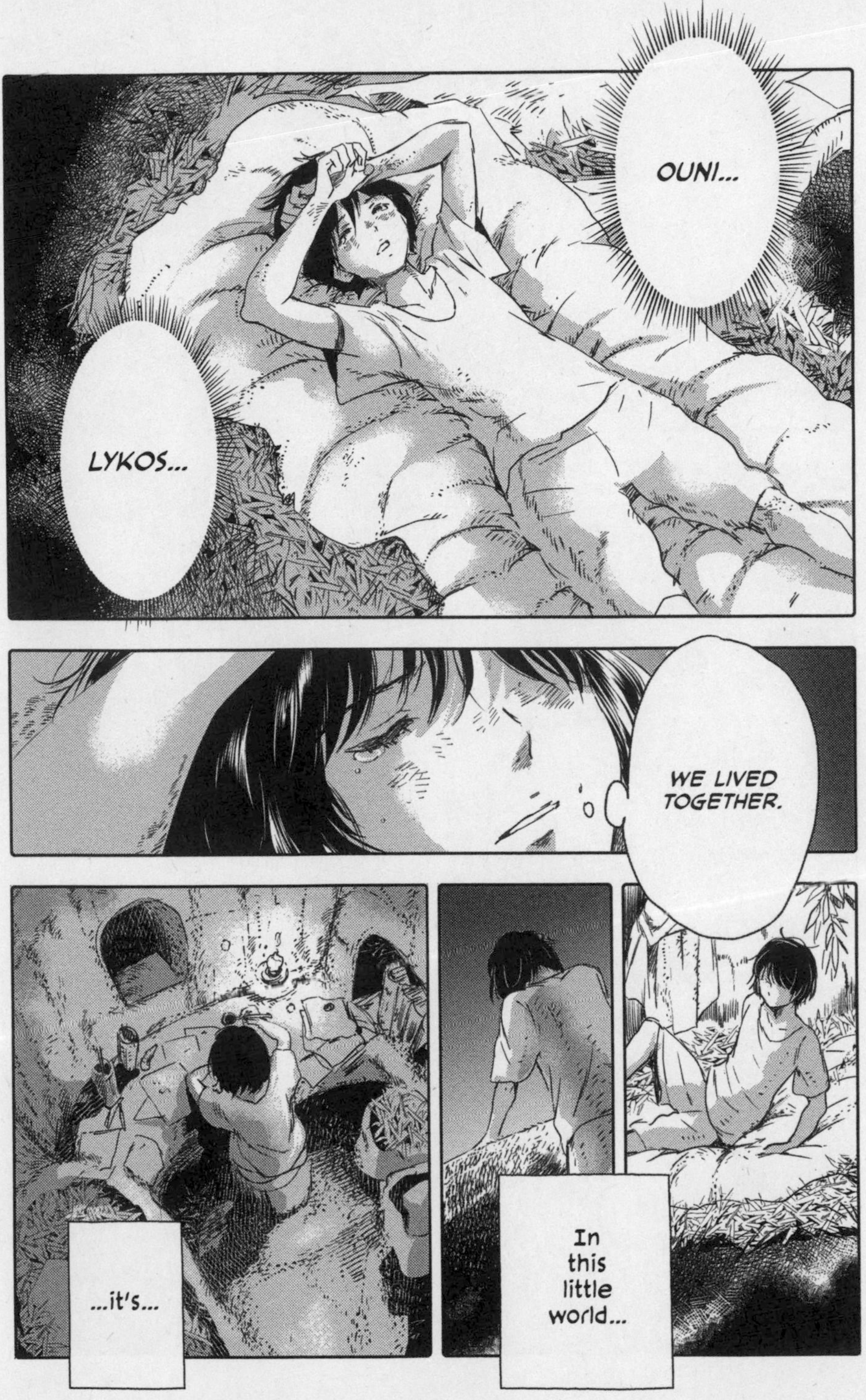
OUNI...
LYKOS...
WE LIVED TOGETHER.
In this little world...
...it's...

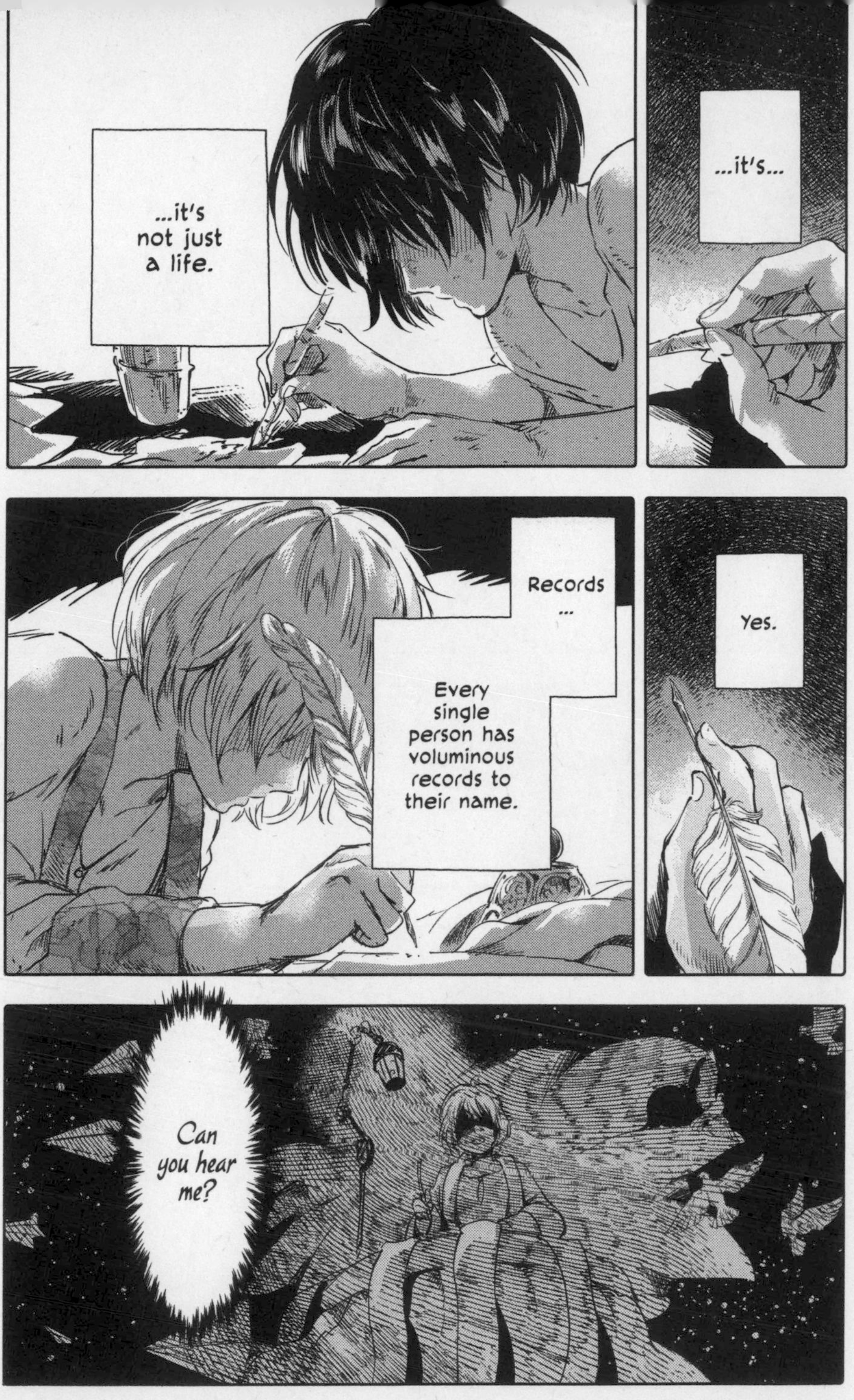
...it's...
...it's not just a life.
Yes.
Records ...
Every single person has voluminous records to their name.
Can you hear me?

Marmarigias of
Karcharias...

I thought
we would
start the
banquet.

Prin-
cess?

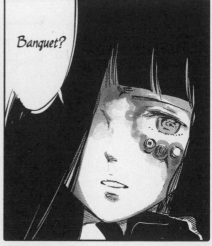

Banquet?

Yes.
It's also
called
"punishment."

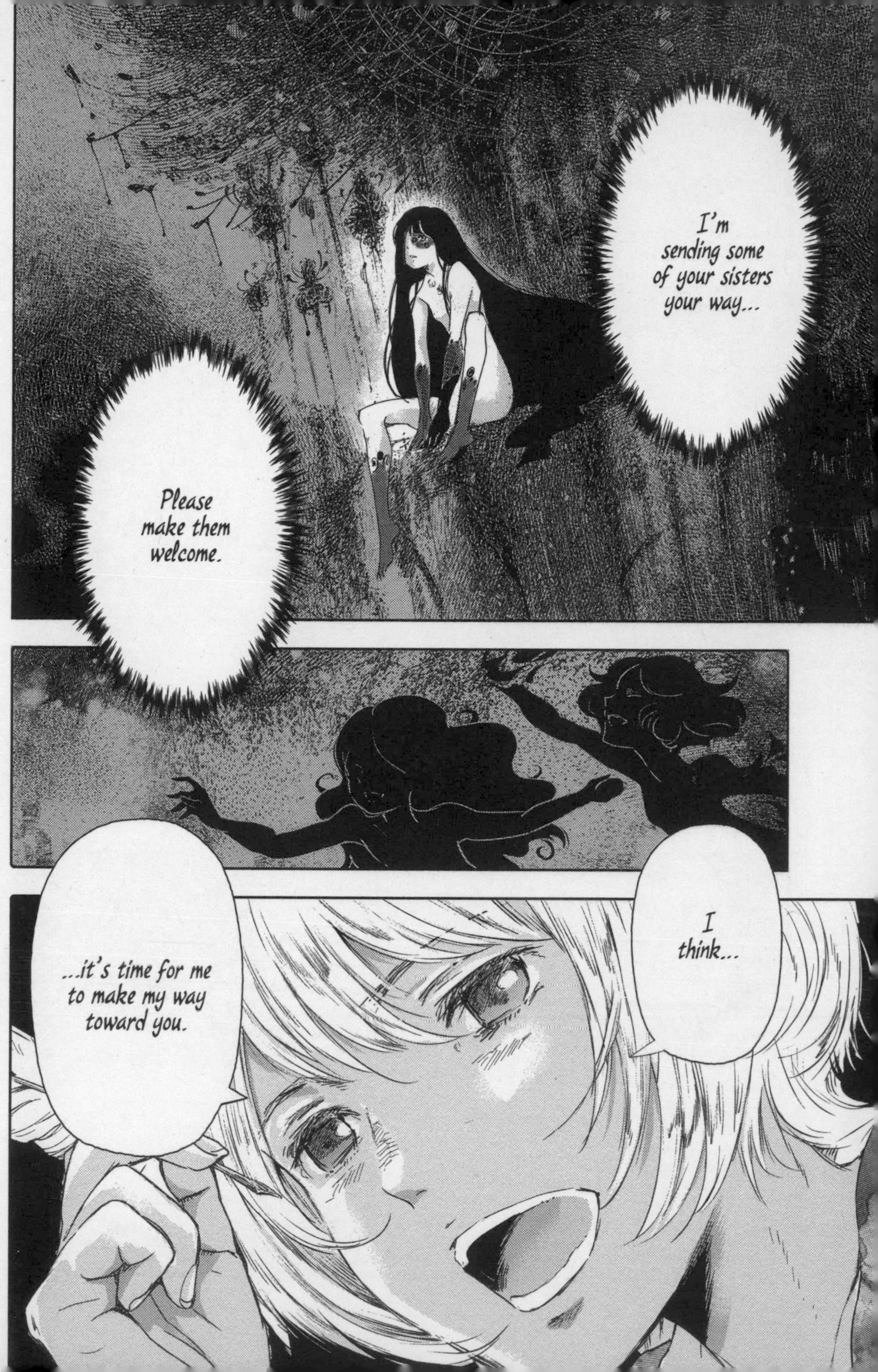
I'm sending some of your sisters your way...
Please make them welcome.
I think...
...it's time for me to make my way toward you.

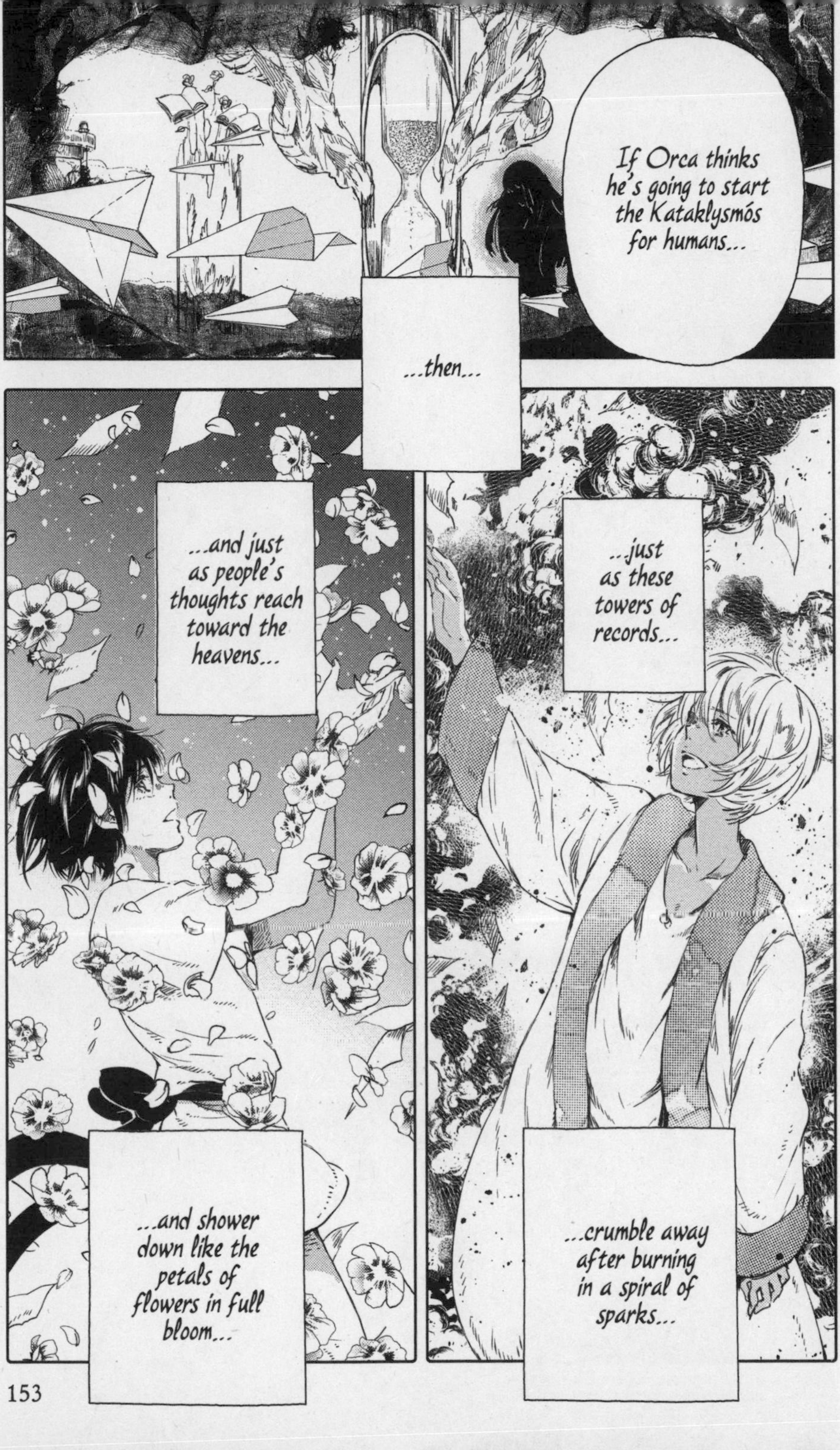

If Orca thinks he's going to start the Kataklysmós for humans...
...then...
...just as these towers of records...
...crumble away after burning in a spiral of sparks...
...and just as people's thoughts reach toward the heavens...
...and shower down like the petals of flowers in full bloom...

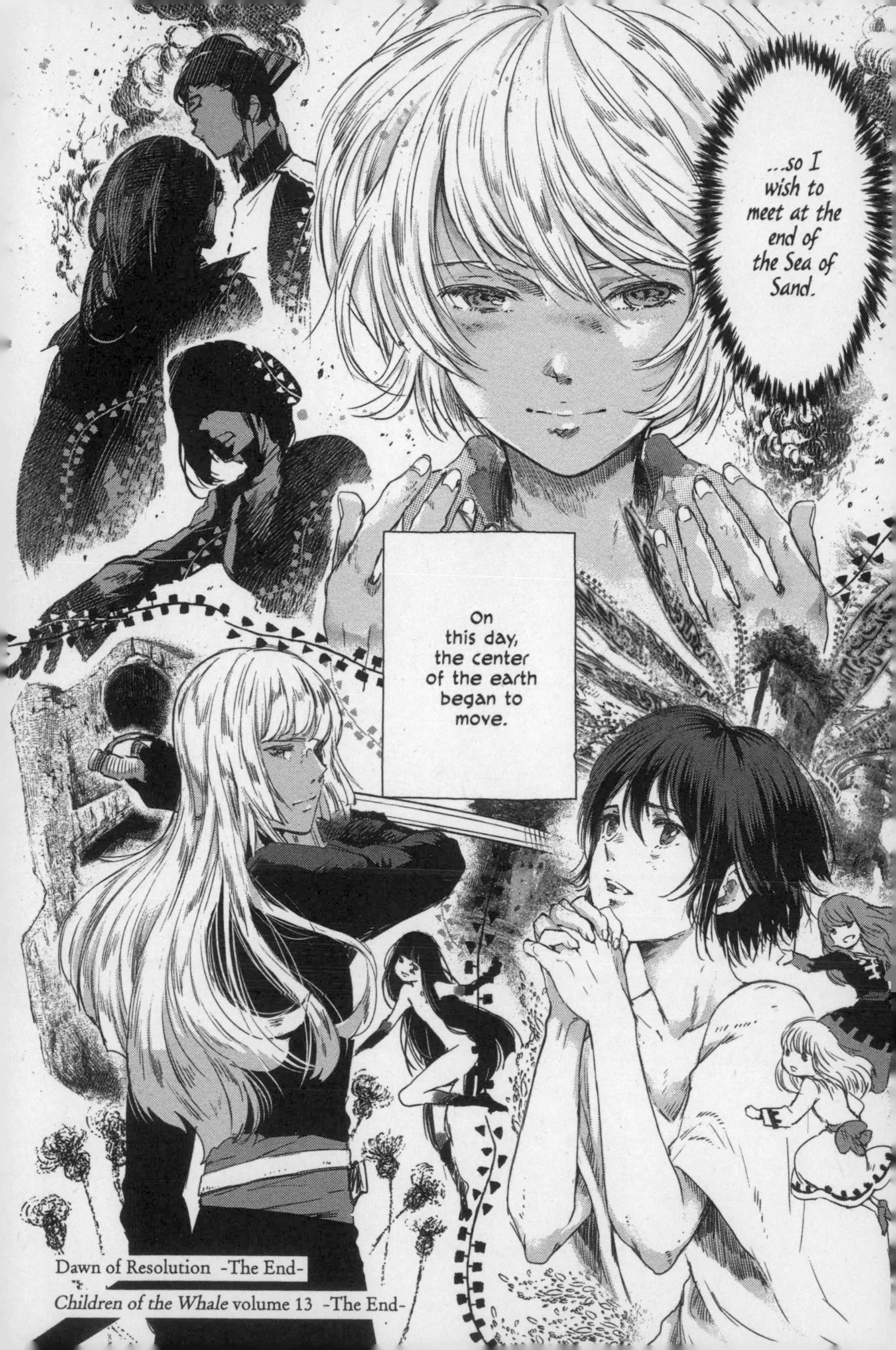
...so I wish to meet at the end of the Sea of Sand.
On this day, the center of the earth began to move.
Dawn of Resolution -The End-
*Children of the Whale* volume 13 -The End-

CHILDREN OF THE WHALES

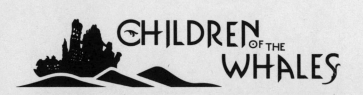

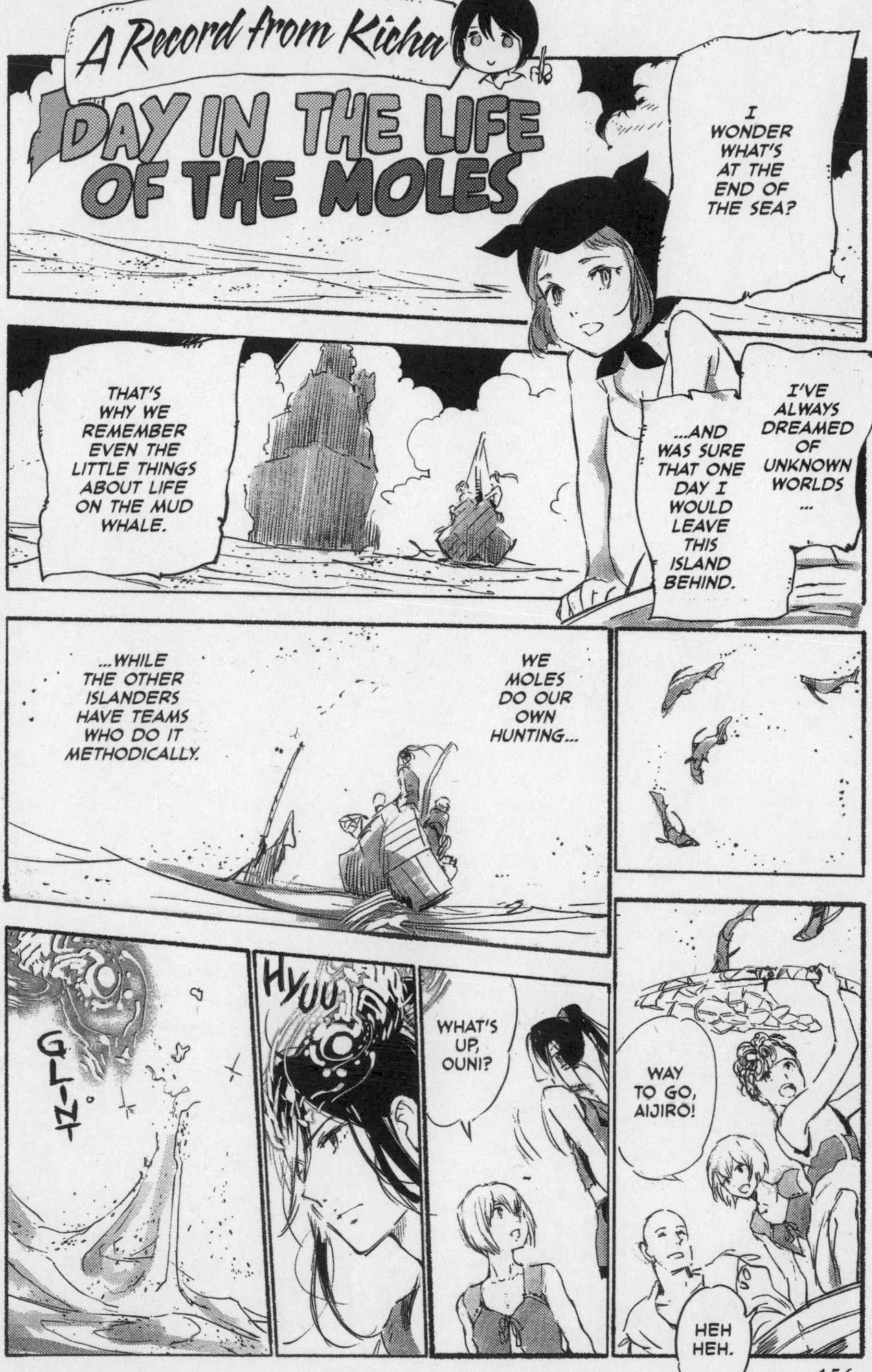
A Record from Kicha
DAY IN THE LIFE OF THE MOLES
I WONDER WHAT'S AT THE END OF THE SEA?
I'VE ALWAYS DREAMED OF UNKNOWN WORLDS ...
...AND WAS SURE THAT ONE DAY I WOULD LEAVE THIS ISLAND BEHIND.
THAT'S WHY WE REMEMBER EVEN THE LITTLE THINGS ABOUT LIFE ON THE MUD WHALE.
WE MOLES DO OUR OWN HUNTING...
...WHILE THE OTHER ISLANDERS HAVE TEAMS WHO DO IT METHODICALLY.
WAY TO GO, AIJIRO!
HEH HEH.
WHAT'S UP, OUNI?
HYUU
G-L-I-N-T

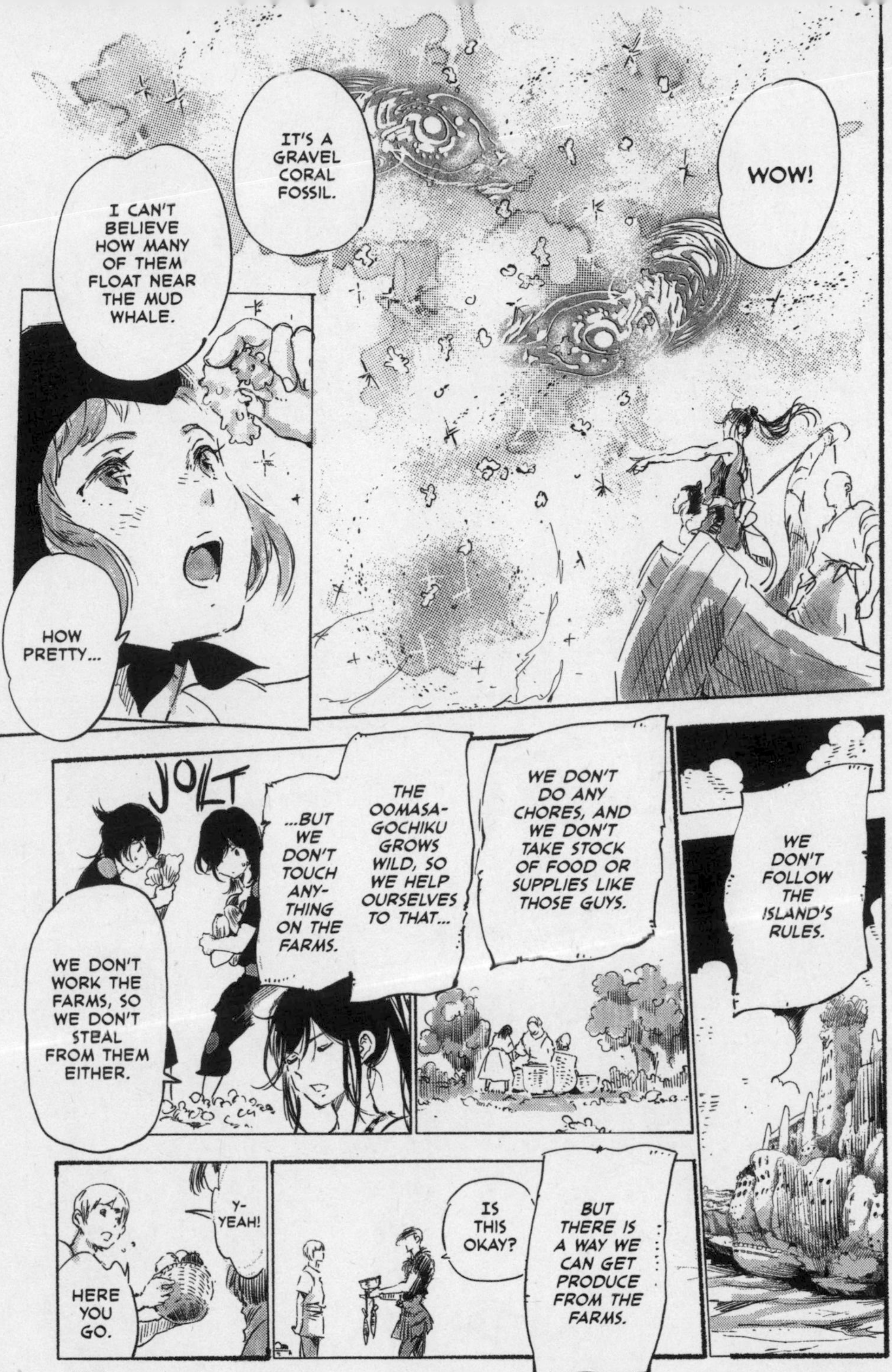
WOW!
IT'S A GRAVEL CORAL FOSSIL.
I CAN'T BELIEVE HOW MANY OF THEM FLOAT NEAR THE MUD WHALE.
HOW PRETTY...
WE DON'T FOLLOW THE ISLAND'S RULES.
WE DON'T DO ANY CHORES, AND WE DON'T TAKE STOCK OF FOOD OR SUPPLIES LIKE THOSE GUYS.
THE OOMASA-GOCHIKU GROWS WILD, SO WE HELP OURSELVES TO THAT...
...BUT WE DON'T TOUCH ANYTHING ON THE FARMS.
JOLT
WE DON'T WORK THE FARMS, SO WE DON'T STEAL FROM THEM EITHER.
BUT THERE IS A WAY WE CAN GET PRODUCE FROM THE FARMS.
IS THIS OKAY?
Y-YEAH!
HERE YOU GO.

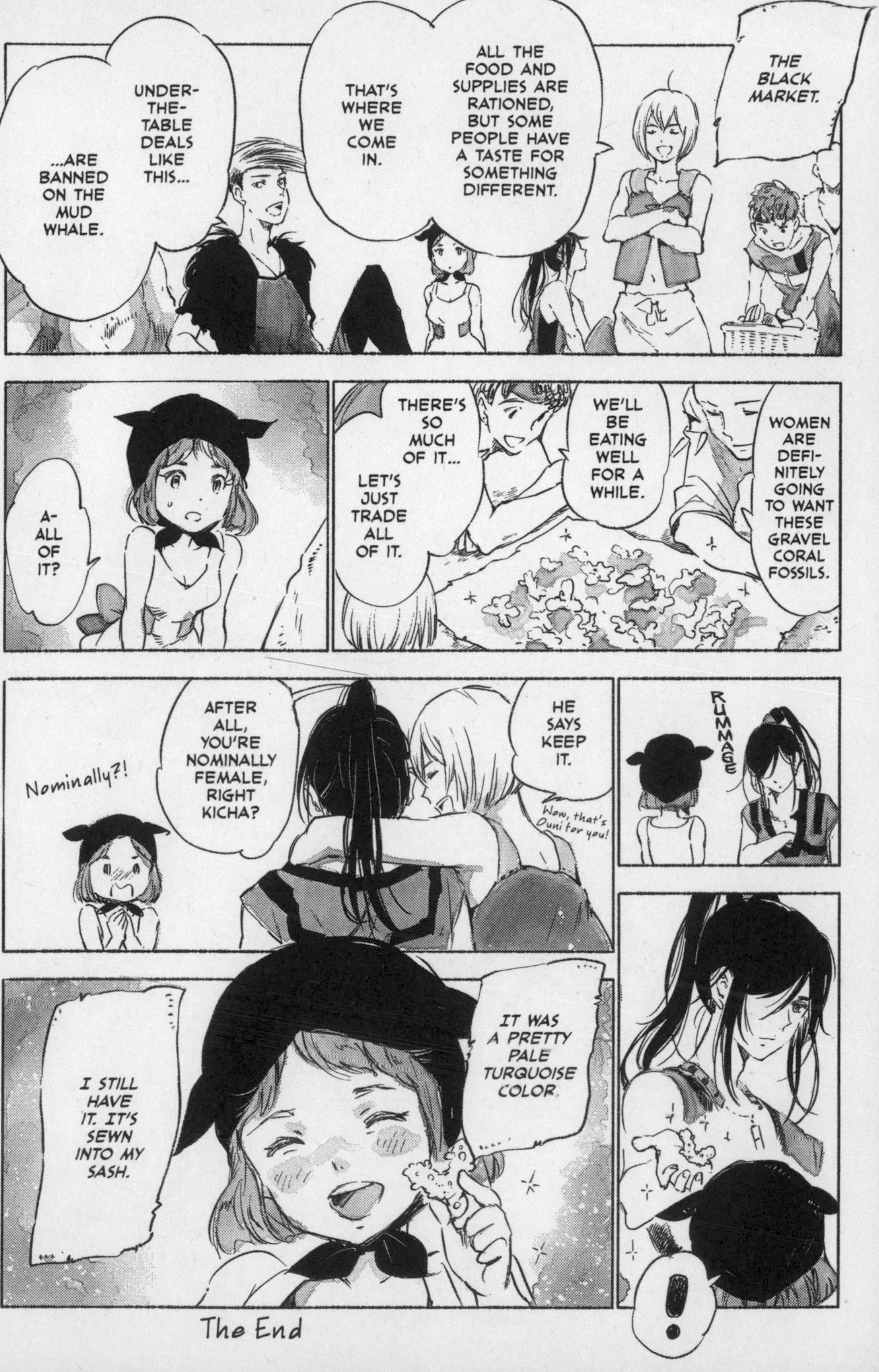
THE BLACK MARKET.
ALL THE FOOD AND SUPPLIES ARE RATIONED, BUT SOME PEOPLE HAVE A TASTE FOR SOMETHING DIFFERENT.
THAT'S WHERE WE COME IN.
UNDER-THE-TABLE DEALS LIKE THIS...
...ARE BANNED ON THE MUD WHALE.
WOMEN ARE DEFINITELY GOING TO WANT THESE GRAVEL CORAL FOSSILS.
WE'LL BE EATING WELL FOR A WHILE.
THERE'S SO MUCH OF IT...
LET'S JUST TRADE ALL OF IT.
A-ALL OF IT?
RUMMAGE
HE SAYS KEEP IT.
Wow, that's Ouni for you!
AFTER ALL, YOU'RE NOMINALLY FEMALE, RIGHT KICHA?
Nominally?!
!
IT WAS A PRETTY PALE TURQUOISE COLOR.
I STILL HAVE IT. IT'S SEWN INTO MY SASH.

The End

CHILDREN OF THE WHALES

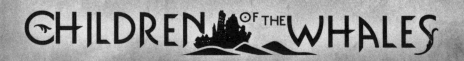

# A Note on Names

Those who live on the Mud Whale are named after colors in a language unknown. Abi Umeda uses Japanese translations of the names, which we have maintained. Here is a list of the English equivalents for the curious.

| | |
|---|---|
| Aijiro | pale blue |
| Benihi | scarlet |
| Buki | kerria flower (*yamabuki*) |
| Byakuroku | malachite mineral pigments, pale green tinged with white |
| Chakuro | blackish brown (*cha* = brown, *kuro* = black) |
| Furano | from "flannel," a soft-woven fabric traditionally made of wool |
| Ginshu | vermillion |
| Hakuji | porcelain white |
| Jiki | golden |
| Kicha | yellowish brown |
| Kikujin | koji mold, yellowish green |
| Kogare | burnt muskwood, dark reddish brown |
| Kuchiba | decayed-leaf brown |
| Masoh | cinnabar |
| Miru | seaweed green |
| Nashiji | a traditional Japanese crepe weave fabric |
| Neri | silk white |
| Nezu | mouse gray |
| Nibi | dark gray |
| Ouni | safflower red |
| Rasha | darkest blue, nearly black |
| Ro | lacquer black |
| Sami | light green (*asa* = light, *midori* = green) |

| Shikoku | purple-tinged black |
| Shikon | purple-tinged navy |
| Shinono | the color of dawn (*shinonome*) |
| Shuan | dark bloodred |
| Sienna | reddish brown |
| Sumi | ink black |
| Suou | raspberry red |
| Taisha | red ocher |
| Tobi | reddish brown like a kite's feather |
| Tokusa | scouring rush green |
| Tonoko | the color of powdered grindstone, a pale brown |
| Urumi | muddy gray |

The Amonlogian streets and scenery turned out differently than I had originally imagined. I hope can use my initial ideas at some point.

—Abi Umeda

ABI UMEDA debuted as a manga creator with the one-shot "Yukokugendan" in *Weekly Shonen Champion*. *Children of the Whales* is her eighth manga work.

# CHILDREN OF THE WHALES

**VOLUME 13**
VIZ Signature Edition

Story and Art by **Abi Umeda**

Translation / JN Productions
Touch-Up Art & Lettering / Annaliese Christman
Design / Julian (JR) Robinson
Editor / Pancha Diaz

KUJIRANOKORAHA SAJOUNIUTAU Volume 13
© 2018 ABI UMEDA
First published in Japan in 2018 by AKITA PUBLISHING CO., LTD., Tokyo
English translation rights arranged with AKITA PUBLISHING CO., LTD. through
Tuttle-Mori Agency, Inc., Tokyo

The stories, characters and incidents mentioned in this publication are entirely fictional.

Printed in the U.S.A.

Published by VIZ Media, LLC
P.O. Box 77010
San Francisco, CA 94107

10 9 8 7 6 5 4 3 2 1
First printing, November 2019

VIZ MEDIA
viz.com

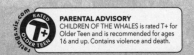

vizsignature.com

I'll tell you a story
about the sea.
It's a story that
no one knows yet.
The story of the sea
that only I can tell...
Children of the Sea
BY DAISUKE IGARASHI
Children of the Sea
DAISUKE IGARASHI
1
Children of the Sea
DAISUKE IGARASHI
Uncover the mysterious tale
with Children of the Sea—
BUY THE MANGA TODAY!
Available at your local bookstore and comic store.
RATED T+ OLDER TEEN
VIZ
viz.com
KAIJU NO KODOMO © 2007 Daisuke IGARASHI/SHOGAKUKAN

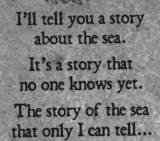

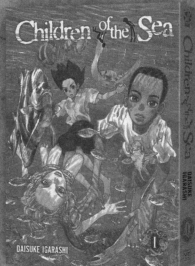

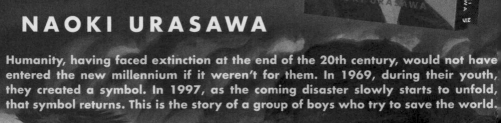

RUBY ROSE

WEISS SCHNEE

BLAKE BELLADONNA

YANG XIAO LONG

# RWBY

# OFFICIAL MANGA ANTHOLOGIES

Original Concept by Monty Oum & Rooster Teeth Productions, Story and Art by Various Artists

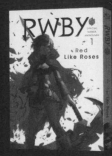

All-new stories featuring Ruby, Weiss, Blake and Yang from Rooster Teeth's hit animation series!

# THIS IS THE LAST PAGE!

*Children of the Whales* has been
printed in the original Japanese
format to preserve the orientation
of the original artwork.